T0128014

SUMMARY & LIFE APPLICATIONS ON THE BOOK OF PROVERBS

L.O. LAWAL

WESTBOW
PRESS®
A DIVISION OF THOMAS NELSON
& ZONDERVAN

WestBow Press books may be ordered through booksellers or by contacting:

WestBow Press
A Division of Thomas Nelson & Zondervan
1663 Liberty Drive
Bloomington, IN 47403
www.westbowpress.com
1 (866) 928-1240

Because of the dynamic nature of the Internet, any web addresses or links contained in this book may have changed since publication and may no longer be valid. The views expressed in this work are solely those of the author and do not necessarily reflect the views of the publisher, and the publisher hereby disclaims any responsibility for them.

Any people depicted in stock imagery provided by Thinkstock are models, and such images are being used for illustrative purposes only.
Certain stock imagery © Thinkstock.

ISBN: 978-1-5127-5496-4 (sc)
ISBN: 978-1-5127-5497-1 (hc)
ISBN: 978-1-5127-5495-7 (e)

Library of Congress Control Number: 2016914158

Print information available on the last page.

WestBow Press rev. date: 09/28/2016

INTRODUCTION

REVIEW ON BOOK OF PROVERB

1) The book of Proverbs was written around 950B.C. It was written by several writers including Solomon, Agur, and Lemuel – Pr. 1, 10, 30:1-31 25:1-2a:27.

2) The book of Proverbs was a collection of wise sayings while some were in the form of Hebrew poetry. Each leaf in the book of Proverbs was a nugget of wisdom for dealing with issues in everyday life for Individual and collectively for churches, families, and relationships. Pr. 1:8-10; 2:1-2, 4:1-4, 6:1-5 6:6-11, 6:12-15, 6:16-19.

3) This book of Proverbs has many wise saying with which if one decided or determine to follow, he will be a wise person; he or she will have peace and eternal life. Pr. 8:35, 9:9-11. Many of these Proverbs have dual meaning or interpretation that express in styles for our understanding. In another hand, these are the four types of proverbs; namely:

    1. Comparative Proverbs: - This explains the truth with experience or nature. Pr. 26:11. 1 Corinth 11:13-14
    2. Antithetical: Proverbs – contrary or in opposite to the first line. Pr. 10:12, 1:7

3. Synonymous: Proverbs – the second line repeats the first line in a different way. 16:18, 4:20-21.
4. Synthetic Proverbs: - This adds more idea or shed more light to the first line Pr. 16:3. In other hand using or applying these steps above will be of the best help in interpreting or understanding the whole Bible in all our daily devotion to Jehovah Elohim.

4) The book of Proverbs is to teach people wisdom and discipline and also to help them understand the wise saying. In other words book of Proverbs is to teach wisdom and common sense. The book of Proverbs is a bag full of truth and it also a precious book of wisdom because you can always find something that will give best effects on your choices of life for the day. It is also a book that teaches or tells you how to choose friends, resolve conflicts, what to do with your money, how to find a wife/husband or God's will in every step and decision in life and how to live your life in the details where things can get the most complicated

CONCLUSION:

The book of Proverbs is the rare gem of truth that teaches a man and woman basic characters and qualities and also it teaches how to have a peaceful, happy and long life on this earth planet of turmoil. The book of Proverbs is mainly base on Wisdom; a Godly wisdom.

THE BOOK OF PROVERBS COVERS ALMOST MANY CONCEIVABLE PROBLEMS AND ALSO GIVES THE DIVINE REMEDY FOR IT.

OVERVIEW

What is Wisdom; one might sum up the meaning of the term "wisdom" with the words, "know how." Wisdom is based upon knowledge. Often, in fact, wisdom and knowledge are mentioned together (see Jeremiah 10:12; 51:15; Luke 1:17; Romans 11:33; 1 Corinthians 1:24; 2:5; Colossians 2:3; Revelation 5:12; 7:12). God knows everything. Theologians use the term "omniscient" when speaking of God's infinite knowledge.

Wisdom cannot exist without knowledge of all the facts applicable to any purpose or plan. For example, The God who is all-wise is also the God who is all-knowing. Though it is possible to see a prophet that gives a word of knowledge without a word of wisdom, I think that was the Holy Spirit trend of the division of Labour and a way of making us see the needs of each other in the body of Christ 1 Corinthians 12:4-26.

LIFE APPLICATION:

I remembered when I was like age 17, I was on the road, going to church weekly service when I heard Jehovah Elohim speaks through His divine Spirit to me and He said "Child when things happen you always think too deep about it for a long time" that's all I heard - Not knowing that I was about to receives the demonstration gift of phenomenal Prophecy in the church service that evening. What the spirit of God release to me that very day of which the church Authority misinterpreted; was later after few days specifically and exactly confirmed by another visiting Missionary Minister that was not even there in the church that very evening.

Meanwhile, before the confirmation, I almost die of despair when the church authority publicly misinterpreted the Prophesy and I was like terribly ashamed. It was then I remembered that God was preparing me ahead of what will happen that very day as per; not to border about it much. We can see here that I was given a word of knowledge of what was about to happen and at the same time word of wisdom not to let the rejection eat me deeply.

God knows everything about everything. He knows what men are thinking Ezekiel 11:5; Luke 5:21-22. He knows everything that is going to happen. He even knows everything that could happen, under any set of circumstances (see, for example, 1 Samuel 23:10-12; 2 Kings 8:10. God cannot devise a bad plan or fail to bring His purposes and promises to their conclusion because He knows everything. His omniscience undergirds His wisdom.

Wisdom is not just knowledge, but "know how." God's wisdom enables Him to "know how" to do anything, 2 Peter 2:9. Wisdom entails the skillfulness to formulate a plan and to carry it out in the best and most effective manner. Bezalel was a craftsman, a man with incredible "wisdom" in the art of making the furnishings for the Tabernacle (see Exodus 31:1-5). Joshua had been given the wisdom to know how to lead the nation Israel Deuteronomy 34.9. Solomon asked for and received the wisdom and knowledge needed to rule Israel 2 Chronicles 1:7-12.

Wisdom does not "know good and evil." Wisdom is a knowing; good from evil. True wisdom, the wisdom which is a "Tree of Life," does not come from below, from man; it comes from above, from God. Too many Christians try to become wise by reading secular sources; not that we should avoid all secular reading, but we should not read these to become wise. Let us desire God's wisdom as a "Tree of Life," and let us look for it in God's Word and pursue it by keeping His commands. Let us not persist in the very thing which brought about the fall.

God's Wisdom Revealed through Israel: Romans 9-11

God promised Abraham that in him, in his seed, all the nations of the earth would be blessed Genesis 12:1-3. It seems this would have taken place through the entire nation, but history makes it clear that the nation will not be subject to God and will persistently resist and rebel against God. It was not through the seed (plural) of Abraham that God brought about the blessing of the world, but through the seed (singular) of Abraham—Jesus Christ:

The Wisdom of God in Christ and His Church:

The divine Godhead is the wisdom and through this wisdom God sent Christ to deliver us all from the fall of Adamic nature brought us out from thick darkness to His divine marvelous light. *God's Wisdom revealed in Christ to the Church, He promised to bring salvation and blessing not only to the Jews but also to the Gentiles. He promised a Messiah who was a man, born of a virgin woman. God's Wisdom is being revealed Through the Church:* Ephesians 3:10-11

God's eternal purpose is to reveal His wisdom to the celestial beings as well as to His church. God is still accomplishing His purpose, which will culminate in the second coming of His Son and the establishment of His kingdom upon the earth. When this purpose and program is completed, the full scope of God's wisdom will have been revealed, and this wisdom will be revealed and so great that it will provide the fuel for the praise of God throughout all eternity.

The purpose of this lengthy History and drama is the demonstration of the Wisdom and Glory of God. In Ephesians 3, Paul speaks of God's purpose as God presently working to display His wisdom through the church. When this actor chapter is consummated, all creation, including the heavenly creatures, will have all eternity to marvel at His wisdom and to praise and glorify Him.

Do we sometimes wonder why God takes so long to fulfill His promises and to answer our prayers? It is because His doings and ways are vastly bigger than we are, and He has chosen to take thousands of years to present it to the enormous Witnesses and audience. Do we wonder why we cannot understand at present exactly what God is doing, how he is using the most unusual circumstances (including man's sin and rebellion, sickness, death, sorrow) to achieve His purposes? God leaves these matters a mystery because He is creating and sustaining the interest of His audience. He, the great author, producer, and director is creating the suspense appropriate to the grand conclusion of the final act. He dares not inform us because we would then not be proven faithful to the degree that we are. And He also dares not inform us because this would dispel the intense curiosity and wonder which holds all of the heavens in rapt attention (see 1 Peter 1:12; 1 Corinthians 11:10).

Do we sometimes wonder why God is putting us to the test in a seemingly private and personal way, a way that no one seems to be aware of but us? Our thinking is wrong! There is, as the writer to the Hebrews informs us, a "great cloud of witnesses" Hebrews 12:1 looking on with fixed attention even this moment. When we endure the tests and trials of this life, without knowing as Job did, for example, we are left with only one thing in which to trust—God Himself. When life simply does not make sense, we must look to Him who is the Author and the Finisher of our faith, to Him who has a great extraterrestrial plan, a plan to reveal His glory and to accomplish that which is good for His people. We must trust in Him who is all-wise and who is also all-powerful.

What a great privilege is ours to be a part of this great drama and to have a part in bringing praise and glory to our all-wise God! "With the goodness of God to desire our highest welfare, the wisdom of God to plan it, and the power of God to achieve it, what do we lack? Surely we are the most favored of all creatures."

Walking in the Wisdom of God

In Solomon's time ruling kings often lived behind the protection of fortified walls. Not only did walls surround their palaces, but walls surrounded their cities. Understandably, many put their confidence in the seemingly impenetrable defense of the city walls, along with the Soldiers who patrolled them. What Solomon is teaching us here is that just one man, equipped with the wisdom of God can figure out a way to infiltrate even the most protected city and to destroy the stronghold (defense] of the king and his citizens so confidently trusted in.

"Wisdom is superior to Violent strength or bully force. A man may be able to build a seemingly impenetrable wall of defense, but there will come along a man who is smart enough to figure out how to invade it. The ancient city of Babylon is a classic example. Belshazzar sat inside the walls of Babylon thinking he was perfectly safe. In fact, there was an inner wall around his palace. He was certain that the walls of Babylon could never be penetrated, and, of course, guards were stationed all along the walls. But the general in the camp of the enemy used his wisdom and figured a way to get into Babylon. A branch of the Euphrates River went through the city, more or less like a canal. He diverted the water back into the mainstream of the river, and then he was able to march his army on the riverbed under the wall where the river had flowed. The Mede-Persian army spread into the city, and the city was taken before the Babylonians knew what was happening."

Those who have earthly power are quick to rely on it: Those who are in positions of authority and who have established earthly means by which to protect their position without God will naturally rely on the protection they have established. However, no matter how much they have invested in their security, earthly wisdom can never truly provide complete security.

Those who have supernatural wisdom can accomplish the seemingly impossible: There is nothing that you cannot do when God is working in and through you. When God's super is applied to your natural, it enables you to operate in the supernatural! The Father – Jehovah Elohim can equip, enable, and empower you to accomplish the seemingly unachievable and in so doing, baffle the world in the process. Just remember to give Him the glory when He uses you this way.

The laws of God certainly play a key role in instruction in righteousness and for men and women to be able to obtain the wisdom of God as taught by His Holy Spirit.

The following texts in the book of Proverbs make reference to the commandments and God's law: Proverbs 2:1-2, 22; 3:1-2; 4:4; 6:20-23; 7:1-3; 8:32; 13:13-14; 16:17; 19:16; 23:26; 28:4, 7, 9; 29:18; 31:5

IT IS OF WISDOM TO RESPOND TO ABILITY IN THE
STRENGTH OF KNOWLEDGE AND UNDERSTANDING -
WISDOM IS SUPERIOR TO VIOLENT OR BULLY FORCE

CHAPTER ONE

SUMMARY

Proverbs 1:1–4

Here, Solomon, the son of David, whose name means "peaceable," begins to reveal the reason for these proverbs. They are "wisdom" and "knowledge." These are keywords in Proverbs, and both are used similarly (1:7; 9:10). "Wisdom" means skill and suggests a right use of knowledge. Many people mistake knowledge for wisdom. A person with several college degrees and qualifications may not have a much practical sense of what he or she studied in disciplines. One may not know how to use the knowledge he or she has until the individual passes through some practical experience that will make he or she a professional. That is the reason many companies send their incumbent personnel to several training sessions on and outside the job. It is possible to hear words of understanding without understanding. This is also true of spiritual things, for it takes special spiritual enlightenment for someone to understand spiritual truth (John 8:43; 1 Corinthians 2:14). The natural humankind can understand the natural but not the supernatural.

The older, the expert, and understanding people have a duty to teach while the younger has a duty to submissively learn. This is how knowledge can be passed on. It baffles me how many organizations put those who are supposed to learn practical wisdom ahead of the professional, who is in the position of passing on knowledge and wisdom. Many pay amateurs, younger, and inexperienced people more than what they pay the experienced professional. A wise person continually learns to reach perfection and knowledge; the fool thinks he or she knows it all. The wise individual is submissive and humble in spirit. The proud and rebellious, in their folly, proudly refuse counsel from others. The more we learn, the more we need to learn, for life's mysteries open up to us as we learn. To stop learning is folly (verses 5–6). In other words, true wisdom is never stationary but always progressive and humble.

Without proper reverence for God, no knowledge will profit much. In the same way, without reverence for knowledge and practicality from the expert and mentor, there is no way the senior individual will happily and voluntarily pass his or her proven experience to upcoming leaders. We all know the outcome of this: plenty of foolishness that leads to loss of property and life.

The word "fear" is used as in reverential trust and love, such as a child has for his or her father. In the Bible, a fool is not a mentally derailed person, but one who rebels against God, who lives as if there were no God (Psalm 53:1), that is, an unsaved person. These people are the real liars in the Bible. They will be damned by God on judgment day (Revelation 21:8).

In verses 8–19, godly wisdom warns us in all ages of the dangers of following the crowd in doing evil and being greedy. Much of book of Proverbs is devoted to instructing children in the truth. Probably the greatest danger to young people is their refusal to be taught by their parents, their guardians, and their true church. The spiritual truth is that almost every other evil is a result of this negligence. We occasionally hear of parents who teach their children only evil, but even bad parents will generally teach their children what is right and good, though they may not set the example. Anciently, most nations enjoined obedience only to fathers, but divine law elevates the mother to a place of honor and respect (Exodus 20:12 Ephesians 6:1). They are to teach what is good to their children, probably with age appropriateness in mind—for example, age one to eighteen or twenty-one—so as to not violate the Word of God in 1 Timothy 2:12 and John 2:3–5.

The ornament of grace is a wisdom to follow the right teaching and godly examples. This is an ornament that gives life. Even adults need a spiritual ornament as opposed to a cosmetic ornament. The ornaments of wisdom and truth are what influence others most (1 Peter 3:1–5). Parents must teach their children all that is right and those that are wrong There comes a time when each child will face the issue of whether to do good or evil. It then left for every person to be accountable for what he or she does. However, God is not going to take a vote on the day of judgment to determine what is evil and what is good. That is already settled. "Every man must carry his own breast" (Romans 14:12; 2 Corinthians 5:10; Revelation 20:12).

It shows good character and Christian teachings for younger ones, and even adults, to flee from all appearances of evil. Natural humankind is so spiritually blind and may not be aware of the possible punishment for their sins in this life. They may not realize there awaits an eternity of punishment for the sins of this life. Escaping punishment in this life only hardens people in sin and increases their guilt—and the degree of punishment in the next world. Heaven and hellfire are real.

Life Application

I remember when I was about nine years old. I was on holiday in a family compound. My grandfather gave one of his brother's wife a position as a head of communities and larger clans. The widow had to stay with him in the compound; her children came from time to time to see her. On the day she died, her coughing woke me up about 12:50 in the morning. She was calling my grandfather. She called him Akowe, meaning clerk or registrar. She started mentioning all the dead before her. She shouted, "Akowe, help! Help! Help! They are beating her. Oh, they should stop beating her, the pain is too much. Oh!" Then she shouted, "Take away fire from me, oh," about six times. She finally gave up the ghost at about 1:05 a.m. What baffled me until now was that this old aunty prayed very often, almost five times a day, and she was more than 100 years old. In other words, I wondered, *Is it true that your good character is the yardstick to make heaven or by following Him in His divine way? Does God Almighty have a particular time He closes one's good deeds book of record* (Ecclesiastes 12:1–3), *as in the case study of my old aunt, or, like some people use to say and or pray, that death would meet them when they are inside church or when doing some piety, even when they know they have not reconciled with their Creator or make restitution of their past lives* (Joel 1:14; Romans 10:9–10).

You can see that God Almighty will not be a respecter of any person on his or her last day on earth. He has shown you the way of life and death through His divine Word, each truth taught with godly wisdom. It is up to you to escape all appearances of evil and those who practice them. Believe and trust in the words of divine Godhead both in Rhema (spoken) and logos (written; the Bible), and principles and patterns (Ecclesiastics 12; Isaiah 55:6–7).

Another example is when my aunt prophet died in 1990. He was a friend to her family and her church. From time to time, she consulted him for insights, and it was like she built trust in him for the accurate prophecies he gave her. I was told that on the day he died, he was crying and lamenting that "Ah! Ah! God, why is he ending it this way," upon all good things he had done. He was in service for the Lord many years faithfully inside the church. I think, so he thought. A tear dropped onto his cheek, and he died. I was somewhat startled by what I heard because all the time I knew this elderly man, he was portrait as a true, kind, and humble man of God (Matthew 15:8–9; Isaiah 29:13; Psalm 50:16–18). On other hands, this adage was true: "Vain is a religion unto salvation." It is not by our good work and righteousness *alone,* so no one should boast. It is through God's divine mercy and our obedience and faith in Elohim. This is what we need to seek all our lives (Colossians 2:20–22; Romans 12:2; Ephesians 2:7–10; Titus 3:5). Based on his experience and statements, I doubted if he made it to heaven (John 3:5).

Dear ones, let us get our priorities right and get serious about the issues of judgment day at the end of this evil world (Matthew 24:2; Hebrews 10:22). In other words, in every second of our lives, let us cry for His divine mercy and always plead the blood of Christ upon ourselves.

Again, the divine heaven and hellfire are real places (Revelation 20:15; Matthew 7:21–23). Let us be sincere with ourselves and develop a personal relationship with the true and divine Godhead, worship Him in truth and spirit, and obey him. Worship Him faithfully, without adding and or subtracting from His divine ways, principles, and patterns. This is for our own good in this present life and life to come in eternity. When you are weak, cry for His divine grace and help. Carry your cross daily, and follow Him until the end. If you fall, do not lie there as if it were the end. Get up quickly, and run to meet Him. He understands and will help you (Psalm 46:1; Matthew 24:13).

Life Application

On a night in November 2011, I went up to heaven, got some information, and came back to Earth. There was no ladder, and I did not fly. It was just like the way airplanes accelerate gradually and then take off and land. A few days after this, in another insight, I found myself going deep down into Hades, near the blazing heat. With terrible fear I shouted—I mean, I cried out—"I am sure to God Almighty, Jehovah. I do not want to go to hell!" In the twinkle of an eye, I was drawn out of that situation and woke up. You too can cry out to Almighty Jehovah for your salvation today (Acts 2:20–21; Romans 10:13).

The value of any material things and all what we try to achieve and or; how will propel along our assignments and living purpose on Earth is due only to God's blessings on it Proverbs 10:22, and that which is gotten in a wrong way cannot have God's blessings on it, but must be cursed and made to vanish away, either in our course of Material things, Positions, Marriages etc. Proverbs 23:4-5, Proverbs 3:5-6. Jeremiah 17:11.

Part of the curse brought about by sin is that we must labor for all that we have, and earn it only by the "sweat of our face," (Gen. 3:19). All robbery, fraud, gambling, Prostitutions, secret societies, love potion, spell, and charm etc., is an attempt to bypass God's curse upon the works of our hands and gets something for nothing. Having a common treasury has never worked because there are always some who will shirk their part of the work and commitment. Even among Christians, this was not long lasting, Acts 4:32, for in Acts 6:1 there was dissatisfaction with the administration of the treasury. I do not know why the issues of money, food and women and relationships of some sorts were so deep in mystery and also a problem with men, and this makes me have a second thought that partnership with someone in business and relationships should not be a rush into without distinctive approval of the Holy Spirit. Many other more issues, especially in the circle of bodies of Christ, have to be managed in the true Spirit and this is part of our commitment and mature state of mind in Christ.

LIFE APPLICATION:

In one of the insights divine Spirit gave to me 2006. I saw a man seeking for Power, Riches, and Fames and he was told that, for him to have all these three things, he has to give up the marriage of all his daughters in exchange, for some time he lied on the bed and thought of it, he got up and made up his mind to do exactly what the world, devil and wicked men suggested to him and I woke up Matthew 16:26. My question is this, is that a good father? The innocent children will be in trouble when the time to settle in marriage comes because of the evil association and covenants with the devil their father had entered, and the most painful thing is this; the friends and associates or whoever entice him and even himself will not be able to amend all of the evil consequences wrought into the life of those children. The acquaintance will then be raising question against God as if God Almighty His their mate, or probably point to some character in the bible that had passed through some trials and temptations, please let us set our priority right, the God Almighty is not to blame Jeremiah 29:11.

The sin of Greed is always destructive, never productive. Covetousness and greed always lead to worse sins, even to murder; as in the case of these wicked men. And afterward, when the calamity comes as a result of this evil, the innocent ones somehow share in it; it is painful. There was a saying that if sinners suffer the consequences of their evil deeds and sin, it does affect the righteous in one way or other, Deuteronomy 5:9, Psalm 11:3. But even Christians can fall into many foolish and hurtful lusts, and can err from the faith through covetousness.

In the circle of Christ today, many Christian compare themselves with another; it mostly come to our hearing this day - brother so and so slaughtered cow and make seven steps of cake during his wedding, I must to the same or sister so and so marry a rich guy I must look for one rich man too, so that she will not be making or feel superior over them. A lot of example of this kind of the Bodies of Christ and we quickly forget that the God Almighty that creates us, He is a God of Timing and Faithfulness, He never owed any man.

If we allow God to lead us in life, we will not miss out any of our living purpose on Earth 1 Timothy 6:9-10. Too much emphasis upon material things is always dangerous at best. No one can be materialistic and spiritual at the same time, (Yeah! We may desire good thing – this is the true will of God but with wisdom and seeking God first) Matthew 6:24. Real faith in the Lord eliminates the need for anxiety and enticement to do evil in the believer, Matthew 6:24-34, 1Peter1:23, 1John 3:9.

In Vs. 20-33 we will discovered that wisdom's appeal to everyman in all ages and the folly of those that reject wisdom, "Solomon, shown to us how dangerous it is to hearken to the temptations of Satan, and more also, how dangerous it is not to hearken to the calls or voice of God for salvation, whether it is in the Bible, in divine preaching, in circumstances, or whatever. In Christ Jesus; are all the treasures of Wisdom, Colossians 2:3, and He is made unto His people a divine and perfect wisdom, 1Corinthian 1:30.

The Godly Wisdom is likened to a person standing in the streets and markets calling out to the passers, appealing to them to turn from their folly unto the wise ways of the Lord. Yet; God do speak to mankind in many ways, but they are all characterized by wisdom, and it is folly of the worst kind to ignore the voice of God. Throughout the Bible, the emphasis is mainly for the public teaching and preaching of the truth; verbally or by writing. The truth is to be publicly proclaimed by us for we never know when the Spirit will take the truth to some heart and cause it to be effectual. No human can apply the truth to another's heart: that is the work of the Divine Spirit alone. However, we can faithfully proclaim it Vs.20-21, Psalm 81:10

Vs. 22 gave three characters of folly: (1) Simple ones, who are negligent about learning the truth, and prefer sinful simplicity to Divine knowledge (2) Scorners who turn serious warnings into occasions of jesting, (Gen. 19:12-14). In Psalms 1:1 the scorners are the third of three stages of wickedness. (3) Fools who not only scorn the truth but actually hate it. In many places the Lord promises to hear and answer the calls of His people on the day of their distress, (Ps. 50:15; Isa. 55:6-7; Jer. 29:11-13). But these are they who have first responded to God's call to them to turn unto Him. Those who spurn the call to repentance can expect to receive no aid from the Lord when calamity comes upon them.

LIFE APPLICATION:

I remembered a friend of mine some year back we both boarded the train to school every morning then, and we are also in Christian communities together. I remembered I used my money to organized coconut for her to be selling during her break time in her school while I go for selling stick meat. Somehow universe smiles on us and we were able to meet some daily need with our younger ones. But, before we rounded up secondary school I notice some way of life that was not part of her as a Christian that she was exhibiting, I decided to openly call her attention to them to the extent; one of the elderly train officers notice this word of counsel and wisdom and pray that she will heed to them 1Timothy 5:20. That very morning, as I was about to cross the main road, this LSTC transport (this olden days kind of long bus in Lagos) almost crushed me; the line between me and the vehicle is just too narrow that people already lose hope and put their hands on their head, I am sure the Spirit of divine God sent His Angel to held that vehicle for me, I do not know what could have to happen. That very day, I heard it vividly and audibly in my inner Man that "don't you know who you talk to" I could not relate to this statement properly until this incident happen.

After we all passed out from secondary school, I suggested that I will still continue with my stick meat by following train to Iddo and Idumota axis to sell, that she should go with seasonal fruits and our third friend could fry Fish at the frontage of their house, so that, we will not lack money. But, this friend of mine rejected the voice of Wisdom and decided to follow the voice of the evil friend that stood as a messenger of love between her and her sinner lover. This messenger of love collected many material things on behalf of this my friend for her own personal use without delivering them to my friend. Then it got to a point that the man asked for a kind in returns for his gesture as per taking her to bed, it was then she remembered that fornication is knocking at her door and she rejected. This angered the man and plan to rape her with other men nearby bush where she was passing to sell her fruits, they found her dead with her neck twisted, I learnt that maybe they could have left her after the raped but she mention one of them she knew, to avoid scandal, they twisted her neck and killed her. A few days later the family started looking for her and they decided to come to my house, that I am the only friend she was closed with.

It became embarrassment one morning like that at about 4:00am the family brought police that I should know where their daughter is, I humbly told them I know nothing about this and I cannot follow them to anywhere that early morning, because I have to prepare my younger sisters for school and that later in the day we shall see. Thank God for the Church and My close Christian brother that stood in the gap for me and attested to my justifications, meanwhile, the news has gotten to the messenger of love and she had run away.

My justification became more real when the train officer I mentioned above testified to my warning her inside the train the other day. To shortening the story, her despair killed her mother, because the poor woman kept coming to train station to wait for her return, as her first born, she could not stand seeing us her daughter's peer group and she died of despair. Though, some said she was from an evil kingdom, that she belongs to the secret world. Then; I remembered that incident of crossing the road after counseled her as I mentioned above.

Dear friends, you can now see that this is an evil enticement that leads to entanglement and eventually to death. Come out of them and touch not unclean things and God in His divine Wisdom will guide you. There are no good things with the devil and his fallen angels Psalm 16:4a, 34:9b and 10b. When it comes to the relationship of any kinds you need to do it in the right way and with the right person, 'you do not ready before you ready'. The person who refuses to hearken to the voice and call of divine God does more than one harm to himself; yea, he shows that he despises his or her own soul.

The man who hates knowledge and does not fear the Lord because sin seems so appealing will have himself to blame because this leads, not only to physical calamity but also to spiritual calamity as well, Proverbs 29:1, Hebrew 2:1-3.

Take, for example, the same way Satan tempted Christ Jesus was the same method he is still using today because that treasure of life originally belonged to you, Satan would pretend as if he is the source and owner of all good things that was meant for you in other to lure people to his sides of destruction – Matthew 4:1-11, and believe me if you can stand his fiery attack on you in whatever ways he wriggle them, God in His divine mercy will send His divine Angels to minister unto you. However, Satan in his deceitful ways entices you with those good things that are your original inheritances from your Creator.

There was a saying that - if you think making a lot of money is because of your money ritual is a big lie; and it further says; it is because you are already destined to make it, because, not all that goes these evil ways succeeded is either that; they are not destined to over rich or retribution just catch up with them Matthew 6:24, James 4:4. God in His greatness as a Creator of the whole Universe has shape and mapped your existence with everything that will keep you as you live with your purpose of life on Earth Deuteronomy 8:18.

In God Almighty alone is the fountain of all life and good, Zech. 7:11-13; Ps. 36:9. Prosperity has destroyed many people than adversity ever has, Deut. 32:15, and those who judge of God's favor solely by outward prosperity are deceived, Mark 10:23-27. Material prosperity is not that much important as is spiritual prosperity, 3John 2. Divine wisdom and turning to the Lord when He calls: gives safety and serenity both for this time and eternity, Isa. 26:3-4; 33:14-16; Jer. 33:6.

Generally, if a person hears with the natural ear long enough, God will bless him with a truly "hearing ear, One's moral purpose must be in harmony with God's will before one can understand the truth, and one of the great laws of rightly understanding the truth is the law of submission to the Divine will of Godhead Romans 10:17. Most people do not have any depth of spiritual wisdom because they treat the Bible as if it had nothing to offer them but myths and fables, entertaining stories, or, at best, some mere moral platitude. The truth is, it is a veritable mine of treasures of wisdom and knowledge, without which no one can know or do God's will. God is a God of order, and all that He does is orderly 1Corinthians 14:40.

WHEN GOD'S SUPER IS APPLIED TO YOUR NATURAL, IT ENABLES YOU TO OPERATE IN THE SUPERNATURAL

CHAPTER TWO

SUMMARY

In Proverbs 2:1-15

Throughout the book of Proverbs, Solomon and other co-writers give evidence of great concern for the spiritual welfare and uprightness of younger ones and even adults. For this reason, Proverbs is a book well adapted for family devotions, Guides and signposts with principles and practice. Juvenile delinquency would almost cease to exist if at least followed. It has always been hard for young people to realize that parents and Spirit-filled elders have at least twenty years more knowledge and experience than they do, and it is quite a wisdom to submit to their teaching in the Will of God and this is the divine order, Ephesians 6:1.

The Word of Truth is not only a preventative to sin, Psalm 119:11, but it is also a producer of God-honoring fruits, Matthew 13:23 - Solomon appeals to his son to both receive his teachings and also hide them in his heart. The ear is the avenue to the heart, unless men stop the avenue, as the Jews did Zechariah. 7:11; Acts 7:51. 'The hearing ear' is God's gift Proverbs 20:11 ask God for it and He will give willingly James 1:5, 17.

Man can by nature, get an education in worldly and human matters, but heavenly and divine things can be understood only by the aid of the Holy Spirit, 1Cor. 2:7-13. God has given this heavenly wisdom orally to His Prophets and Apostles, not in some nebulous thought inspiration such as the modernist thinks to find in every poet and philosopher.

God spoke to Moses and the other inspired writers of the Bible, and it is from their writings that we too may have this heavenly wisdom, but in no other way, for God's revelation of Himself and His will for us has long been closed. He who rejects this wisdom will be eternally unwise, dammed and on his or her own (OYO), 1 Corinthians 14:38, Acts 4:12, Revelation 22:19. It is certain that not only are there wisdom laid up for those who are upright, but also there is safety.

"If we depend on God, and seek him for wisdom, he will uphold us in our integrity, "He will enable us to keep the paths of judgment; for He preserves the way of His saints.

When God's "sound wisdom" is operative in the saint, it will not only keep him or her safe, but will also give him or her understanding of these right principles and practices, both as regards Godhead and man. God's Spirit and God's Word are harmonious in the direction that they lead.

One may have knowledge in the head when there is no wisdom in the heart, for wisdom is the right application of knowledge: knowledge is theoretical, but wisdom is practical. Too many people do not have wisdom because they only give superficial glances at Divine truth, so that it never gains an entrance into their hearts, and so never enlightens them Psalm 119:130. God keeps His people, Deuteronomy 32:10; Isaiah 27:3, but He does so through teaching them the truth, and moving them to believe the truth, 1Peter 1:3-5. We can have this security only if we submit ourselves to the truth 1Peter 1:3-5. Rejection of the truth always leads to delusion and often to damnation, 2Thess. 2:10-12.

A person is known by his practice, not by his profession, and some, who have not the courage to do the evil but delights in the evil that others do, are partners and associates in corruption that leads to damnation; 'Bird of the same feather flock together' Vs.14-15. One's thoughts can be hidden from man, but God knows the heart and judges accordingly, Jeremiah 17:9-10; Revelation 2:23. No amount of human works or flesh piety can ever change a man's sinful nature. God alone can do this. The sin of fornication and adultery has been from time memorial and it a great mystery between God and man.

A woman has a sort of spiritual springs or what we can term as a fountain of life that was like two edges sword that could either be a life when practices in the holiness of God and massive damage to life when practice with a strange or demonic woman. There a lot of mysteries around the sexuality of man (Anthrop) that I keep on wondering an alarming destruction it caused to man.

There are many passages the Word of Living God warned tensely about keeping purity in our sexual life and we could see this every day in our society, media and the world; - the untold agonies it brought to those that do not regard the warning in Leviticus 20:10-21, like as it is in Vs. 18- If a man lies with a woman during her sickness (Menstruations) and uncovers her nakedness, he has exposed her flow, and she has uncovered the flow of her blood. Both of them shall be cut off from their people, no one knows exactly why this should be wrong even with one's wife; yet; God Almighty said He hates this.

Sexual intercourse during menstruation also defiles and it an abomination unto God. Even though Leviticus 18:19 is in the law and Christ is the end of the law and righteousness for everyone who believes Romans 10:4 and Ezekiel 18, further reveals that sex during menses is indeed ungodly.

Notice how the Lord describes a "just" man in verses 9, in Ezekiel 18:5-9: But if a man is just and does what is lawful and right; if he has not eaten on the mountains, nor lifted up his eyes to the idols of the house of Israel, nor defiled his neighbor's wife, nor approached a woman during her impurity; Ezekiel 18:5-6. Along with several other things that depict a "just" (righteous) man, is one who does not approach "a woman during her impurity." God says this man "shall surely live!" Ezekiel 18:9. Several other sins are listed off in Leviticus 18, sex with nearer kin's, marrying a woman and her sister, adultery, idolatry, homosexuality, and bestiality. These are all identified as things that defile and are things that God hates.

In Proverbs 2:16-22.

A strange woman and prostitutes refer to a demonic possess; and or a woman forsaking her husband and practice unfaithfulness to the marriage vows made before the Lord. As here, the unfaithful wife is rebuked, so in Malachi 3:14-16 the unfaithful husband

Marriage vows are made before God who instituted marriage in the beginning, and who is the unseen party in every marriage, and the unseen head of every family, 1Corinthians 12:3. To believe the flattery of an unfaithful man or woman is to be deceived. "What faithfulness can the youth look for on the part of a man or woman tempter who has been unfaithful to their natural friend and true love? "Lust and idolatry are the spiritual adultery into which they entrapped the once wise king Solomon and until today there was a debate among the scholar if King Solomon actually makes it to heaven.

Vs.18 "For her house inclined unto death, and her paths unto the dead." This is very similar to Proverbs 7:6-27. This is a good reason to warn people about this strange woman if her house is the door to death. Her house, as described in Proverbs 7:16-18. She seems to promise attractive and flashing things so much, but its real products that are of death and damnation—were not advertised. How craftily Satan works today by picturing sin in such beautiful and alluring ways, when its end is always eternal death, Rom. 6:23a; Rev. 20:14. The word "Death" has to do with the act of dying, while "the dead" refers to the departed; those who have experienced death. Thus, the adulteress' house is where the death occurs, but it is the doorways to the hereafter from whence none return to this life, for example; think on those that have gone through her by much calamities, nemesis and Thunderbolt (Magun).

Vs. 19 None that goes unto her return again neither takes hold of the paths of life. For all her promises are nothing but damnation, this pathway is a one-way street to death and when one begins this slippery downward path, there is no stopping apart from Divine Grace intervening. Thus it is written of sinners generally that "Their foot shall slide in due time," Deuteronomy 32:35, and this sin is specifically said to be against one's own body, 1Corinthians 6:18, for it tends to physical death, having neither justification nor excuse in the eyes of the offended husband, Prov. 6:30-35. Many murders are committed because of a strange woman.

In Proverbs 2:20-22.

There are only two pathways through the present life: (1) The one that God dictates in His Word, and (2) Satan's erratic and evil way which leads to perdition. One is extremely narrow and so unpopular and not crowded; the other is extremely broad, popular and many people are therein, Matthew 7:13-14. It takes much self-denial to walk in a narrow way, but it is, ultimately, the only way of all good—eternal good. The materialist, the opportunist, the self-seeker, etc., will not have the faith to wait for this, but in seeking present pleasures and possessions, will miss out on true good.

There is a great and encouraging prophecy given in 2:21-22. It is the final triumph of the righteous over the wicked. The righteous that possess the divine wisdom here are described and may walk in the ways of good men also dwell safely in the land, but the wicked are doomed to defeat and final banishment. The parable and example are taken from trees being cut down or plucked up, as in Matthew 3:10 and 15:13. Whatsoever is not rooted in truth is of short duration and destined for the eternal burning, in another hand, the gratification of sins dies at a gasp, yet; the consequences could linger for life 1Corinthians 3:11-14, Revelation 20:15

MAN IS A SOCIAL UNIQUE CREATURE AND UNFORTUNATELY, IN SOME CASES, HE IS IMITATIVE OF OTHERS.

CHAPTER THREE

SUMMARY

Proverbs 3:1-10.

In this chapter, Wisdom continues the appeal to sons to take heed to the Divine law and wisdom which is so necessary for God's blessings. "A brief outline of this chapter is - Our duty to God; 1-12 the happy state of them that have wisdom 13-26 Man's duty to his fellow man 27-35.

Forgetfulness of God's law is the fault of the heart, not merely of the head. When the heart keeps God's precepts as a precious treasure, the memory does not easily forget them," Since the Law of God (Bible) is a manifestation of God's will for men, a standard conduct and that by which every person is going to be judged, then it is certainly an act of wisdom to know and keep it to the best of our ability Revelation 20:12, 19. The essence of sin is the transgression of God's law, 1John 3:4, and transgression of the law always originates in the heart, for no one ever yet acted out any sin but it was first incubated and meditated in the heart, which is the spring of all our actions, Matthew 15:19.

God is the source of life, peace and good; how then can men have these if they, by their wickedness, constantly antagonize Godhead and His Word;

the great Giver of all good, James 1:17. Often; God promises long life and joy for obeying His law, Deuteronomy 8:1; 30:19-20; 1Timothy 4:8. Most of the sickness and death that assails mankind is due directly to the transgression of the dietary laws that God gave in ancient time to Israel, and if these were carefully followed today, *much sickness would be eliminated. It is well known that most of the heart trouble, high blood pressure, cancer, etc., are due to abuse of the body. S. I. McMillan, a medical doctor, wrote "None of these Diseases" based on this idea. I recommend this book to you Exodus 15:26.*

If we would enjoy mercy and see good in our life, however, we must exercise it, and the truth is always to be exercised toward others Matthew 5:7 for to do otherwise is to be like the devil, John 8:44, and to be a candidate for hell, Revelation 21:8, 27; 22:15. But these are not to be mere ornaments about the neck; they are also to be the coded nugget of the heart. Only if they are in the heart will they be exercised outwardly Luke 6:45.

Divine wisdom is justified of all her children, Luke 7:35 because they practice the precepts of wisdom toward God and man. Our Lord alone fully realized the picture here, for He alone perfectly manifested mercy and truth as a man, Luke 2:52. It is the Lord's mercy and grace alone that many are saved from sin and its penalties, Ephesians 2:8; Titus 3:5. This truth must be transplanted in man's heart, and this is done in the new birth. John 3:5 Head faith is not a saving faith, but a heart belief is, Romans 10:9-10. This is to be a total trust "with all thine heart." Divided hearts are faulty in their faith toward God, Hosea 10:2. Hence, David prayed for his heart to be united to fear the Lord, Psalm 86:11-12. This, however, does not apply solely to salvation, for many heresies have been brought in because men tried to reason out doctrinal truth—leaning unto their own wisdom—instead of simply believing God's Word in all that is says.

Most of our failures are due to pride, for we think that our own wisdom, strength, and piety are sufficient, and so we do not acknowledge Him as necessary in all things. We need the knowledge that Jeremiah had, Jeremiah 9:23-24; 10:23. We need God's direction in everything, for this alone is a safe path to tread. Pride was the devil's own sin, and many humans have fallen into it also, 1Timothy 3:6; Isaiah 14:12-15; Ezekiel. 28:17. Pride is always hateful in God's sight, Proverbs 6:16-17; 16:5, 18. This is because pride always exalts itself against the Lord and tries to idolize self. The fear of the Lord is the beginning of wisdom. A right attitude and honor toward the Lord; i.e., a reverence for Him, makes for a healthy person mentally, morally, spiritually as well as physically. To honor the Lord with the firstfruits is to acknowledge His ownership of all things; to refuse to do so is to deny His ownership of all things. He blesses those who honor Him. God shall be no man's debtor: He shall repay that which is given to Him in Hundred folds when it is given with the proper attitude. It is to be carefully noted that this promise is not given just to him who "gives" to the Lord, but only to him who "honors" the Lord with His possessions. There can be a great difference.

V. 11 My son, despise not the chastening of the Lord; neither be weary of his correction. this shows that this chastisement is a lot of every child of God, and its absence betokens that God does not claim one. How comforting then is chastisement even while it smarts upon our backs. We should not despise it because of what it manifests about God's love for us. God's chastisement is always severe enough to turn the willful person back from sin, even if physical death is necessary, for He will not suffer the spirit to be lost, 1Corinthian 5:5. Since the body is but the "house" of the spiritual nature, it is not so important what happens to the body as it is what happens to the soul. We thank God for His loving chastisement.

All true happiness is based upon knowledge of, and submission to, the divine will of the Godhead, it is spoken of here as wisdom, since it is an act of highest wisdom to be submissive to God, who is the source of all good James 1:17. God delights to give good things to His children Matthew 7:7-11, but there are a correct order and way of obtaining all these goodies from Him Matthew 6:33. Silver and gold can only purchase with worldly things which are temporal at best, but this Divine wisdom can obtain for our eternal life, for it brings us into harmony with the Divine will. Job discussed this same matter and came to the same conclusion, Job 28:12-28. True Wisdom is considered to be a queen, to be desired above all things that any person could possibly possess. Alas, how few people really desire true spiritual wisdom: it is generally one of the last things to be desired to some people? Why is this? Because it directs us away from earthly things and selfish gratification, and points us rather to the Lord and to heavenly things, which the natural man has no concern for, and which even the truly saved person desires only as a last resort, and when he is cut off from the things of earth. Divine wisdom holds out both hands full of blessings to those who seek her: with one hand she holds out a long life, but this alone would not be worth anything unless there was the enjoyment of life as well, Ecclesiastics 6:3. God's way is the best for all it supplies for all a person's needs. The way of the world may be pleasant, but not safe, and some professed Christians hold to a way that is safe but not pleasant, but Divine wisdom shows a way that is both enjoyable and safe.

Vs. 18 -26

Divine Wisdom is a tree of life and much more to them that lay hold upon her: and happy is every one that retained her." The "tree of life" has always been man's hope of living on forever, and it has always been God's provision to be desired. "The fruit of other trees appeases hunger for a time: meanwhile; this tree of life is forever. It saves not merely from death, but from disease Revelation. 22:2, 14; 2:7; Ezekiel 47:12.

Salvation and service to God are the most personal duties in the world: no one can act for us. The Lord by wisdom hath founded the earth; by understanding hath he established the heavens." Here it is the recommendation of this wisdom, the original creation was brought about, and by consideration of the magnitude of that great work, and we can see how this wisdom will be all sufficient for our little petty needs. It also suggests why God has never had to revise, repair or otherwise change His original creation, it is because the original plan was "very good" in its origin, Genesis 1:31. Any imperfections now found are due to man's sinful disruption of the universe. Today the heavens operate with such perfect precision that all the clocks in the world are set by and corrected by the precision of the heavens, and time can be calculated to the precise second several thousands of years backward or forward by this precision. By His knowledge, the depths are broken up, and the clouds drop down the dew." And the dew in some dry areas of the world serve for the needs left lacking by the scarcity of rain. Dews in Israel are especially copious at times, Judges 6:38. Our great God knows how to supply every need of His people.

To keep sound wisdom and discretion, God in His everlasting love must continually sound forth His warnings and admonitions to us through various means and sometimes individual. Yet, if we do not have these things continually before our eyes, we forget them, Joshua 1:8. This is but a part of the ravages of sin—that we so easily let slip away spiritual things, Hebrew 2:1-2. One of Satan's favorite tricks is the stealing away of the Word, Matthew 13:19. Thus, while Divine wisdom is necessary for one to have eternal life, discretion is necessary for one to act out that life in such a way as to ornament the Christian life. Some truly saved people are very indiscreet in their ways so that they do not show grace by their actions.

We are saved by grace, Titus 3:7 and need grace to discreetly serve, Hebrew 12:28. In other words, there is safety for those who walk in God's way, but not for the rebellious, Proverbs 10:9; Psalms 91-11-12. Divine wisdom will prevent a man from stumbling over Christ, for it will only lead him to submit to Him and when he lies down, he shall not be afraid; yea, thou shalt lie down, and thy sleep shall be sweet. The night is the time when we are most defenseless for there is darkness to cover our enemies, and unconsciousness in sleep, yet there is safety even then for God's people, Lev. 26:6; Ps. 3:5. He will not be afraid in the night neither of the desolation of the wicked when it cometh." "Sudden fear" is panic—perhaps the worst kind of fear, for it attacks us when we are least prepared for it, yet not even this can permanently harm the follower of Divine wisdom. But for the "wicked," "Wicked" means to act impiously toward God in reversed order. For the Lord, Almighty is the confidence of the righteous, and He alone shall keep their foot from being taken." To trust the Lord is to be confident, for He has never betrayed the trust of any of His saints so that neither the snares of the world, the flesh, or the devil can take him who is directed by Divine wisdom. As the saints have security, Ps. 66:8-9, so there is an insecurity for the wicked, Deut. 32:35. "Feet" suggest the daily walk, so that there is promised protection for those who daily walk with Him, Prov. 28:26.

Proverbs 3:27-35

Here begins the last of the three divisions of this chapter—that which deals with man's duty to his fellow-creatures. "Here Solomon passes from general recommendations of wisdom to particular precepts. "Withhold not good from them to whom it is due when it is in the power of thy hand to do it." Many are guilty of defrauding their neighbors simply because they have not recognized that the Bible teaches that we are to love our neighbors "as ourselves," Matthew 22:39. We all have a duty to love one another, which is a fulfilling of the law, especially in the latter six commandments, Roman 13:7-10. We are therefore obligated to do good to all men, Gal. 6:10 and the failure to do so is a sin, James 4:17. The ancient Greeks had an adage: "A slow-paced favor is a flavorless favor

"Who is my neighbor?" is used as an excuse by many, but Jesus taught a parable to show that they are neighbors where one has a need and another has the remedy for that need, Luke 10:25-27. After having praised benevolence toward neighbors, Solomon passes on to forbid malevolence toward one's neighbors. If refusal to do good when one has the ability is sin, how much more is it sin to do evil to one's neighbor; yea, it is of two folds wickedness when that one (neighbor) is innocently and unsuspectingly dwelling peaceably by him.

The true Wisdom enjoins us not to strive with our neighbor without cause if he has done us no harm." Alas, how many of man's strife's have had no adequate cause, rather, most arising from pride, greed, touchiness, evil ambition, lust, unconcern for others etc? The divine command is for us to live at peace if at all possible, Romans 12:18-21. When strife arises, it is general because two people are both too conceited and proud to admit that they might be wrong. It always takes two to make a fuss. If only one is cantankerous he will soon become known for what he is, and will be shunned by all wise people. Sometimes strife is necessary and has good cause, but this is not often the case. Certainly, it is not justifiable when one has not been really harmed. Most fancied hurts are more the result of excessive touchiness and vivid imaginations than of real hurts. Envy thou, not the oppressor, and choose none of his ways. Solomon here made us understand that Envy is generally based upon the conceited idea that we are not receiving the fame or fortune that we really deserve, and that someone else is receiving more than he deserves. It has its roots in self-righteousness Psalms 37:1-2. "Oppressor" is literally "a man of violence" and it suggests that he gets what he wants anyway that he can, with no compunction even if he has to hurt someone in doing so. The only sin could so blind man that he puts more value on things than upon people.

The froward, for all of his seeming prosperity in this life, is not to be envied, for he is under the Lord's frown and in due time will taste of the wrath of an offended God, Psalms 37:16-20. The righteous, though they may seem to be greatly disadvantaged in the present life, yet; they have God's secret with them, and they shall see the fulfillment of His covenant promises, Psalms 25:14.

The Lord shall bless the justified man, though it does not always so clearly appear so in this life, for God has most of His blessings stored up for eternity. His household (i.e., his descendants) shall continue to grow numerically and spiritually so long as they are taught the truth, but the house of the wicked, like a leper's dwelling, shall be pulled down and destroyed lest the plague of sin spread, Lev. 14:44-45; Zech. 5:3-4. The greatest mansion is like a foundation which is built upon just principles. However, "house" and "habitation" here probably are more in reference to families than they are to material buildings.

In parallel to v. 32 and the explanation of its meaning; to be an abomination to the Lord is to have His curse upon one's house. Evil men are almost, and or always a curse to their whole family for their evil teachings and their example is so often followed by their families so that the curse must also fall upon them. None suffer unjustly, for when the children of an evil man recognize his evil and turns from it, God's blessings come upon them, Ezekiel 18:14-23. God reacts differently to those who humble themselves under His Almighty hand: He gives them the necessary grace to do His will. It is characteristic of the proud to scorn God's people because of their humility, but in the end, God's people will be exalted, and the proud will be held in everlasting contempt, Isa. 66:23-24; Dan. 12:2. How often is man's condition reversed at the moment of death, Luke 16:19-23, we see this reversal in both Lazarus and the rich man. Death strips a man of all their pretensions, possessions, and promotions, and only the promotion that God gives shall remain. "When glory shall be the promotion and peculiar and permanent inheritance of the godly wise, shame shall be the only promotion that ungodly fools shall have," "The wise shall inherit glory: but shame shall be the promotion of fools."

TRUE HAPPINESS IS NOT FOUND IN ANY OTHER REWARD THAN THAT OF BEING UNITED WITH GOD – CHRISTIANITY GIVES LIFE A MEANING

CHAPTER FOUR

SUMMARY

Proverbs 4:1

"Hear, ye children, the instruction of a father, and attend to know understanding." "Ye children … a father," being somewhat abstract, may mean that Solomon is acting the part of spiritual father: i.e., an instructor. Paul contrasted instructors and fathers in 1 Corinthians 4:15, for an instructor, only teach the truth, but a father is the instrument of the new birth. Solomon seeks to instruct his hearers so that they come to accept divine wisdom which is necessary to salvation.

Note: the proper order: "hear … know understanding." The reason so many know so little truth is that they refuse that whereby faith comes, Rom. 10:17. For I give you good doctrine, forsake ye not my law." "Doctrine" means teaching or that which is taught. Because some doctrines are deep and mysterious, many people assume that all doctrine is incapable of being understood by any but theologians and philosophers. "Good" implies that some doctrine is not good, as the N.T. teach Matthew 15:9; 16:11-12; Eph. 4:14; Col. 2:20-23; 1 Tim. 4:1; Heb. 13:9; Rev. 2:14-15.

Vs. 2-10-14,

"Only beloved" does not mean that Solomon was the only son of David and Bathsheba. Though there were others, 1 Chron. 3:5, not that these were slighted by their mother. Isaac was also called Abraham's "only son," though several other sons are named, Gen. 22:12, 16. The Hebrew word that appears in these three places appears only twelve times. It signifies one peculiarly beloved, as occupying a special place. Bathsheba certainly knew that Solomon was to succeed David as King, 1 Chron. 22:6-10; 1 Kings 1:15-21, and so that he was a special person in God's sight. David used almost the exact words here of Solomon in 1 Chronicles 29:1. It is natural for parents to love their children, but when God has chosen to use one in a special way, this especially endears that child to godly parents.

Good practices ought to be passed on from generation to generation. Apparently, David had been less strict with his older sons 1 Kings 1:6, and they turned out badly, Absalom and Adonijah both trying to usurp his kingdom, 2 Sam. 15:1; 1 Kings 1:5. But, he was stricter with the younger sons, and Solomon especially turned out well, 1 Kings 3:3.

There is little evidence of any real piety in Absalom or Adonijah. Later Solomon will emphasize the value of early training and teaching of children, Prov. 22:6. The good old way is still the best way for the souls of men, Jer. 6:16, for there, is no new truth. Someone has well said, "If it's new, it can't be true."

In fact, God places parents as a fundamental teacher for children. Godly parents ought to be able to pass down the godly truth and moral facts to the children. Though young people, as they come into their late teens, they tend to think parents were very ignorant and old fashion, but they learn shortly that parents are not so dumb after all. Again wisdom is personified and treated as a beautiful and desirable woman whose presence guarantees one's safety. Indeed, 2Thessalonians. 2:10, love of the truth is shown to be necessary for salvation. What then of those who are contemptuous of this Divine wisdom? In rejecting and forsaking all Truth about Divine God, that is to sin against one own soul, 8:35-36.

The wisdom of God, having the omniscient (all-knowing), and being directed to man for his good, cannot but be a blessing to all who receive it, for it saves men from temporal and eternal harm and destructions.

There is Nothing that is as important as the pursuit of wisdom and understanding: with wisdom, all good things will eventually come: without it, though one may have many good things, they will eventually be lost and give one no lasting benefits. Conversely, the world thinks that riches is the one needful thing but wisdom gives so many things that money cannot buy—pardon, peace and paradise, to name three, (see Prov. 16:16). On the other hand, how much would the whole world worth if one lost his own soul because he was not wise unto salvation? Matthew 16:29.

Promotion and praise are gifts of wisdom to those who receive it, and this promotion and praise are of the lasting kind. Satan, because this world is under his domination, Luke 4:6, can give men worldly promotion and the praise of men, but this is all so very temporary, and then eternity shall reveal their degradation and shame. It is not enough just to pay lip service to God's wisdom: we must exalt and embrace it. See the similar statement in 1 Samuel 2:10 which simply traces this principle back to its source.

The gift that wisdom bestows on us was the present life, while the second of this kind is the life to come. Certainly, it is true that we receive grace now and glory to come, whether this is the present meaning or not. But Psalm 84:11 shows both grace and glory as present possessions of all who walk uprightly.

Vs. 11- It is natural for parents to be concerned that their children live long and well healthy. Unfortunately, children often think they know better what is best for them than their parents do, but it is always "want—to" instead of "know—so. Book learning, however, extensive it may be, is not as valuable as learning by experience, and most parents have at least twenty years more practical knowledge than their children. In another word, though; good counsel may not be Godly counsel it is apparent for each man to whose counsel to accept. I have taught thee in the way of wisdom; I have led thee in right paths." Here are the two sides of right teaching: instruction and example. Both are necessary. Many people teach without setting an example: "Do as I say, not as I do," but this is hypocritical, and produces a worse generation of hypocrites. This was what was wrong with the Pharisees, Matthew 23:1-4.

"Way" and "path" are both suggestive of the daily walk so that this has to do with practical knowledge, not merely with the theoretical. So far from one's pathway being narrow and dangerous, the Lord will enlarge it for those following wisdom's teachings, Ps. 18:36. Wisdom both smoothes and broadens our pathway for us.

One of Satan's favorite ploys is to steal the true Word away from us, Matthew 13:19. Hence; there is a need to continually refresh our knowledge of the truth, and practice it daily. People are not saved by keeping the law, but they are saved by Christ who kept it for us, and who is our Wisdom, Righteousness, Sanctification and Redemption, 1Corinthians 1:30. "Obedience to God's law is life; every departure from it is a step towards death. The child of God has no business walking in fellowship with the wicked, for their ways will become his if he does. The man is a social creature, and, unfortunately, in some cases, he is imitative of others.

Vs. 4:15-21.

This and the preceding verse contain no less than six warnings to keep clear of evil. One is not to hang around with temptation, nor to debate about whether it is really evil or not, nor to delay to flee from it. It is a wise maxim that says "If it's questionable, it's wrong." 1 Thessalonians 5:21-22 plainly obligates us to: (1) Test all things. (2) Retain the good. (3) Reject all that even appears evil. It doesn't have to be clearly evil: if it appears so, it must be rejected. Joseph wisely practiced this rule, Gen. 39:10-12. The best remedy for all temptation is to flee from it. Sadly, sinners always try to talk others into joining them in their sins. Sin, like leaven, is permeative.

This is similar to Psalm 36:4, it is common for men upon their beds to make plans for the next day, and the character of those plans will be determined by the character of the man himself. The children of darkness make sin their element. The children of light should learn similarly to give themselves no sleep till they have done or devised good Ps. 132:4; Prov. 6:4. So vicious are the wicked that they often "eat up" the righteous by their violence toward them, Ps. 53:4. Not only do they enjoy wickedness and violence—it is a refreshment to them—and also; their livelihood is also by them.

The danger of fellowshipping with those who delight in wickedness is such terrible that one cannot win with them, for, as Matthew Henry says: "Thou wilt ruin thyself if thou dost concur with them (chap. 1:18) and they will ruin thee if thou dost not." Sin pays wages, but they are the wages of eternal death, Rom. 6:23. But the Lord came that His people might not walk in darkness but have the light of life, John 8:12, for in Him there is no darkness at all, 1 John 1:5, and the more we trust Him and follow Him the lighter He leads us. He is the Day the Sun, 2 Pet. 1:19, who enlighten us as we follow Him, 1 John 1:5-7. Salvation makes us children of light and of the day, 1 Thess. 5:4-8.

Those who walk in spiritual darkness are but a step from tumbling into the bottomless pit of hell, yet how merrily and unconcernedly do they go tripping through life. As the path of the just shines more and more unto brightness, (v. 18), so the path of the wicked is one of increasing darkness until it ends in the blackness of darkness forever, Matthew 22:11-13; 25:30; 2 Pet. 2:17; Jude 12-13. Vs. 4:22.

The truth shown here were of two uses: and they are similes (1) Food that gives life, as Jesus taught, John 5:39. (2) Medicine that purges sickness and promotes health. The truth has a cleansing, purging effect, Ps. 119:9; Eph. 5:26. Because Satan does his best to substitute other things for Truth, for he well knows that this is the only instrument for healthy spiritual life, salvation, sanctification and edification, 2 Tim. 3:15-16.

Alas; how many preachers and churches have allowed the Word to be taken away and some worthless pattern, philosophy and man-made doctrine substituted for it, to leave the heart unguarded is to surrender the whole citadel of the soul. Sin has so corrupted some hearts, however, that it cannot perform its ordained function until it has been cleansed and changed in the new birth. This will be the result of keeping the heart with diligence: it will control man's whole life and conduct. All sin stems from a bad heart, Matthew 15:19; Acts 8:21-23. Lips only speak what is in the heart. People sin quicker and easier with the mouth than in any other way, James 3:2.

Vs. 4:25-27 Lay emphasis on the different parts of the body in verses 20-27. These can be used either for good or for evil and if they are not sanctified to do good they will naturally turn to evil uses. Jesus warned about lustful looks, Matthew 5:28-29. The right use of the eyes is declared in Isaiah 45:22; Hebrews 12:2; 2 Peter 3:12-14. And the right use of our feet we are not to rashly and thoughtlessly walk through life: to do so is to end up in hell. In other hands "Walk cautiously, Ephesians 5:15, and walk uprightly, Galatians 2:14.

Many think only of present momentary pleasure, with no regard to the end of the matter. Remember Jesus' warning about the straight and narrow way, Matthew 7:13-14. All temptations are attempts to turn us aside into sinful byways instead of walking in the King's highway of righteousness. Wisdom leads us into right ways: sin turns us to the right or to the left hand unto evil. Let us ponder the path we tread.

WHATSOEVER IS PURE, TRUE AND LOVELY ALWAYS THINK ON
ALL THESE THINGS STRIFE FOR CLEAN HANDS AND PURE HEART

CHAPTER FIVE

SUMMARY

Proverbs 5:1

Sex drive is a powerful force in most people, and the temptation to a misuse of it is a very common one. Here is a warning against this. "Solomon's lectures are not designed to fill our heads with matters of nice speculation, or doubtful disputation, but to guide us in the right paths for ourselves

Once again there is an appeal to the young ones to take heed to the wisdom of the parents and godly elders, who have much more experience and learning in the ways of the world. In every temptation, we need to think beyond the momentary pleasure and consider what will be the consequences if we yield to it. Here the thought is the same as in Proverbs 2:11, 16. Discretion and knowledge are needed to overcome the subtle and flattering words of the immoral woman who allures with smooth words, as in verse 3.

The agents for sin always picture it in beautiful hues, as it were between Eve and serpent in the garden of Eden Genesis 3: never in the awful blackness that it's real characteristic. A sample of this found in Proverbs 7:7-21.

Alas, how many have been persuaded by the sweetness and smoothness of a tongue given over to the service of sin and Satan. Only the oil of the gracious Spirit's leading and daily walking in the Word can counteract the appeal of this sweetness and smoothness.

The sin of fornication in reality, and are bitterly poisonous, yea, so fatal in many cases, for the sin of fornication is a sin against one's own body, 1 Cor. 6:18, but God's Word, is the only antidote to temptation, is sharper than any two-edged sword, Heb. 4:12. Immorality leads to death. "Death" here means the destruction of the body, and "hell" the destruction of the soul; it is not profitable either physically and or spiritually. Sin, of whatever sort it is, be it Wickedness, evil societies etc., is always a downward path that grows more slippery the further one goes in it, Ps. 73:18-19; Jer. 23:12. The Fornicators, Armed bandit, and witchcraft generally are characteristically using flattery, deceit and violent to gain their own ends, Prov. 2:16; 7:21. This characteristic they receive from their father the devil, John 8:44.

LIFE APPLICATION:

In 1989, there was a day I was in the kitchen preparing stick meat I was selling during break time at school. It was during the evening time the Spirit of God told me that one of the tenants was an adulterous and a witch, she was using that her apartment a place of slaughter for men. I left what I was doing to preach Christ and salvation to her and to let her know what the Spirit of God said about her. I was surprised she did not say anything, she was just quiet. I did not know that she was thinking a revenge on me.

The very second day of the scenario, I caught the train in motion and the train was dragging me on the track, then, I had no strength in me, but; God Almighty gave me strengths and I shouted for help, a man heard me and quickly shout back that there was a girl on rail, please help!! and people came to lift me up, they were like questioning me what is my problem; I could not give a reason, but I know that I do not want to miss the train may be because I do not have an alternative and also to sell my stick meat cause me to do that.

I came back home with 7:30am train because I lost one of my sandals, immediately this strange woman saw me she ran inside and my spirit man told me she was the one that project that attack, I then went back to school with after 9:00am train – all this happen just because I minister Christ to her, and within few days she packed out without even seeing each other again. I pray she found Peace.

Another of this kind was when my mummy's friend told me how her Christian mother, someone to like be her role model sold away her offspring to wickedness. She killed her daughter's husband, caused her boys to become highway armed robber and the girls' prostitutes and yet this woman mere seeing as a Christian woman, May good God deliver us from this kind of wolves. Dear reader, you can see that spirits of wickedness, revenge, armed robbery and prostitution cob round the terrible spirit of witchcrafts

Proverbs 5:7-20 In these particular verses; Two dangers are here expressed: (1) Refusing to hear the warning. (2) Hearing, but forsaking it by yielding to the entreaties of the immoral woman. Hearing alone is not enough: the advice must be acted upon, else it is worthless. Yet, how quickly is advice spurned from our parents because we conceitedly think that we already know it all? We harm ourselves most of all when we refuse to hear vs. 7, James 1:22.

The nearer we approach temptation, the more alluring it becomes, and the weaker becomes our spiritual strength. Our safety is in flight. Therefore, we are often admonished to "flee" from temptation, 1Corinthian 6:18; 10:14; 1Timothy 6:11; 2Timothy 2:22. Sin often comes about by first admiring it, then lusting after it, and then committing it. We can cut it off in its first stage by fleeing from it, and this shows our honor to God and man.

An honorable person is one who does not transgress or violate his or her neighbor, property or the rights of others. The adulterer destroys his own honor when he violates his own or others' marriage vows, for he shows himself to be totally selfish, with concern only for his own pleasure regardless of whom he hurts. An adulterer is not really interested in the honor of his or her partner in crime or persons, but rather in their wealth.

Thus, this sin tends, not only to take away the honor and the life but also the estate of life. In our modern world, blackmail of adulterous business men is commonplace, and there are numerous schemes to accomplish this. Remembering that adultery was a capital crime in Israel, Leviticus 20:10, this was a weighty tool for a wronged husband to hold over a transgressor.

In a very recently, venereal diseases ravaged without check, and many lives were destroyed or at least made worthless and miserable, and while penicillin has cured many of these, yet new strains have developed recently which are immune to it and many inmates of insane asylums are there because of venereal diseases. Folly can only be covered up so long, and it will finally be manifest, but the longer it is denied and covered up, the greater it becomes and his own folly will, at last, convince the sinner. Better to be informed and reformed now than to be conformed to the world until one is spiritually deformed. One of the terrors of hell will be the many appetites that men have created for themselves which will be impossible to satisfy in hell. So long as one is ashamed of his or her sin, there may be hope for him, but there is little hope for the one who sins openly and unashamedly, only judgment and final irremediable humiliation await such.

In Vs.15 our desires resemble thirst, to drink water means to gratify a desire, and the woman is compared to a well. It then shows that lawful Marriage and its pleasures are the divine antidotes to fornication and adultery, 1Corinthian 7:1-2. Cisterns and wells were generally the only two sources of water in the East, and almost every house had a cistern to catch rainwater, 2Kings 18:31. Jesus used "drink" in a spiritual sense of satisfying spiritual thirst, John 6:35, 53-56. As the wife is likened to a well, or to a cistern, so "fountains" and "rivers" represent children, which are regarded as special blessings from the Lord, Psalm 127:3, 128:3; Zechariah 8:3-5, and barrenness was considered as a reproach, 1Sam. 1:2, 5-11.

Godly children are always a credit to their parents, but sinful children are a curse to them, Proverbs 10:1, 5; 15:20; 17:25; 19:13, 26. The mother is said to be "saved," i.e., to live on and on, in her children "if they continue in faith, love, and holiness," 1 Timothy 2:15, but if they are wicked, then she would be better not to have lived at all than to have produced a brood of evildoers. Since children are waters that issue from the fountain of a man and a woman, what they reflect back are directly from their parents, for the waters shall be as the fountain is, James 3:11. Children are to honor their parents, and in no better way can they do this, than by godly living. Yet; the first duty of parents is to see that they have none but legitimate children, by remaining faithful in marriage. Illegitimate marital affairs are almost always an indication of immaturity and insecurity, and we can see the deadly outcomes of this?

There is no justification for the common practice of a man leaving his wife of his youth neither for a younger companion nor even for temporary unfaithfulness to her. See the reference to the "wife of thy youth" in Malachi 2:14-16. Clearly, throughout the Scriptures, marriage is meant to be a happy state for both parties. If thou would go to excess, let it not be with a strange woman, but with thy own wife. Satan beguiles people into believing that forbidden things are always sweeter, Prov. 9:17. That was his lies from the beginning, the cost is so high, and there can be no profit in its Genesis 3:1-11.

LIFE APPLICATION:

In 1991, one of my daddy's in the Lord had a layman friend who was in terrible sickness; he was just losing weight without good reasons even, after many series of tests. He then came in contacts with this man of God for prayers of deliverance. They were getting ready to go on the mountain when a prophesy came that his problem was as a result of strange and adulteress woman he had as a lover and or partner in sexual sin. She made him signed his *Will* out and some other documents of his Estates and properties; this woman passes this horrible sickness through charmed vegetable soup, in other to kill him gradually.

Proverbs 5:21-23

There is nothing that goes on anywhere in the world, of which the Lord did not know all about it. Many people act as if God was confined to His temple in heaven, outside of which He knew nothing of what was going on in the heart of man, but not even the darkest night can hide men's activities from the eyes of the all-seeing One, Ps. 139:1-16. It is folly to sin when one cannot be hidden. The sinner will not forsake his sins: but he hopes that his sins will forsake him in old age, but it never works that way. Sin persisted and forms a sinful character which binds him in his wickedness.

God needs no prison for the wicked, for they are bound in their own darkness and wickedness which can be taken away only by the abounding grace of God, Rom. 5:20-21. If this is rejected by men, there remains no more remedy for sin, but only certain judgment, Heb. 10:26-29. It is part of the deceptiveness of sin, that man is always led to believe that there will always be time for repentance later on after he has fully drunk of sin to the full "He shall die without instructions; and in the greatness of his folly he shall go astray 2Corinthian 2:6B, 1John 5:16.

The world is full of human leeches who are willing to take advantage of the good-hearted, but gullible, and they often use the Christian's natural desire to do good to defraud him. They often profess to be friends (in need) when in reality they are strangers (to honesty). The Christian is not obligated to give to every request for help; sometimes it is a sin to do so, if it encourages laziness, sloth, dishonesty, etc. "Surety" is one who stands in good for, or guarantees someone else. Its first appearance, in Genesis 43:9, shows its meaning. "There is a warning here, as elsewhere in this book, against all kinds of suretyship. Compare 11:15; 17:18; 20:16; 22:26-27; 27:13,"

We must always stand by our word when once it is given, but we must also use wisdom and discretion in giving our word lest we are bound to a debt that we cannot pay. Youth, being not as experienced in the evil ways of men, would be easily engaged to stand for a seeming friend, who being without conscience, would use him then forsake him.

LIFE APPLICATION:

How many Bank Managers and or Business entities were in prison just because they trusted a friend and or seemly good customers? The tenacious ones without conscience will even go to the extent of charmed off the payments of their loan and as a result of this, whosoever stands as a surety will be in trouble. What about Marriages vow and oaths taken on the D-days, all was forgotten just because of unfaithfulness and divorce and all the witnesses and surety blame themselves for involvement. Many of these kinds of confusion in the world Romans 13:8.

AN INHERITANCE QUICKLY GAINED AT BEGINNING WILL NOT BE BLESSED AT THE END

CHAPTER SIX

SUMMARY

Proverbs 6:3-5

Do this now, my son, and deliver thyself, when thou art come into the hand of thy friend; go, humble thyself, and make sure thy friend." It is natural to try to proudly force one's way out of such a situation, but the better way is to humble oneself to either the debtor or to the judge so that he could get released from the responsibility he had incurred.

There is an ancient proverb that applies here: "While the word is unspoken, you are master of it; when once it is spoken, it is master of you." Humility is not enjoyable, but often it is the only way of escape from a self-induced problem such as this. "Give not sleep to thine eyes, nor slumber to thine eyelids." That is, rest not until you have delivered yourself from this responsibility. Under these circumstances, delay only increases the chances that one will not be able to get free of the bond one has taken upon himself.

Sometimes we may like to think that if we ignore the problem and go to sleep, it will go away while we are asleep and or some think it is when they get drunk, but it seldom does. "Deliver thyself as a roe from the hand of the hunter, and as a bird from the hand of the fowler." The roe (a type of gazelle or antelope) is a symbol of swiftness, 2Samuel. 2:18; 1Chronicle 12:8. The bird (possibly a sparrow) suggests a readiness to fly away at the first sign of danger, for it seldom takes more than one or two bites without looking around for signs of danger, and the least unusual sound will send it winging away. Tarrying in the face of danger is a quick way to get caught. Hence the wise thing here advocated is to seek deliverance from this legal bondage as soon as it is possible to do so; - to flee in alarm from it.

In Proverbs 6:6 the bible forbid slothfulness and laziness "Go to the ant, thou sluggard, consider her ways, and be wise." There is a sermon to us in every part of nature if we will but consider it, for God has created it all, and has designed it to testify of Him. Yet, though man is the highest of God's creation, and has almost infinite potential for wisdom, sin has so degenerate him that he needs to be taught by the lowliest of insects. "The ant does not borrow or beg, nor is it starved by neglecting to provide for its wants in time, but of its own accord burns with zeal for toil, without anyone urging it. All the ants move on the same path. The ants that are without a load make way for those most laden. The burden which would be too difficult to carry they divide … They construct their houses and cells underground, and fill their stores with grain, and have channels sunk to drain off the rain, and if their food becomes wet, they bring it out to dry, this is great and Marvelous natural wisdom.

Study the Ants careful, they have no guide, overseer, or ruler." Some people must be the leader or they will not work at all: others must be, like wheelbarrows, constantly pushed; else no work is done by them. Both classes need to consider the ant and learn from it, for it has no ambitions to lead, yet all are ambitious to work for the common good. What a wonderful world this would be if everyone cooperated in this way. Nothing is more orderly or busier than an ant hill or bee hive, yet neither requires rulers with whips to get the work done. Common needs prompt to common concern and common effort. They gather their meat in the summer and gathered their food in the harvest. The lesson here is preparedness in the time of opportunity; make use of good opportunities available to you Proverbs 30:24-28. Alas, how many people are neglecting the opportunity to become children of the light and to walk in the light until one day they will no longer have the opportunity, John 12:35-36.

The whim of Delay is one of Satan's best tools in the damnation of souls. Our duty is to work while it is the day before the night comes when no man can work, 1Thess. 5:4-8; Ephesians 5:14. The sluggard is the slothful man, and this same Hebrew word is also rendered "slothful" more commonly. He is simply the man who refuses to labor, Proverbs. 21:25; 24:30-31. From the time that sin entered the human race, labor has been a lot of each of us, Genesis 3:17-19, and a part of the curse. Churches, which were originally the ones responsible for feeding the poor and the needy, were commanded not to feed any who would not work, 2Thessalonica 3:10-14. Earning our food by labor being a result of the curse brought about by original sin. Vs.10 "Yet a little sleeps, a little slumber, a little folding of the hands to sleep." Note the descending gradation from deep sleep to the lighter slumber to just the preparations for sleep. Scientists now know that there are stages of sleep ranging from deep sleep bordering on total unconsciousness up to very light sleep which is almost wakefulness. We all know how hard it is to wake up sometimes, and how easy it is to drift back into a sounder sleep.

There is a danger of becoming both a physical and a spiritual sluggard by yielding to this physically and spiritually. If we promise ourselves a little more ease before we rise up to our work, we may slip into a deeper sleep than we think and fail to awaken when we think through and it will be unprofitable and too late. In another hand; consequently and literally poverty set in, he becomes as one that travelleth, "one that travelleth" as a highwayman" which would seem to be a better parallel to "armed robber," vs. 11. Therefore the Spirit of Wisdom warns of loss by becoming surety to another, or by being slothful in work. God shows us how to prosper even in business for He is graciously concerned that we have the best of this world, as well as that which is to come. Jehovah Elohim deserved our Praises and worship.

Proverbs 6:12-19

A naughty person, a wicked man, walked with a froward mouth. To act without Wisdom is naughty, wickedness is an evil as the Hebrew word suggests. Most commonly it is rendered as "Belial" as in Deuteronomy 13:13; Judges 19:22; 1Samuel 2:12, all of which show the depth of wickedness that this practice. "Froward" is the same word as in 4:24, and means "distorted" or "perverse." It is not the physical shape of the mouth that is meant, but rather what comes out of it that is perverse and distorted. "He winked with his eyes, he speaketh with his feet, he teaches with his fingers." By subtle and secret signs the man of Belial manifests the evil that is in his heart, (v. 14; also see Job 15:12). The different terms, mouth, eyes, feet, and fingers, all show that he is wholly given over to wickedness.

The froward man is he who is idle in righteousness, but busy in evil. This was the cause of Sodom's sin, Ezekiel 16:49. "Frowardness is in his heart, he devises mischief continually; he soweth discord." Anyone can fall into sin, but the man of Belial lives in sin, delights in it, and devices it continually. It is the characteristic of his life. He delights in it whether it is profitable to him or not. Alas, how evil must he be who delights to do evil simply for evil's sake? Sin has always been the great disrupter of the universe, and Satan the great sower of discord between brethren. But there is justice for such: judgment shall find those who love and practice wickedness; Isaiah 33:1, suddenly shall he be broken without remedy." "Without remedy" means without healing, Proverbs 29:1; Jeremiah 14:19; same word.

One of the deceptions that Satan practices is in telling sinners that they will always have time to repent just before judgment falls upon them. It is true that God hates all sin, but some seem to be especially odious to Him, and thus; draw forth a speedier judgment.

A proud look, a lying tongue, and hands shed innocent blood. Pride is always hateful in the eyes of God because it partakes of the nature of self-worship, which is idolatry, 16:5. Haughty eyes (margin) simply evidences what is in the heart, and so are also hateful, Psalms 18:27; 101:5; 131:1.

The lying tongue is a direct agreement of the ninth commandment, Exodus 20:16, as well as being an imitation of the devil, John 8:44. The truth is always pure, and needs no misrepresentation to establish it: he, who will lie, shows that he is not of the truth, 1John 2:21. The third of these hateful things is blood-thirstiness, which is always characterized by a supreme love of self, and disregard of others. Men of blood are guilty men, Genesis 9:4-6, their prayers go unanswered, Isaiah 1:15; and they shall be given blood to drink as a judgment, Revelation 16:6. The heart is the fountain while the feet carry out the thoughts of the heart, like a stream, carries out the waters of the fountain.

A false witness that speaks lies and him that sows discord among the brethren, there are at least three distinct sins committed by this one: (i) in being a false witness, one sins against God, whose name is invoked in giving witness. (ii) The lies are directed at others, whose characters are besmirched by the lies. (iii) The lies told alienate the brethren from him who is lied against so that they are led to feel hard toward him without cause. The false witness must answer to God for all three of these, for it is his words that have multiplied sin. The distinction in faithful and false witnesses is drawn in 14:5, 25. Satan uses malicious tongues to sow discord among those who should always be unified, for his philosophy is "Divide and conquer." An American statesman said in Revolutionary times: "We must all hang together or we shall surely all hang, separately."

Proverbs 6:20-34,

My son; keep thy father's commandment, and forsake not the law of thy mother. 1:8; 3:1. For one thing, to dishonor parents is to shorten one's physical life, Ephesians 6:1-3, for it is only right that parents be obeyed since they occupy the place of God in the child's mind until he is old enough to understand the concept of God. How parents live and act will determine how the children think of God in later years. Parents' teachings shape and mold their children's minds and manners. If truth has been bound upon the heart, then there will not be wicked imaginations in the heart. But the meaning here is simply that men were to learn the law, and to bow their necks to its teachings. Contrast Proverbs 29:1; Jeremiah 7:26; 17:23; 19:15.

A stiff neck in the Bible symbolizes rebellion against the Word of God. The Word of the Lord is not only a command, it is also a counselor to lead us in the right way, a controller to keep us safe from evil, and a companion to converse with on our journey through life. He who is always led by the Word of the Lord will never walk long in wrong paths, nor will danger be able to over-take him, since the Word prescribes the way of escape from temptation, 1 Cor. 10:13 and it always a comfort to hear its blessed promises which it speaks to us.

How much sorrow would be averted if people would but hear and heed the Word? But; the very fact that the Word is the antidote to so much sin and sorrow, this is the very reason Satan tries so hard to divert people from God's Word. "For the commandment is a lamp, and the law is light, and reproofs of instruction are the way of life." The soul of man is, by nature, in darkness: it needs an external illumination to lighten its way so that it can find the way of life eternal, and this need is supplied by the Word of God. Any law, but especially the Law of God, is given to direct man into right paths where there is no condemnation because of transgression.

The Word of God is often likened to that which gives light, Psalms 19:8; 119:105. But neither this nor any other text ever implies or means that men are saved by keeping God's law, for none can do so to perfection, which is what is demanded. The law does not save except by condemning sin and sinners and then directing men to the Saviour who alone can save, Romans 3:19-22; Galatians 3:11-13, 19, 22-24. However people may dislike being reproved by the Word, it is still the way of life. The Rhema (spoken Word of God through His Divine Spirit and Logos – Bible) are to keep thee from the evil woman, from the flattery of the tongue of a strange woman." Solomon seems to dwell upon this particular danger, which is one of the most common dangers to youth also.

The more we read the warnings in the Word of God against this sin, the less likely we will be deceived into yielding to it as if it were some great good that we could not do without, which is always Satan's persuasive pitch. "Lust not after her beauty in thine heart; neither let her take thee with her eyelids." Here Solomon, in agreement with our Lord in Matthew 5:28; 15:19, traces this sin ultimately to the heart where it is first harbored and incubated before it is acted out, but it is real even when it is in the heart, and so it is guilty. Thus, many sins—lust, pride, unbelief, etc., —that are never seen by any man, are recorded against the man by God. "Take thee with her eyelids" probably refers to a woman's flirtatious looks by which she captures the male attention. In ancient times, even as now, women often painted their eyes to accentuate them so that they could better catch the attention of men as they flirted with them, 2Kings 9:30; Ezekiel 23:40.

The devil's mode of operations is always (i) Look, (ii) Lust, (iii) Enticement, (iv) Sin, (v) Death (vi) Damnation James 1:14-15. The secret of escape is, never dwell upon forbidden things. "For by means of a whorish woman a man is brought to a piece of bread: and the adulteress will hunt for the precious life." "Intercourse with the 'whorish woman' —i.e., the adulterous 'wife of a man' is bought at the cost of losing not only one's substance, but even one's life—the life of nature, of grace, and of eternal bliss.

In the old Testaments, the detected adulterer was put to death," The thought here seems to be that a man's transgressions with such a woman may reduce him to utter poverty—so that he possesses no more than a single piece of bread. (Read some Life Applications in my other Inspirational book Titled: The Divine Godhead with Divine Principle and Pattern – under Asmodee). And it is true that sinners, both male, and female, would rather entice a Christian to do evil, than another unsaved person, for a sinner is a so-called churchgoer Christian that makes the law of God Jehovah no effective by knowing the right things to do but decisively refuses to do them. Apostle Paul made mention of them, they ever learning, but they never measure up to the truth 2Timothy 3:2-8. "Can a man take fire in his bosoms and his clothes not be burned?" Just as a person could not wrap up a hot coal in his robe to carry it without it burning his robe, so one cannot take sin unto himself without bearing the marks of it Proverbs 6:27. There is a high cost for a careless and low living. The heat of unholy passion will certainly burn the individual, man or woman, who transgresses God's commandments in this matter.

It would take a greater miracle for the adulterer to escape judgment than for one to walk on hot coals without being burned, for in the case of the adulterer, the very holiness and justice of God are involved: God cannot close His eyes to sin: it must be reckoned with in judgment. See the results of David's sin in 2Samuel 12:7-14. It is interesting to note the likeness of fire to adultery in verses 27-28, for adultery, is considered a consuming fire in Job 31:9-12 and was indeed punished by burning at times, Genesis 38:24.

There is no way that any person can commit this sin and still be innocent in God's sight, for he is transgressing the property rights of another, violating marriage vows, scorning God's commandments, both concerning adultery, Exodus 20:14, and concerning covetousness, Exodus 20:17 he is destroying family relationships and setting evil examples for children, and only confusion and evil can come from it. Little wonder that even to touch a woman in a carnal way is forbidden, for "petting" is the first step toward fornication, 1Corinthian 7:1-2. Seldom people plan to commit fornication when they begin to touch one another familiarly, but it leads to it all too frequently.

Men do not despise a thief if he steals to satisfy his soul when he is hungry." Men do not despise the thief if he steals to satisfy physical hunger, yet he is still answerable to justice for his stealing, for it is wrong, yet it is not of the same nature of sin as the man who takes the wife of another man. The sex drive is also a hunger, yet it is one which has legitimate outlets, and he who violates the laws governing must answer for it. There are no excuses when it comes to breaking of Law and justice. It is far better to flee all appearance of evil before it consumes you without remedy.

Not even desperate need justification for breaking the law: how much less is there justification for breaking the law simply to fulfill one's lusts? No excuse is possible for the adulterer, for God has made provision for the legitimate exercise of desire, for "every man" and "every woman" is granted permission to have "his own wife" and "her own husband," 1 Corinthian 7:2. Whatsoever is otherwise than to this is a sin.

Adultery is often committed in the name of great love, but the marginal reading "heart" for "understanding," shows that the adulterer lacks even the capacity for true love. Those who are guilty of this sin are generally immature, insecure, self-centered persons who lack any depth of feeling for others, being primarily selfish in their desires. Fornication is a sin against one's own body and life, Job 331:9-12; 1Corinthian 6:18. There would be no overpopulation today if this law was enforced.

Vs 6:34-35

For jealousy is the rage of a man: therefore he will not spare in the day of vengeance. Husbands and wives may rightly expect the other to remain faithful to them, and jealousy in the good sense of expecting total affection and love from one's mate is right and good. Even God is jealous in this sense, Exodus 20:5; 34:13-14. There was even a special jealousy law ordained in Numbers 5:11-30. As water cannot quench the fire of love, so neither can money be sufficient for the alienation of a spouse's affection, Song of Solomon 8:7. Sometimes only the blood of the guilty party will suffice to satisfy the aggrieved person.

LIFE APPLICATION

In my teen years, I had a friend, her father wants her to close to me as a friend since I and her father were both in children's department in my church. I was really close with her and we are a good friend. One day, I had not seen her in our Christmas carol practice and I decided to go look for her. When I got to her house, it was like giving me a flinch excuse and her mother was like asking if I have come to call her for the church? I answer 'yes ma' and she said, she should quickly go to where she send her before we go and we both left for the message and we got to a slaughterman in a market and he gave my friend some amount of money, and I was like asking what sort of money was that and she said the money was for her and that the man was her mother secret lover and he always giving them money and meat and that was that.

After few year I was passing through a street in one of populous street in Lagos and another friend ran to meet me up I looked backed and I saw her we exchange greetings and trust, as a long time old friends, we started to gist and there she relayed to me how this my friend mentioned above snatched a principal of her school and drove out the principal's wife with five children. I do not get it in the first place; I was like how did she do it? She then told me that her big sisters and their friend took her to one terrible godfather and what they do was that they incise women face, back of the hand and private part for the sin of fornication and adultery. The one for face is to drag a rich man to themselves, the one for back of the hand work to together with one for face and if by discussion they found out that the man was rich in money and properties, they would lure the man to bed and afterward anything they asked the man to do he will do without hesitation.

We can see here that Godly parents and Divine principles are very vital in cultivating the life of the young ones.

AVOID GODLESS CHATTER BECAUSE THOSE WHO INDULGE IN IT WILL BECOME MORE AND MORE UNGODLY

CHAPTER SEVEN

SUMMARY

Vs. 7:1-3 "My son, keeps my words, and lay up my commandments with thee." 2:1. The first five verses of this chapter are introductory to the parable in verses 6-27, and are very similar to 6:20-24 and are put to the same use. The main thought is that the Word of God is an antidote to sin. Someone has very wisely said: "Sin will keep you from the Word of God, or the Word of God will keep you from sin." There is no neutral ground in this matter, for these two things are mutually exclusive. Most people who sin are doubly guilty for they first neglected the Word of God before they fell into the sin they committed. However, the law had many capital punishments attached to it, and other violations of it led to sickness and early death, so that obedience promoted long life and through the law is the entrance of spiritual light more also; bidding the Law of God upon one's finger would be to constantly be reminded of His love, as well as to have that sign of the authority of God by which every thought and deed of ours is to be tested.

Vs. 7:4-5 "So unto wisdom, Thou art my sister; and call understanding thy kinswoman." Here Divine wisdom is to be treated as a beautiful and delightful kinswoman. And these verse calls for a closeness and affection such as is found in close-knit families. Men often do not understand women, nor women men: thus, the counsel of a sister or brother could warn one of the snares of a flatterer of the opposite sex. Human wisdom and understanding often are put to work to try to justify sin, but divine wisdom and understanding will keep one from sin, and from its subsequent punishments. Note carefully that God's Word is never given to keep the youth from having a wife of his own, but only to keep him from the strange and immoral woman. God's Word does not forbid pleasure, 5:19, but it does forbid illegitimate pleasures.

Vs 7:6-25 "For at the window of my house I looked through my casement." Seeing through "casement" means literally "pattern," Judges 5:28. We may learn many lessons simply by observing other people's mistakes and profiting from them. Lack of discretion and self-control is characteristic of immaturity. Manhood is manifested by self-control and understanding of what is right and proper, and acting accordingly. If giving in to unrestrained lust evidence manhood, then most animals are manly, for they follow no rule but lust. Clearly, then the giving in to lust without regard to the consequences is evidence of beastliness, not manhood. When one toys with temptation, he is more guilty when he falls into sin, the circumstances which give an occasion to sin are to be noticed and avoided. Lust hates the light, and sin hides in darkness Job 24:15; John 3:20.

The sinner thinks no eye can see him in the dark; but God's eye is upon him Psalms 139:12 A great deal of crime is committed under the cover of darkness in order to escape the detection of human law, but no darkness is dense enough to escape the detection of Divine law. Any youth that sought fellowship with the unfruitful works of darkness: will only lead himself or herself to the blackness of darkness forever.

When men foolishly seek for occasions of sin, they shall meet with them. A woman or a man, that is unfaithful to their spouse, can certainly not be trusted to deal more faithfully with one she is not married to. The Eastern women were generally kept secluded from men and did not generally talk with strangers, and among some people, for a woman to talk publicly with a man was to compromise her reputation as a chaste woman. Even in

N.T. times, women were commanded to be "keepers at home," Titus 2:5, and they were warned against wandering about, 1Tim. 5:13-14, but were commanded to be diligent home-makers. Vs. 11 give a description of the loudness, stubbornness, and home duty forsaking woman as a reminder to us, about some of the women's liberation advocates of our day who betray their husbands, children and themselves in their quest for personal liberty. The only true liberty for man or woman is to be in subjection to God's will for them: anything else is not freedom but is the worst kind of bondage—the bondage of sin.

Note: the stages of her departure from her own place: "without," then "in the streets," and finally "lieth in wait at every corner," and that with evil in mind. This was Tamar's sin, Genesis 38:11-26. Restless wives easily get into trouble and sin when they go to places they ought not to go because they have left their God-given place of service and blessing. For both man and woman, God's wisdom is very plain when the place of blessing is for each. May God help us to understand this and to get into our places and be content there? It is so today that many people profess to worship and give thanks to God even while they are in the midst of offending Him by their sin. This is inconsistent and hypocritical. Some seem to think that mouth worships excuse sinful manners and disobedience to His divine Commandments.

True love is from heaven - Yes, but most of what goes under the name of love in our day is straight out of Satan domain. True love always desires the best for the beloved: it never degrades or disgraces the beloved. It is a very selfish "love" that has no interest but self-gratification, yea; it is nothing more than pure animal lust. Alas, how many strong men have been so "forced" because their desires agreed with the temptation? But such "force" never justifies anyone in yielding to it, as I mentioned above, no excuses for sin and judgment for no one—not even the devil—can force anyone to yield to sin; the yielding comes from inside, not from the outside. "The devils made me do it!" is a false teaching.

In sin, things are never as they seem to be for Satan paints sin in the deceptively beautiful colors that please men's pride and unholy desires, not in the black color that they truly are. The youth follows this adulterous woman to what he thinks will be the fulfillment of his desires, not knowing that it leads to death. When ones go into the ways of sin, he necessarily lays aside the breastplate of righteousness, Ephesians 6:14, and so he is open to the judgment that follows sin.

This is, therefore, the application of this story and the summary of what Solomon began in verse 1. It is better to listen to counsel, however, it may go against one's desires, and to heed to the enticement of a deceiver is to finally be brought to Judgment. Vs. 7:26 for she hath cast down many wounded: yea, many strong men have been slain by her. One of Satan's very effective tools is human pride. He appeals to it by telling the tempted one: "Do not fear" Only the weak succumb to evil. You are strong. You may walk by sin and look upon it, but you shall not be caught by it." So he ensnares many, for sin is always more powerful than human strength and wisdom when men foolishly toy with it.

Those who are destroyed by this evil woman were not just the ignorant and weak, but were the wise and strong. Satan's snares are all by very gradual steps away from truth and right; each so subtle that man does not realize he is approaching the brink until too late. The school of experience is a hard one, but many people will learn in no other for they reject the wise counsel of fathers—both physical and spiritual fathers. The youth thought this woman's house was the house of delight, but it turned out to be the house of damnation, and instead of being the way of happiness, it turned out to be the way to Satan domain. All sin must be judged, either in the sinner or in his Surety. Where is yours judged?

IF JEHOVAH ELOHIM MARK SIN AND SINNER, NO ONE; I MEAN A SINGLE SOUL WOULD NOT BE JUSTIFIED; ONLY EVERY MINUTE OF YOUR BREATH PLEAD AND CRY FOR MERCY.

CHAPTER EIGHT

SUMMARY

Proverbs 8:1

Doth not wisdom cry? And understanding put forth her voice? This has already been stated in Proverbs 1:20-21, so that here it is but a call for the hearers to acknowledge this fact that has already been declared. How does Wisdom cry? (i) personally, as Jesus Himself taught. (ii) Verbally, in the written Word of God. (iii) Providentially, as God speaks through His works, Psalms 19:1-6. (iv) Ministerial, in the preaching of His ministers. (v) Evidentially, in the lives of the saved. "The things revealed are easy to be known, for they belong to us and to our children Deuteronomy 29:29, for they are proclaimed in some measure by the works of the creation Psalms 19:1.

The divine "Wisdom" is the chief subject of this chapter, and several of the things predicated of it make it evident of none other than the Lord Jesus Himself. And this only harmonizes with the N. T. which also refers to Him under this term, Luke 11:49; compare with this Matthew 23:34; 1Corinthian 1:24-30 and perhaps 2:7-8; Colossians 2:3. The gates of a city were the place where one could reach the most people with a message, for everyone entering or leaving had to pass through here. Here the prophets often proclaimed their messages of rebuke to the people, Isaiah 29:21; Jeremiah 7:2; 17:19, etc. As "gates" suggest the way into the city, so "doors" would suggest the way into the house, for the appeal of the Word of God is not just to men's public lives and conduct, but also to their most private lives and conduct as well. Thus, Wisdom appeals to man's needs in every area of life and does so in the plainest and positive ways. "Those who will go astray and be lost do so in the face of the plainest warnings and invitations of love,"

Where danger exists, true love must cry vehemently. (Compare the 3rd Life Applications above in this book). Thus, Wisdom is shown to be needful for the great as well as the small: for the fathers as well as for the sons. Wisdom is sufficient for the needs of all classes of sinners, and there are none who are exempted from needing it.

The design of Wisdom is to make men wise where they are simple, and it is capable of even giving understanding to fallen, sinful man. Vs. 8:8 "All the words of my mouth are in righteousness; there is nothing froward or perverse in them." Again, no one but Jesus Christ could honestly make this claim. Because Men often twist and distort the truth for their own purposes, but, Christ also spoke in righteousness for He perfectly practiced what He taught; He never had to twist His teachings to make them harmonize with His life. Spiritual things are generally dark and mystery to lost people simply because their minds are blinded through their unbelief, 2Corinthian 4:3-4. Most people, who claim not to understand the Bible, really do understand it, but they are unwilling to obey, and so they claim not to understand it to avoid being obvious rebels against the truth.

To receive instructions is better than silver; and knowledge rather than choice gold." Though this does not mean an absolute rejection of silver and gold, but this shows the relatively greater importance of spiritual truth to earthly treasures, and that spiritual wisdom is the most important thing. But the time to choose wisdom instead of wealth is before death takes one away from both. So the rich man learned his folly after it was too late Luke 16:19. Divine wisdom is better than rubies, and all the things that may be desired are not to be compared to it. How clearly this shows the importance of knowledge of Divine truth. Gold, silver, jewels and all other forms of wealth must be left behind when this short life on earth is over, but wisdom, being an acquisition of the mind and the heart, will endure throughout all eternity. Man, because he is a carnal creature until he is born again, always desires things that pertain to the flesh, but these things, like the flesh, are so very temporal and fleeting. Only the soul, and what it has accumulated to itself, will last on and on and on. How we ought to feed and beautify our soul with imperishable truth.

Proverbs 8:12-16 I wisdom dwell with prudence, and find out knowledge of witty inventions. "Prudence" is a practical knowledge. It takes more than a merely theoretical knowledge of the Lord to have His indwelling us. Since his fall, man has sought out many inventions, Ecclesiastics 7:29, to flatter his ego and promote his own welfare, but the Divine Wisdom judges these in their true light and determines their worthlessness in the light of eternity. We must submit to the Divine diagnosis of these in order to have the right outlook on things and to prevent displeasing our indwelling Instructor and Teacher. Wisdom preserves men, but wealth often destroys a man for more people have died as a result of luxury and its influence, than have died because of poverty.

The fear and love of the Lord involve the hatred of evil: there is no room for compromise in this, for evil sets itself against the Lord. Here are three categories of evil: (i) Pride and arrogance are mental evils. (ii) The evil way has to do with evil actions. (iii) The froward mouth is vocal evil. Evil is either in thought, word or deed. Not only is Christ the Wisdom of God, 1Corinthian 1:24, but He is also the Wonderful Counselor, Isaiah 9:6, for His counsel, is always that which does us good. "Sound wisdom" is contrasted with the wisdom of the world, 1Corinthian 1:20-21, which is not sound. Being understanding personified, He is also the source of all understanding, 2Timothy 1:7 But He does not unscrew the top of the head and pour in understanding regardless of one's attitude: NO! He gives it through the hearing and obeying of the Word of God. With Christ the Divine Wisdom kings reign, and princes' decree justice." Many texts show that God alone raises up and puts down the rulers of the earth, Psalms 18:35; 75:6-7; Jeremiah 27:5; Daniel 2:21; 4:27-37; Romans 13:1-2. Because it is always of God's directive and or permissive will that anyone reigns, believers have a duty to pray for all who are in authority, 1Timothy 2:1-3, even for thoroughly wicked rulers, as Nero was at the time Paul wrote this. "If even 'kings' owe their authority, and their power of reigning wisely and happily, to Wisdom, whose embodiment is Messiah, the King of kings, much more may we, as private individuals, depend on her for guidance in all our concerns," Vs. 15-16 show that all governmental offices are ordained by God, and men only come to occupy them by God's permissive will. This is why we have a duty to honor them, for they represent God, even when they do not personally know God.

Proverbs 8:17-31 I love them that love me; and those that seek me early shall find me. Here is shown that there is a reciprocal love between Christ and His people. "Early" may be applied several ways: (i) Early in life. (ii) Early in each day. (iii) Early when problems first arise (not as a last resort). (iv) Early, in the sense of earnestly, without delay. Riches and honor are with Christ the true Wisdom; yea, durable riches, and righteousness." This does not justify the idea that every believer will become rich in material possessions.

God has never promised more than just a sufficiency of our needs, Psalms 37:23-26; Philippians 4:19. Nor does this mean that the believer will have much worldly honor; quite the contrary, John 15:18-21; 2 Timothy 3:12. These promises deal with spiritual riches, honor, and righteousness; hence, they are "enduring" riches. Everything of the earth will eventually pass away, but he who seeks the Lord's righteousness will endure forever, 1John 2:17.

The fruit of Wisdom is the benefits that flow to those who receive it and submit to it. However, men may value gold and silver, in the final analysis, no material thing can deliver one from death: righteousness, which comes from knowledge of the Lord, alone, can deliver from death and damnation, Proverbs 10:2; 11:4.

The Lord's leading is always in the way of righteousness: it is only the devil who leads the way to unrighteousness. The way of truth is, as Jesus taught, a straight and narrow way, Matthew 7:13-14. The broad way that allows people to wander far astray, though very popular, is the way to eternal destruction. Divine Wisdom leads men to the way that is righteous, and that produces righteousness and fruits of the Spirit. Galatians 5:22-25. Worldly possessions and riches are but shadows that are here today and gone tomorrow, Proverbs 23:5. But spiritual blessings, though seen only by the eye of faith, are the real substances, for they have God's own power operating in them, Romans 8:28.

Note: that not only does the Lord Promise substance to them, but He promises to "fill" their treasures. See the greatness of this promise in 1Corinthians 2:710; Ephesians 3:18-29; Revelation 21:7. Nothing is eternal but Divine Godhead (Elohim) God in all three persons of the Trinity is "I AM THAT I AM," Exodus 3:14 —the eternally existing One, to whom there is no past or present or future. He is above time, and He alone compass the World. "Compass" is "a circle" as the marginal reading and shows that the Bible taught the spherical of the globe long centuries before the first scientist thought of this.

The Bible is always accurate in all realms and science 1Timothy 6:20. Clouds are a mystery even to meteorologists. Anytime I travel up the sky, I like the window sides and I always marvel at the creations; as the cloud moves and fly.

All that God does is orderly, and every part of the creation is bounded by laws and decrees, but for the law of gravity which constantly presses the waters into the pores of the earth, God in His infinite Wisdom also appointed foundations to uphold the earth.

Proverbs 8:32 Now, therefore, hearken unto me, O ye children: for blessed are they that keep my ways. "Therefore" suggest a reasons to love God because of His love for us, 1 John 4:19 and love are always manifested to God by obedience. Wisdom appeals to the sons of men to obey and keep her ways that they might be blessed. Christ apparently refers to this very verse in Luke 11:28, 49; 7:35. So far from Wisdom's counsel causing one to lose out on some desirable thing, it actually promotes happiness, for it withholds one from dangers, and directs one to that which is best for him. No one really loses anything of real value by obeying the Word of God. It is a part of Satan's deception to imply that God withholds good from people, Genesis 3:1-5.

There cannot be any wisdom without the hearing of God's Word and accepting it. Hence, Satan attempts to out off wisdom at its very source by stealing the Word from men. Note how he does this in Jeremiah 23:29-32: (i) by withholding the Word, verse 30. (ii) By misinterpreting it, verse 31. (iii) By substitution of falsehood for it, verse 32.

This has always been a common way of keeping people from obeying Wisdom's precepts for false happiness. "Blessed" always has to do with happiness, and source of true happiness is obedience to Christ. Vs. 35 "For whoso findeth me findeth life, and shall obtain the favor of the Lord." "Life" is plural, for the promise is both of the life that is now, and that which is to come. Both of these find their fullness only in Christ, for in Him alone is the life that is the light of men, John 1:4. Eternal life is alone in Christ, and this is through the grace (favor) of God, for we are only accepted in Christ, Ephesians 1:6. Whoso neglects the salvation that is in Christ alone, shall not have life, Acts 4:12; Hebrew 2:2-3. The Lord's promise to seekers is that they shall find, Matthew 7:7-8.

There is no promise but of wrath to come for the unconcerned and negligence, (Rom. 1:18; 2Thessalonica 2:10-12. It is a simple choice: we must choose Him who is the Truth or we shall be deceived by him who is the Lie. But he that sinneth against Christ wronged his own soul: all they that hate Him effectually, love death. This is no one's fault but the one who neglects to hear. They ruin themselves, and Wisdom will not hinder them because they have set at naught all her counsel remember the warnings of Proverbs 1:24-33. May Divine grace tender our hearts to hear and receive the Divine Word of Wisdom?

THE NATURAL MAN CAN UNDERSTAND THE NATURAL, BUT CANNOT UNDERSTAND SUPERNATURAL

CHAPTER NINE

SUMMARY

Proverbs 9:1-9.

This chapter concludes the first division of Proverbs. It "consists of two parts, in which wisdom personified (vv. 1-12) and folly (vv. 13-18). "Wisdom hath built her house, she hath hewn out her seven pillars." If Wisdom refers to Christ, then doubtless this is prophetic of the N.T. church which He has been building since He spoke Matthew 16:18. "Her 'house' stands in contrast to the house of the harlot (Prov. 7:8). The seven pillars of this house would be the seven great truths upon which the true churches rest, of which The Divine Christ is the head, (Eph. 5:23 27, Col. 1:18-19. Any other 'gospel' is under the curse, (Gal. 1:6-9). (6) The Christian hope symbolized by baptism, Rom. 6:3-5, and the Lord's supper, 1 Cor. 11:18-26, and a democratic form of church government, wherein all are equals, Matthew 23:8-12.

Vs. 9:2 "She hath killed her beasts; she hath mingled her wine; she hath also furnished her table this qualification refers to Christ's voluntary death as an atonement for sin, John 10:16-18. "Wine" is the same Hebrew word as in Genesis 49:11, which shows that this wine is neither alcoholic nor fermented, and yet it symbolizes the cleansing blood of Jesus Christ. Some think that "mingled" is a proof that it was fermented and so was so highly alcoholic as to need to be watered down. Not so! One of the ways of preserving grape juice without fermenting it was to boil it down to very thick syrup which was incapable of fermentation. Then when used, it had to be mingled with water to thin it to a drinking consistency. "Table" refers prophetically to the Lord's supper which pictures Christ's death, but also to the marriage feast that is yet to come for the people of God, (Matthew 22:1-14).

As Wisdom is represented under the image of a pure woman, so the ministers of heavenly Wisdom are represented as pure maidens. The minister is to wait upon His Lord, 'as the eyes of a maiden look unto the hand of her mistress' Ps. 123:2; cf. 2 Cor. 11:2; Matthew 25:1.

Those who has little reasoning ability, lacking understanding, and so, one that are easily misled or deceived; thus Wisdom's invitation is for one to enter into her house for the cure of ignorance of spiritual things and this is an invitation to the empty to come and fill himself with God's truth. Vs 9:5.

Jesus Himself interpreted the symbolism of bread in Matthew 16:6-12, and in John 6:35-58. Wisdom has all-sufficient nourishment in spiritual things for all who will turn in unto her and receive her counsel. "Mingled" suggest: water was mixed with the thick syrup to give it drinking consistency, so the Lord teaches His own according to their ability to understand.

The wine was something mingled with spices to make it more pleasantly aromatic, and the Lord makes the truth pleasant to those who are of the truth. Conversion is always of a two-fold nature: we turn from sin and all its folly to Christ in all His fullness. Skeptics like to characterize Christianity as the refuge of the ignorant, but it is a fact beyond all disputation that salvation gives men greater understanding in many realms, but especially in spiritual matters. Indeed, the scorner and natural (unsaved) man cannot understand the truth because it is contrary to his very nature, 1Corinthian. 2:14; Rom. 8:7.

Scorners are often incorrigible and hopeless as human wisdom is concerned. Of course, none are beyond the reach of divine grace, but a scorner is seldom saved since he refuses to even listen to that alone which can remedy his condition.

The command is to preach the gospel to every creature, (Mark 16:15), but no one is obligated to continue to preach to those who harden themselves against the truth. Our Lord Himself spoke of some who were to be left alone in their unbelief and scorning, Matthew 10:12-15; 15:14. And Paul practiced this, for he never continued to try to reach those who had hardened themselves against the gospel, but he always went on to more receptive people, Acts 13:45-46; 18: 6-7; 28:25-29. All Scripture is profitable to reprove and to instruct us that we may be fitted to serve God, 2 Tim. 3:16-17. Are we heeding the invitations of Wisdom?

Proverbs 9:10

The fear of the Lord is the beginning of wisdom: and the knowledge of the Holy One is understandable, 1:7. Here is a very important principle that is little understood today by most people: without a reverence for the Lord, wisdom and understanding, will, for the most part, be lost, for one will not apply it to the heart.

The fear of the Lord leads men to depart from evil, (Prov. 16:6). It is the rash and self-confident that rushes in where angels fear to tread and is ensnared in sin. "Holy" is plural, causing some to think that it refers to holy things, but the parallel to "the Lord" makes it more likely that it refers to "the Holy Ones," being a reference to the Trinity. "Holy" (Heb. Kedoshim) has the same plural ending as God the Trinity (Heb. Elohim).

Many things said of God, apply to all the Person of the Trinity Through the divine Wisdom, thy days shall be multiplied, and the years of thy life shall be increased." The practical importance of submission to Wisdom lies in that it promotes longevity. However, long life is not necessarily desirable; but wisdom not only promotes long life but also makes it enjoyable. Almost all cases of early death result from a transgression of some natural law; Man's natural tendency to be rebellious against God's laws in the natural and spiritual realm is the cause for most of his early deaths. Remember: the early men often lived for almost a thousand years because sin had not so firmly invaded the race.

Sin is principally against the Lord, though; does not actually hurt Him: its principal hurt is the one committing it, for he alone must bear the responsibility for it: there is no passing of the buck, however, one may try, the one that scorns, alone shall bear it consequences, Genesis 3:12-13. Satan subtly tricks men into believing that they can shift the blame for their sins and make others partly bear them. Hence the excuse so common today was that "Everyone is doing it." Leviticus 19: 15, II Chronicles 19: 7.

In Proverbs 9:13

It gives an illustration of some kind of women that lack divine Wisdom. "A foolish woman is clamorous: she is simple and knows nothing. Who is the temper—a foolish woman, Folly herself, in opposition to Wisdom? "Clamorous" is more commonly rendered "roar" or "make a noise," for fools are often the loudest and longest talkers of all, being enchanted with the sound of their own voices and their supposed wisdom. "'She is simple,' not artless Prov. 7:10, 12, 21, but utterly destitute of true wisdom, answering to 'she knows nothing.' One can know much about worldly things—even hold several degrees—yet still know nothing about spiritual matters, which are hidden from the natural mind.

As Wisdom cries in the high places of the city, v. 3, 8:2, so this foolish woman imitates her, but with the purpose of counteracting Wisdom's good desires for those who pass by. "Seat" is literally "throne," so that it suggests that she assumes authoritativeness about her teaching. Women who assume authoritativeness among the Lord's people is always affliction to the Lord's house, never a blessing, Rev. 2:20-23. (Read my other book titled: Divine Godhead with divine principles and Pattern – under woman).

It has been suggested by some commentators with plausibility that in as much as "Wisdom" refers to Christ, so there is a long range prophetic reference in this foolish woman to the Antichrist who shall also pompously sit upon a throne, claiming for himself honor that he does not deserve, 2 Thess. 2:4; Rev. 17:1-9; 18:7-9; the Antichrist's kingdom.

Pride and ambition, as seen in the desire to sit in high places, is characteristic of the unsaved and unspiritual, and while ambition is not necessarily wrong, it is often wrongly used; probably, to the detriment of others and her appeal is to those who are making right their ways, and seeking to walk in the way of righteousness.

Satan has never been too concerned about the openly wicked and rebellious, for they already are under his domination; but he delights to ensnare those who are seeking to do God's will, for those alone causes much trouble to his kingdom. His greatest temptations are always directed toward those who are trying conscientiously to serve God, for these have the most influence with men for God's glory.

Notice how this foolish woman imitates the very words of Wisdom, (v. 4). Satan has always been the great counterfeiter, and he apes (mimics) that entire things that God does, for he desires to be like the highest, (Isa. 14:13-14), yet for the wrong reasons. Satan has his churches, (Rev. 3:9), his ministers (2 Cor. 11:13-15), his false gospels, (Gal. 1:6-9), and he has a false charity and benevolence which his people practice, so that it takes no little spiritual discernment to recognize Satan's workings.

However, it is not in the invitation that the difference is to be discerned, but at the end of that invitation: is the invitation to obey God, or is it to disobey Him by seeking personal pleasure in forbidden things? This foolish woman's appeal is to partake of forbidden things, hers; is an invitation to rebellion and sin.

God's Wisdom does not forbid any real good to anyone, Ephesians 1:3, but it does regulate that good, and requires that it be sought according to His will and His rules, that is the primary reasons, you have to seek Him for all your daily needs Mathew 6:33. In other words, you are not of your own; that is why you are His beautiful creature, you can't just go anywhere you feel like going, you cannot work anywhere you think you can quickly make it nor marries anyone just because you can 1 Corinthian 6:19b-20a.

All things have to be regulate by Him alone He is All-Sufficient God and He alone reigns in the affairs of Men for good. The same things may be sought by individual, yet the way in which they are sought reveals the character of the seeker. Notice also the difference in the quality that each offers: while Folly only offers bread and water, which are sufficient to sustain life only, yet Wisdom offers flesh to eat, and wine to drink, (v. 2), yea, spiced wine of high quality, as well as bread, (v. 5). God's provisions far surpass the very best that the world can offer. Folly may proclaim her food to be sweet and pleasant, but this is but false advertising. Only Wisdom's food is truly sweet and pleasant, and it leaves neither bitter aftertaste nor upset stomach, Prov. 5:4; 20:17; 23:6-8; Deut. 32:31-33. Folly promises much, but it produces only more folly.

God's Word warns that death is the end result of following forbidden pleasures, (1 Tim. 5:6), and it is possible for people to be twice dead, (Jude 12) —spiritually dead in sin, and mentally dead to the danger they are in. Folly's house has a trapdoor that opens directly into hell itself, so that those who enter, seeking pleasure, find perdition instead.

The final warning as to the results of yielding to her is given in verse 18. Sin's enticements are never as they are represented: they are presented in the rainbow hues of desire, but they are really in the somber hues of death. Let us all carefully examine every invitation to pleasure, as to whether it is Wisdom's call to us, or the call of sinful pleasure and folly. Wisdom leads to life eternal, but Folly leads to death eternal, Daniel 12:2, Matthew 25:46. It is a considerable part of wisdom to know when to speak, and when to be silent.

EVERY MAN'S LIFE IS A TALE WRITTEN BY GOD'S FINGERS

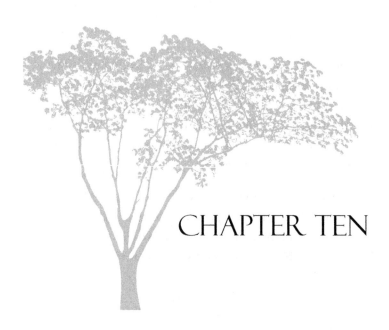

CHAPTER TEN

SUMMARY

Proverbs 10:1-16.

The proverbs of Solomon; a wise son makes a glad father: but a foolish son is the heaviness of his mother." This proverb teaches the responsibility of both parents and children alike. V.2 "Treasures of wickedness profit nothing: but righteousness delivered from death." So it was with the rich man in Luke 12:19-21, and a number of other biblical examples of this could be cited. But to live righteously promote long life, for there will be no cause for judgment to fall upon the individual.

This does not promise that the righteous will never hunger physically, for saints have hundred of this kind at times, 1 Sam. 21:3; 1 Cor. 4:11; 2 Cor. 11:27; Heb. 11:27. However, the Lord's promise is that they will not utterly starve, Ps. 37:25-26. However, the primary thought here is that one shall not spiritually starve, for the righteous possess both the bread and water of life, John 6:35, 48-51. But just as God works for the good of the righteous, He works against the good of the wicked. Wickedness can never be allowed to be permanently profitable, for that would teach men to be evil.

In other words, God's promised of provisions toward us is not meant to encourage sloth and idleness, for diligence in our labor is God's means of giving us our needs. Someone has wisely observed that God generally gives more to the most diligent and most faithful workers, Matthew 25:24-29. Parallel teaching is found in Proverbs 13:4 and 19:15. Hard labor has been man's decree lots since he sinned in Eden, Gen. 3:17-19, but it can be blessed to the enrichment of man by the Lord when a man's ways please the Lord.

All attempts to get rich without honest labor are simply man's denial of his sinfulness, and his attempt to bypass the curse. Labor is meant to remind man of his sinfulness and to seek out empowerments of Divine Spirit of God for wealth, Isaiah 48:17, Psalm 84:11.

One of the characteristics of the wise son that makes glad his father in summer, v. 1, is his diligence in the time of opportunity, while this is meant to primarily illustrate natural things, yet "summer" also has a spiritual meaning of the opportunity for salvation, as Jeremiah 8:20 shows. No one lives unto himself, and the child that causes shame, not only dishonored himself, but he also dishonors his parents who have taught him. This also suggests that God's blessings shall guide the just; the wise son in their activities. For the wicked, there will be violence instead of blessings, and his mouth, by which he dishonored God, shall be silenced. Many godly people have lived and died without a fitting memorial of them being preserved by man, but God has a book of remembrance containing the names and deeds of all His people, Mal. 3:16-18. Often wicked people think that their fame will live on forever, but how quickly people forget the deeds of men even when they are great. On the Day of Judgment, instead of their names being honored, the sinful deeds they have done will cause their names to be execrated as those of rotten sinners, Matthew 25:30.

Some people are wise in profession and pretense that are not truly wise in heart. But real wisdom is practical: it will be seen in its obedience to God's revealed will (Bible). He who refuses to obey God's commands shows his real character, whatever his profession may be. Their gross rebellion, while it may flatter their proud hearts, will be against their own best interests.

A person manifests his character by his response to God's Word either Rhema (Spoken) or in Logos (Bible). V. 9 "He that walks uprightly walks surely: but he that perverted his ways shall be known." The upright walk is the sure walk because it is pleasing to the Lord, and so is blessed by Him. "Walk" suggests the daily life and way of a person, while "upright" means "in perfection" or "with integrity," as in Genesis 20:5-6 and 1 Kings 9:4, etc.

The upright walk is the daily life that is characterized by right living as regards both man and God. It is the life that is in harmony with the Lord's commandments, (v. 8), which are His standards of right and wrong. "Perverted" has to do with that which is crooked or twisted, winks with the eye and prattling to cause sorrow: Winking in the O.T. is always associated with doing evil to someone, Job 15:12; Ps. 35:19; Prov. 6:13; 10:10.

If men could but learn to control their lust and fallen natures, how much sorrow they could avoid, but those that decided to be rash in their ways will always be punished. The character of the tongue is traced back to the character of the heart. It is shown that a person often reveals what he is by what he says. Few people realize the deep hurt that a loose tongue can inflict.

It is striking how often Solomon dwells upon sins of the tongue; Solomon emphasizes the fact that the character of a man will be shown by what proceeds from his mouth: the foul-mouthed, slanderous and blasphemous person shows that he has a heart that is defective toward God and man.

On the other hand, he who regularly speaks the Word of life, shows a heart controlled by the Spirit, and desires to do good to man. "Violence," i.e., violent words, will be the characteristic of the wicked. Hatred in the heart is the source of the violent words that issue from the mouth of the wicked. Christians ought to diligently guard their mouths lest any unchristian utterances should belie their profession, for our mouths are to be the instrument of building up, not tearing down, Eph. 4:29. Hatred and love are contrasted as to their consequences. "The great mischief-maker is malice - Hatred stirs up where there is quietness: but love soothes and quiets where there is uproar. Our love to others is no atonement for our own sins, as some think, Isaiah 64:6, but our love for others will effectively cover their sins in our eyes, so that we will not be offended by them. This does not mean that we are to condone others sins, which are to be rebuked, Lev. 19:16-18, but it is to be done in love, Matthew 18:15; Eph 5:11.

In other words, Man's lips were made to proclaim Divine Wisdom to others, but the fool, because he is "void of heart," (uses his lips rather for slander, stirring up strife, lying, blaspheming God's name, etc.. Because of his misuse of the lips, he must be punished by the Lord. A "rod," i.e., punishment is "for," i.e., ordained, for the back of him who has not understanding. Hence it is both wise and profitable to learn spiritual knowledge.

It is part of true wisdom to be able to distinguish between true treasure, and mere junk. So many are treasuring up earthly wealth, and other things of this world which are to pass away, Matthew 24:35; 1 John 2:15-17, which they ignore the true treasure of Divine wisdom which is to endure eternally. This refers to the mind, which is the storehouse of knowledge; the lips, (v. 13), are but the setters forth of this knowledge, and they cannot bring forth what has not been laid up in mind.

The mouth of the foolish is near to destruction because it so often sets forth and causes destruction by what it says. Even right words can be spoken at wrong times, and so can do great harm. The foolishness of man has be revealed in much of his abundance, hence; the rich man's riches become a snare to his spiritual growth, 1 Tim. 6:6-10. Generally speaking, poverty has done more to keep people humbly trusting the Lord, than wealth has, which is often substituted for faith.

As has been often in Proverbs, "instruction" has to do with disciplinary instruction = correction, chastisement. He who desires instruction in theory only, without its corrective force, is not in the way of life, but is deceived. The way of life is that which teaches one with a discipline that corrects the faults of his life.

Alas, how many rejected all such instruction simply because they have no desire to be corrected. One's refusal to be corrected often affects others as well—family, friends, acquaintances, etc. Just as no one lives unto himself, so no one sins unto himself." Hatred is often cloaked underlies, and one pretends to be a friend when he is really the arch enemy of enemies. This is hypocrisy, how many people regularly practice such sins, yet still flattered themselves that they are saints. He attempts to hide his hatred for others, but his hatred often breaks out as slander. Even idle words are accountable, Matthew 12:34-37, for idle words are often sinful words. It is a wise saying of this adage which says: "Better to be silent and to be thought a fool, than to open one's mouth and to confirm the fact." The tongue of the justified man is valuable because it is the instrument of praise to God and the preaching of the gospel. It is good because it is directed away from self: it is used for the glory of God and the good of man. The wicked man's tongue is used wholly for self, for his heart is yet wholly bound up with his own purposes. Better to be a fool in the world's eyes because we believe and follow heavenly wisdom, than to be worldly wise, yet reject the true wisdom that gives us eternal life.

True riches consist in having the blessings of the Lord, for there is no sorrow attending the Lord's enrichment. But often the riches of the world are accompanied by great sorrow because they may have been obtained in a wrong way and become the cause of erring from the faith, 1 Tim. 6:6-10. Wealth is not the key to happiness. One of the deceptions of Satan is to get people to treat sin lightly, for thereby they lose their fear of it, and are easily ensnared by it. Proverbs 10:24-34

"The fear of the wicked, it shall come upon him: but the desire of the righteous shall be granted." Basically, this teaches that the righteous shall be blessed by the Lord, but He will cause evil to come to the wicked, no one can lose serving the Lord, and no one can win while rebelling against Him: it is that simple. The everlasting stability of the righteous is due to their relation to the Lord: by faith they are partakers of the Divine nature, 2 Pet. 1:3-4, and as this cannot perish, they have a sure foundation.

The sinner's days may seem to be prolonged at times, but they are still as a shadow, Ecclesiastes 8:12-13. Many blessings in the present time are the lot of the righteous, yet their chief portion lies in the future, and so it is a "hope," Rom. 8:24-25. Eternal gladness awaits all the saved, regardless of what the present life has given them, (Isa. 35:10). On the contrary, the wicked shall have only frustration for all of his expectations.

This is what Satan domain shall chiefly consist of—eternal frustrations without hope of relief. A wicked man, by his rebellion, frustrates God's purpose in his life, so God shall frustrate all the hopes and good of the wicked.

God uphold the righteous: but destruction shall be to the workers of iniquity." While at this stage in God's revelation to man, "the way of the Lord" had reference only to the practice of holiness, which indeed is strength to anyone, yet God's fuller revelation shows that Christ is the "Way," John 14:6, and so He is the true, spiritual strength to all the righteous. Curiously, and surely not accidentally, the name given to the angel of the bottomless pit (Abaddon in the Hebrew and Apollyon in the Greek), Rev. 9:11, signifies destroyer.

As men will not receive God's Way in Principles and Pattern, they are left unto the Destroyer. The choice has always been simple for God or Satan.

The stability of the righteous is because his righteous is not his own, but it is the imputed righteousness of Christ which can never fail, Rom. 4:3-5, 22-24; Isa. 61:10. It is on the basis of this that God's people are promised an inheritance that fades not away and they shall never be removed 1 Pet. 1:3-5. But the wicked, because all his righteousness is a self-righteousness, which is polluted, Isa. 57:12; 64:6, has no part in the new, sinless heaven and earth that is to descend from God to be the eternal home of the saved, Revelation 21.

In James 3:9-11 the mouth was likens to a spring which is known by its outflow. Truth must be the product of the mouth of the righteous, and those whose mouths produce only evil shall be silenced. Anciently, rulers would sometimes cut the tongue out of one who had spoken something they did not like. Though the wicked now may do much rebellious boasting, yet the time will come when the law of God will silence every mouth that speaketh lies 1 Sam. 2:9; Rom. 3:19; Ps. 107:42.

Note: the silence of man in Revelation 20:11-15 at the great white throne judgment. See also Revelation 8:1 just before the judgment trumpets begin to sound. But in a true righteous person, the lips will automatically speak right, and restrain wrong just as if they had knowledge of what is acceptable. They do so because they are controlled by the spiritual man of the heart. In like manner, the lips of the wicked speak evil because of the abundance of evil in the heart, Luke 6:45. Generally speaking, a man's own mouth will tell what he is in heart.

HYPOCRITES ARE IN CONTINUAL DANGER AND ARE IN FEAR OF THEIR SECRET AND WICKEDNESS BECOMING KNOWN

CHAPTER ELEVEN

SUMMARY

Proverbs 11:1

This chapter continues the miscellaneous proverbs which began in chapter ten. Here, reference is made several times to the folly of trusting in riches, and there is the frequent contrast between the righteous and the wicked.

"A false balance is an abomination to the Lord: but a just weight is his delight." In ancient times, scales for trading purposes were simple things, which could easily be manipulated. Stones of given weight were often used to balance against the item sold. Crooked dealers would have a large stone for buying purposes and a small one for selling purposes, Prov. 20:10; 23; Deut. 25:13-16. "A false balance is here put for all manner of unjust and fraudulent practices in dealing with any person, which is all an abomination to the Lord.

Proverbs 11:2

When pride cometh then cometh shame but with the lowly is wisdom, pride is always hateful in God's sight, Proverbs 16:5, 18, for it always tends to exalt self against all others, including even God. One of God's spiritual laws has to do with this, Luke 14:11. Wisdom humbles self and leaves it to others to do the honoring if any is due, Luke 14:7-11. Both right and wrong principles have their just consequences and it is better to walk in straight paths that the Lord can bless, though this world of storm and rage around us, than to be destroyed by the Lord. Vs. 4 At best, riches serve men only in this world, but the closer men come to death, the fewer value riches have. Righteousness—a right relation to God—has eternal profit, 1 Tim. 6:5-7; 4:7-8. It is the privilege of the righteous not to be hurt of the second death, and so not much hurt by the first

Righteousness is better than riches, for while riches can deliver from the death of want, only righteousness can deliver from eternal death. The saints are perfect only through the righteousness of Christ, Heb. 10:14, but every sinner is trapped through his own wickedness. None can be righteous except by an imputed righteousness, but all can be wicked by themselves. Imputed righteousness is a principle of life which guides and directs those who have it so that they are delivered from death. It is also a shield, Eph. 6:13-14. True righteousness is heavenly in source and directions through the empowerment of Divine Spirit of Jehovah Elohim. And individual can always ask for this grace and empowerment from God Matthew 7:7-11, but wickedness always tends downward destruction through the spirit of pride, flesh, and lust.

Saints are perfect and upright because they are so viewed by God, not because of what they are in themselves. They are accounted so by God because of the association they sustain in Christ by faith, Romans 5:1, but the main thought is that the person who toys with sin is going to be bitten by it sooner or later to his own destruction. Nothing is revealed to be as hopeless as the eternal destiny of the wicked.

The righteous is delivered out of trouble, and the wicked cometh in his stead." 2Peter 2:9. How often has this occurred before and even in our present day to day life, Daniel 6:24; Esther 7:10; Psalm 7:15; 34:19; Exodus 14:27-31. The promise of deliverance comes as a result of prayer to the Lord, Ps. 50:15, but the wicked, through his unbelief, refuses to call upon the Lord, Ps. 53:4. Boldness and presumption in sin get many people in trouble from which they cannot be delivered. It is better to trust the Lord, not that concoctions and charm of protection made by mere man Jeremiah 17:5, Psalm 118:8.

The pretenders with evil mouth - "Mouth" may refer to bad counsel, lies, slanders, blasphemies against God, false religious and teachings, etc., (Prov. 29:8), all these; is capable of—destruction: of characters, of peace, of health, even of life. Ignorance is more often revealed by the mouth. It is general wisdom to be silent until one has carefully thought through the whole matter. Someone has wisely said, "Count ten before you speak, and then do not speak." And what makes this sin even more atrocious is that it is not done to a stranger, nor to an enemy, but to a neighbor.

The "hypocrite" is a pretender, and the suggestion is that he pretends friendship but practices evil toward his neighbor. Often God blesses the whole community simply for the sake of the few godly in it, and at times the utter destruction of wicked people is recognized as a blessing to the whole town. The righteous may not be liked because of their testimony, but they are respected generally as being conducive to the good of a community. God's people are always a blessing to those among whom they dwell, but the wicked always tend to the destruction of their city because their way of life causes the judgment of God upon it, Genesis 29

Vs. 13 "A talebearer revealed secrets: but he that is of a faithful spirit concealed the matter." Gossips delight to exchange their wares abroad. The "Faithful" keep the secret revealed to him by his friend. The gossipers tends to reveal their pretentious character by even twisting that which was true into lies, so as to cause strives, but the faithful concealing a matter does not denote that he is a partner to evil but he will rather find out the truth about all things and hold on the truth as to keeping it. V. 14 "Where no counsel is, the people fall: but in the multitude of counselors there is safety." (Prov. 15:22).

Blessed is any man who has many wise counselors to aid them in making decisions, for almost everything done hastily and without calm thought will result in trouble. Though; good counsels at a time may not be Godly counsel, yet; the danger in having too many opinions given always lies in those who are not really wise or qualified to give advice. Unfortunately, those most ambitious to advice are often those least qualified to do so. It is an act of wisdom to hate being a pledge for anyone, but especially for a stranger. This is the only sure way of not being defrauded by strangers, and of not losing one's good friends.

v.16 "A gracious woman retained honor: and strong men retain riches." "Gracious" is the same Hebrew word rendered "grace" (It's more common rendering) in Genesis 6:8, so that the gracious woman is not just the woman who is kind and helpful, but rather is the woman who has found grace in the eyes of the Lord (been saved). Such a woman will hold on as tenaciously to her honor and virtue as the strong man does his riches, for honor and virtue are more valuable than any material riches.

The carnal and selfish man fears to do good to anyone else, lest by that act he loses something himself, but no one ever permanently loses by doing good to others. On the other hand, many have suffered a great loss by being too selfish, v. 24-26. The man is typically selfish, and he often works deceitfully in order to give himself the advantage, yet this never works to his advantage, for God must curse the work that is so done through that way. His delight is in righteousness and He always blesses this, so that we may always be sure that there will be rewards to this, however, circumstances may appear at the time to deny this. It is both a natural and a spiritual law that the reward will correspond exactly to the labor, and the crop to the seed sown, Hosea 10:12; Gal. 6:7-9.

God never withholds anything from anyone except what would not be good for him in the long run. While every sin is primarily against God, it is also detrimental to the well-being of him who commits it, take for example; adultery and fornication that lead to many dishearten situations or a young school pupil that get themselves pregnant in school; automatically their education hampered, and or even stop for a lifetime.

"Abomination" appears 21 times in Proverbs, three of which are in this chapter, (vv. 1, 20, 22). The frequent use of this word in the Bible shows that God has some very definite feelings of hatred toward many forms of evil: how then can He let it go unpunished, as many think and hope that He will do? He delights in righteousness, yet there could be no real love for righteousness without a corresponding hatred of evil.

Justification from guilt is not a matter of majority belief and practice; many seem to believe that if "everyone does it," God will be compelled to excuse it, since He is supposedly so desperate to be liked and accepted by men that He will compromise on truth and righteousness. Alas, how tragically Satan has deceived men into thinking that they can be sinning with impunity. Think of the story of Babel.

For the fact that Jehovah love unity, does not made Him condones disobedience and foolishness of men in the name of "we are in dispensations of Grace" or rather; He delay His judgments on men as to give room to their repentance. The mightiest and least conspiracies in evil will not escape, but even the seed of the righteous, because they are generally influenced by their righteous parents, will be delivered.

A jewel cannot do anything for a dog, for all its washing, it still prefers the mud, 2Peter 2:22. So a woman, though she is ever so beautiful, if she has no sense of right and wrong, her very beauty will be a snare to her. True beauty is never an outward fairness, but is rather an inward graciousness.

The old man of the flesh is good for only a few years at best, but the hidden man of the heart is made for years at best, the hidden man of the heart is made for eternity, 1Peter 3:1-6. Dependence upon outward beauty is of all things, one of the most foolish. v. 23 "The desire of the righteous is only good: but the expectation of the wicked is wrath." "Desire" and "expectation" are not to be taken subjectively; i.e., of the inward hopes, for often saints wish for that which seems not really good in the sight of the carnal men, and the wicked always flatters himself that he will not really receive wrath for all his atrocities, but will in some way escape. This is meant objectively; i.e., that only good will finally comes to the righteous and only wrath will finally come to the wicked. So is the rules and law of sowing seeds v. 24, he who would reap largely must scatter the seed far and wide, with no grudging, though; others may count him mad, The more he cast away, the more he had, he who thus bestows his good upon the poor, shall have as much again, and ten times more,

It is a truth that is hard for all to grasp and gather yet; give to God's glory, we cannot out give God. Many are afraid to trust Him with their all, and He certainly tests us, even asking us to trust Him down to the last handful of meal in the barrel, 1Kings 17:10-16. Here again is the divine law of sowing and reaping. We are to be liberal in benevolence, not in dogma. We are not to make exorbitant profit off others. God has condemned such practices, Exodus 22:25; Deut. 23:19-20; Amos 8:4-7.

A reasonable profit is approved of by the Lord, but not excessive charges. We must not only do well, but do it seasonably whilst the opportunity presents itself, and diligently; our Lord promised success to seekers, Mathew. 7:7-8. v. 28 "He that trusted in his riches shall fall: but the righteous shall flourish as a branch." Jer. 9:23-24. This is so because riches are so undependable, but whosoever trusted in the Lord shall not only be righteous but shall flourish in his righteousness.

The evergreen tree has long been fitly used as a symbol of the saint, Ps. 1:3; Jer. 17:7-8. A branch does not live of its own intrinsic life, but must be attached to the root, Col. 2:6-10. Christ is our all in all and our redeemer but those who slacked in business dealings will soon be so poverty-stricken that he must become servant to the prudent man, Lev. 25:47-48. V. 30-31 the fruit of the righteous is a tree of life; and he that winneth souls is wise." Some build a whole system of theology on this verse, believing that they can win men to Christ by their own powers of persuasion. But nowhere else in the Bible is this taught. Conversely, many texts teach that God alone draws men to Christ, since one must be born again by God before he is able to saintly believe. Truly God's people are to witness of Him to others, but the Spirit alone can win them to Christ.

The present life is the only time and place where the righteous will be chastised for their sins, and they may enjoy rewards on earth now, but chiefly their rewards will be on the new earth. The wicked will "much more" be punished hereafter than now in the present time during which they may have comparatively little punishment. Judgment is to come for both, but of a different sort for the unsaved, 1 Pet. 4:17-19. Compare the Life application given above, about my 130 year old aunt

WE TURN TO GOD WHEN PROBLEM COMES - ONLY TO LEARN IT COMES FOR OUR CARROT OR STICK

CHAPTER TWELVE

SUMMARY

Proverbs 12:1

This chapter continues the several subjects that have been previously dealt with and the main idea is the contrast between the righteous and the wicked.

Whoso loveth instruction loveth knowledge: but he that hateth reproof is brutish. "Instruction" here as in Proverbs 1:2 and other places, means "discipline" or "chastisement," so that it is shown that knowledge consists in more than merely theoretical or "book" learning: it involves the development of practical "horse sense" in holy living. No discipline is loved for itself, for it is unpleasant, but a saved person will love it for its fruit—development in holiness, Heb. 12:11. The unsaved person, like an animal, looks no further than the feelings of the moment, and so he hates anything that hinders his lusts ... All Biblical reproof is designed for our good, and should not be despised 2Timothy 3:16.

V. 2 "A good man obtained the favor of the Lord: but a man of wicked devices will be condemned." No one loses anything by being kind and good to others: God Himself will see to it, for His very nature obligates

God to reward the doer of good so that good may be promoted. This does not mean that anyone can ever earn the grace (favor) of God, but it does mean that every truly good deed will be rewarded by the Lord. Sometimes, however, our "good" deeds are done only for selfish reasons, in which case, they are their own reward, and God will not reward them, Matt. 6:1-2, 5, and 16. By the same token, God must condemn all wickedness so that it will appear to men that He hates evil, in whatever form it may be.

Note: that not only does He condemn the wicked devices, but also the man who devises them and partner with them. Many people live their whole lives out by wickedness and gather many material possessions, but in the end, they must die and face the judge of all and give an answer for their deeds. For any person to try to live by his own wits is an admission that he does not trust in the benevolence of God. The following texts suggest the importance of being rooted in righteousness, Matthew 3:10; 13:6, 21; 15:13; Eph. 3:7; Col. 3:7. Both wickedness and righteousness result from a corresponding "root" in the heart. What a person does and speaks results from what he is in the heart.

In v. 4 Solomon turns to the discussion of good and bad women. A virtuous woman - Ruth 3:11; Prov. 12:4; 31:10, 29 is always the chief ornament of a husband, and so is considered a favor from the Lord, Prov. 18:22. "Husband" is literally "lord," emphasizing the divine order of the sexes, which the Bible teaches throughout. This in no way justifies the abuse of a woman by a man, for the husband is always to love his wife as Christ loved the church—with a deep, self-denying, sacrificial love, Eph. 5:23-29. v.5 "The thoughts of the righteous are right: but the counsels of the wicked are deceit. One's thoughts are the index to his character.

The words, as well as the thoughts of men, will manifest the true character of them. The words of the wicked are their plotting against others whose blood they plan to shed violently, either literally or figuratively. v. 7 "The wicked are overthrown and are not: but the house of the righteous shall stand." Ps. 37:35-36; Prov. 10:25. "House" often refers to the descendants of a person and the overthrown of the wicked shall be the judgment of God in various form; that will deal with the wicked in due time. Obedience to the divine wisdom will commend a person not the wisdom of this world, which sets itself against Christ, but the wisdom here meant is that simple wisdom of the gospel and its doctrines, 1 Cor. 1:19-31.

A perverse heart is a wicked, unregenerate heart, which, though it may have great worldly wisdom, yet, because it is in rebellion against Christ and His ways, this shall be despised in the Day of Judgment Proverbs 8:35-36. v. 9 "He that is despised, and hath a servant, is better than he that honoureth himself, and lack bread." "Despised" here is a different Hebrew word than in verse 8. Some men try to make themselves be great when they possess nothing: it would be better to be thought light of, yet possess enough to own a servant than to vainly praise oneself. v. 10 "A righteous man regardeth the life of his beast: but the tender mercies of the wicked are cruel." Deut. 25:4. Lordship over the brute creation does not give anyone the right to mistreat them.

A righteous man, because he has become righteous through an act of mercy on God's part, is also obligated to show mercy—even to soulless beasts. But even what the wicked considers to be tender mercies are, by right standards, still cruel. Balaam was rebuked for mistreating his donkey, Num. 22:28. The way some people are cruel to their domestic assistant and or neighbor, is even worse than animals, not to talk of meeting commendation of this verse.

Diligent labor shall be satisfied by the fruits of labor—a sufficiency of food. But no promise is given to the idler and loafer, or he who follows such. Every community has some who are lazy and who expect others to take care of them. But he who cannot take care of his own household has no business trying to lead others. He who follows such persons reveals his own lack of understanding.

Proverbs 12:12-14

"The wicked desire the net of evil men: but the root of the righteous yield fruit." "Net" may also be rendered "fortress" Ps. 18:2 or "bulwark," Eccl. 9:14. Perhaps it means that he desires the cunning of evil men whereby they are able to ensnare men. Or it may mean, as some think, that he desires the fortress or defense of evil men. But the righteous, so far from taking from others, produce fruit for others. "Thus, the righteous yielding their own fruit, for the good of others as well as themselves, stand in contrast to the wicked desiring to entrap in their net other evil men, so as to gain their goods. "Many men have paid dearly in this world for the transgression of his lips and have felt the lash on his back for want of a bridle upon his tongue. A man sins quicker with his lips than in almost any other way, James 3:2, 8. One who is careless in his talk will almost certainly ensnare himself sooner or later. But the just shall be delivered, 2 Pet. 2:9.

We need not human wisdom to escape if we are the Lord's: He will deliver us, Ps. 50:15. He who speaks the truth can be satisfied with it, and will not need to constantly tell different stories. The sad thing about liars is that they must constantly revise their stories to make them harmonize with other lies they have told. A liar must have a good memory so that he will not contradict his own words. By a man's words, he will either be justified or condemned, Matthew 12:34-37. There is a fitting recompose for all that one says or does. This is the Divine law of sowing and reaping.

Proverbs 12:15-2.

"The way of a fool is right in his own eyes: but he that hearkened unto counsel is wise." This is why the fool is always so argumentative: he thinks he cannot be wrong, for they make learning almost impossibility by their proud assumption that they are always right. On the other hand, the wise man does not feel he must immediately defend his own views, but he listens to others, and so is teachable. "None is so wise as not to need good counsel, especially in the concerns of the soul. A fool makes his wrath known immediately by speaking out every time anyone seems to contradict his ideas, but the wise man, in refraining from getting into an argument, keeps from making himself ashamed by speaking unwisely. James 1:19-20 is wise counsel. A proud unwillingness to learn always brings shame, Prov. 11:2; 13:18; 18:13. Shame is the one thing of all others that the proud man does not want, yet it is the thing that pride most surely brings about. God always makes the punishment correspond to the sin. Thus, the man who continually breathes out truth shows that he is a righteous man, while the false witness will show his true character by the deceit that he speaks. The mouth is truly the index of the heart and shows the condition of the heart, so here the working of the mouth in the cases of the righteous and the wicked is seen in its results upon others.

The one speaks cutting words: the other curing words. "The tongue is death or life, poison or medicine, as it is used. To be only a boneless member of flesh, it is amazing how sharp and cutting the tongue can be if it is not kept under control. Men may twist and distort facts in an endeavor to establish a lie, but it cannot be permanent; sooner or later the refuge of lies will be swept away, Isa. 28:17. Since truth cannot long be eclipsed, nor falsehood long be established, how wise it is to build solely upon the enduring foundation of eternal truth.

It has long been one of Satan's lies that "The end justifies the means," and so, those who imagine evil conclude that any sort of deceit is justified to accomplish their desired end. However, evil always tends to sorrow, as the contrasting statement suggests. To those who counsel peace instead of devising evil, there is joy, for joy is the fruit of real peace. V. 21 Momentary evils often happen to the just, but this rather means that no permanent evil shall befall them and that they shall ultimately triumph through faith in the Lord, (1 John 5:4-5). One's inward character shall determine whether or not evil comes to him, and this inward character, if it is good, comes from the Lord. To the evil, not only will evil come, but he will be filled with it. Sin is always permeated— it grows and spreads and takes over. Every lie originates from Satan, who is the father of lies (John 8:44). Lying is one of the seven abominations of Proverbs 6:16. In the light of this teaching, how can anyone think to prosper through lying, unless he is atheistic and thinks there is no God, Ps. 53:1? Lying lips lead to lying deeds, just as those who deal truly do so because they also think and speak truly. He that is wise communicates his knowledge when it may turn to the edification of others.

V. 24 Diligence is the way to success in almost any realm, for it is approved of by both God and man. "Slothful" is more commonly rendered "deceitful" or "deceitfully," as in Jeremiah 48:10. Often the slothful use deceitful practices in order to dodge honest and diligent labor, but this is never permanently success, for God's curse must be on all that is not honest and upright. So long as the slothful trying to defraud others, he will find himself under a debt to others. v. 25 "Heaviness in the heart of man maketh it stoop: but a good word maketh it glad." Despondency and discouragement do more to stop the work of the Lord than almost any other things, for these strikes at the very motive center of a man and it is only "a good word that can help." How easy it would be for us to cheer up the heavy-hearted around us. Alas, too often we are guilty of rather adding to their sorrows than lessening their load. Lifting burdens are the way to fulfill the law of Christ, Gal. 6:1-2. This was Christ's ministry, Isa. 50:41; 61: 1-2. v. 26

"The righteous is more excellent than his neighbor: but the way of the wicked seduced them." "Excellent" is rendered "abundant" by some. The righteous have an abundance that moves them to generosity with others.

Men generally do not follow the way of the righteous because the wicked lead them astray by appealing to the lusts of the flesh. But time will reveal that the way of the wicked is the way of death. We may freely use the things of this world so long as we do not abuse them, nor let them abuse us, 1 Cor. 7:31. The world and all its substance are to pass away: only spiritual riches will abide, 1 John 2:17. Our Lord Himself spoke of the narrow way that leads to life and the Broadway that leads to destruction, (Matthew 7:13-14).

He who walks in the path of righteousness shall never die because by this he becomes a possessor of Christ Who is Life, John 8:51; 14:6. Jesus promised that those who live and believe in Him shall never die.

CHRITIANITY IS NOT A THEORY OR SPECULATION, BUT A LIFE; NOT A PHILOSOPHY OF LIFE, BUT A LIVING PRESENCE

CHAPTER THIRTEEN

SUMMARY

Proverbs 13:1-25

A wise son hears his father's instruction: but a scorner heareth not rebuke. "Instruction" refers to more than mere teaching; it means instruction accompanied with chastisement. "There is little hope for those that will not so much hear rebuke, but scorns. Yet; it is good to mention one's faults in other to mend it. v. 2 "A man shall eat well by the fruit of his mouth: but the soul of the transgressors shall eat violence." The tongue is a deadly poison, Jam. 3:8, with much potential for evil. "No wonder that the Holy Spirit and Apostle of Christ labors so much for the reformation of the tongue; Rom. 3:13.

The judgment that comes to the sinner is not a mere outward judgment but reaches to his very soul. We must always be careful what, to whom, and in what manner we speak. He that opened wide" refers to one who does not govern his speech. Some people seem to have a direct connection between their brain and their mouth, for they speak whatever comes into their minds. Others seem to speak at times without even thinking. An ungoverned tongue brings destruction—of reputation, character and soul. The tongue cannot be tamed; Jam. 3:7-8, but it can be caged.

In v. 4 "The soul of the sluggard desired, and hath nothing: but the soul of the diligent shall be made fat." The desire for wealth without the willingness to work for it is characteristic of many people both older men and young ones, but God gives no promise to the lazy and slothful. Even in Bible times, there were those who desired to be fed without working, but the Bible does not countenance such, John 6:27; 2 Thess. 3:7-12. They were not to be fed by the church, and neither should welfare feed them today. Churches are to take care of their own poor when they cannot support themselves, but it is sinful to encourage the lazy and the slothful.

The diligent is "made fat," meaning being blessed by the Lord and made to prosper. Idleness finds it root in pretentious and lies and cometh to shame." Since all lies originate from Satan, John 8:44, the righteous man, who is related by his righteousness to Jesus Christ, cannot feel otherwise toward lying than to hate it. He hates lying, not only in others, but especially in himself, since this causes him to come to shame and evil-doing reflects back on the doer of it, he may be able for a time to hide his evil, but sooner or later it will be known for what it really is.

Righteousness is a great defense to those who have it, for it keeps the upright safe and secure, both in this life and the life to come, for true righteousness is appreciated even by the world, 1 Pet. 3:12-13. In one sense, wickedness is its own punishment, for it overthrows all those who commit it in the end.

True riches is not in giving to other, though; this is good but this is only because we leave out the unseen factor—God—who blesses all true benevolence, and curses all selfishness. To be rich only in this world's goods, which are to pass away, 1 John 2:17, is to be, of all men, the poorest. To be rich and poor have their advantages. The poor man is never in danger of being kidnapped nor robbed if he is known to be poor, but the rich are almost constantly in danger of these. The divine counsel concerning riches is given in 1 Tim. 6:6-10, 17-19.

The more spiritual enlightenment that we get, the more it rejoices our hearts, for the more we realize God's grace all that it has done, is doing, and shall yet do for us, the happier it makes us. The difference in the light of the righteous and that of the wicked is that the one is as the light of the sun—a great natural, all enlightening light, while the other is as a candle—a man-made, artificial light that is easily extinguished, and which will eventually die of itself. v. 10 "Only by pride cometh contention: but with the well advised is wisdom." If it were not for pride there would be no contention, as those well advised is opposed to the proud, Lowliness promotes peace and fellowship Prov. 15:1.

v. 11 "Wealth gotten by vanity shall be diminished: but he that gathered by labor shall increase." "By labor" is literally "by the hand." "Vanity" means emptiness or nothingness. Those who try to live by their wits generally can't hold on to the money they get. Only that which is honestly acquired has God's blessings on it so that it will go further than one expects. For example, the nine-tenths left after God's tithe is paid, always goes further in paying bills than the ten-tenths when God's part is stolen. God can make wealth be insufficient for needs, or He can make it more than sufficient.

We ought to pray diligently to Him for our desire, and then rest in His will concerning it. v. 13 "Whoso despiseth the word shall be destroyed, but he that feareth the commandment shall be rewarded." Here are the consequences of one's reaction to God's Word: In every case of despising the Word, there comes a time when wrath without remedy befalls the sinner, 2 Chron. 36:16, and none can foretell just when this will be, or on sometimes, it comes quicker than on others. No one hears and remains neutral: one will either hear or obey, or he will hear it and rebel against it. To hear and fear the Word of Jehovah Elohim is to be rewarded with His promises, Ps. 19:11. To obey God's Word always tends to life, for it leads to right principles, and so it leads men away from sins which lead to death. If man were able to perfectly keep God's law, he could have life by it, but only one failure is enough to be guilty of breaking the whole of it, Jam. 2:10, for it is a perfect unity, and so man's sinful failures to keep the law perfectly and continually, put him under its curse, Gal. 3:10-12, therefore, every man needs a saviour from the broken law, which is Christ's office, Gal. 3:13. Jesus suffered those "snares of death" as our substitute, Ps. 18:5, so that believers might not have to endure them, and God's Word leads us to Him so that we may be justified by faith in Him, Gal. 3:24. Every sin is an attempt to take a shortcut to some desired good, and it is always based on ignorance, the wrong teaching of the Word of the right way to achieve that good, precisely, in order to get good results and favor.

Transgression of the revealed will of God leads only to "despair" in which it is hard to walk without stumbling Deuteronomy 21:4. Sometimes the evil man also deals with knowledge, but he puts it to an evil use, not considering all things in the light of judgment and eternity. The obedient and the prudent in a positive sense stands in an even place, Ps. 26:11-12.

The faithful Ambassador is a messenger of divine truth, not serving his own belly, but the wicked man, thinking to turn his position into a profit for himself, only falls into evil himself, for he transgresses right principles when he proves false to his duty and lies, instead of faithfully delivering his message. Disciplinary instruction is necessary for any profession, most especially in the Christian walk. To refuse instruction is to proudly assume a state of perfection, while heeding reproof admits one's sinfulness and attempts to rectify it by the Word. The benefits of divine chastisements never come to those who continue in sin, and only the lies of Satan make people believe that they can continue in sin, yet still receive eternal good. The desire of the wise accomplished by their departing from evil and this is sweet to their soul; but as it is an abomination to fools to depart from evil, their desire being not accomplished is not sweet and they know no peace Roman 6:1-2a. Those that would be good must keep good company, which is an evidence for them that they would be good (men's character is known by the company they choose). Multitudes are brought to ruin by bad company," [Henry].

We are all influenced by association more than we realize which is why we must choose our company carefully 1Corthians 15:33, Proverbs 22:24-25. Evil always returns upon the one doing it, and its natural end is death, Rom. 5:12; Jam. 1:15. Denial of the Lord is the mother sin which begets almost all others, and while men may seem to prosper in their unbelief, yet their condemnation slumbers not, but shall find them in time, 2 Pet. 2:1-3. But just as evil shall be rewarded, so also God's own justice requires that He repay every truly good deed done by the saved, Heb. 6:10, Revelation 22:11-12. Part of God's rewards to faithful ones is to leave inheritance for their upcoming young ones and nothing is so great an inheritance as godly teaching. There are hidden ways whereby God sustains the godly, though they do not see it with their eyes, nor can comprehend it with their minds. He often pays the righteous out of the pockets of the sinner. It is also true that God often destroys the work of men's hands because the work has been done dishonestly. He cannot consistently bless evil.

v. 24 "He that spareth his rod hateth his son: but he that loveth him chasteneth him betimes." Some people claim to love their children too much to spank them, but the Bible belies this claim. The truth is, they love their children's esteem too much, and would rather have their esteem, though it destroys them eternally, than to have the child's anger momentarily when it tends for their good both for time and for eternity. They must be corrected and established the heart of obedience as like from age of six years, because there is going to be small ones on the Day of judgment, no one know exactly the age bracket of the 'Small" Revelation 20:12 but some Scholar said as from Seven years old, because when the trumpet sound as Christ declared in His Word; some various activities will be going on in the world Matthew 24:30, 36-41

True love will teach children to obey, even if it means numerous spanking, so as to develop strong and good characters V. 25. The entire world is not enough to satisfy the selfish man, but part of Christian discipline is to be content with what God gives, 1 Tim. 6:6-8; Heb. 13:5. The wicked, now often complaining against God for not giving more, will one day enter perpetual want of all good.

A WISE MAN WILL CONTINUALLY LEARN TO PERFECTION AND KNOWLEDGE-THE FOOL THINKS HE KNOWS IT ALL.

CHAPTER FOURTEEN

SUMMARY

Proverbs 14:1-30

This chapter, like the past ones, is made up of diverse subjects, ranging from the care of the home to the farm to public matters such as the courts, and the government, contrasting good and evil.

V. 1 "Every wise woman build her house: but the foolish pluck it down with her hands." In a spiritual sense, "to build a house" always means to edify or to build up in the trust, Acts 20:32; 1 Cor. 3:10, 12, 14; Jude 20. In a physical sense, "To build or make a house" means to give descendants, Ex. 1:21; 1 Sam. 2:5; 2 Sam. 7:11, 13, 27, 29; 1 Kings 11:38. However, numerous offspring become a curse if they are not well taught and trained, and a woman's life is either blessed with her children if they are good, or shattered if they are evil, 1 Tim. 2:15. One's walk is his habitual way of life, and it will reveal his attitude toward God, either as a reverence for Him, or contempt of Him. "Perverse" means to depart from accepted standards, and so it suggests that he shows his despite for God by transgressing His commands which are the standard for all men's conduct, Matthew 7:16-20.

A fool is full of empty words, and so his own boasting becomes a rod of chastisement upon him, for the worst thing that can happen to a proud man is to be humiliated by people finding out what he really is. The wise man's words, on the other hand, because they are truth, shall preserve him from most troubles. Many people want the wealth without the work that is necessary to attain it, and many think that it is beneath their dignity to get a little dirt under their fingernails in common labor. Some people are also so ignorant of how to grow wealth and are so fearful of lowering their dignity to learn that they could be placed in a perfect garden of good.

v. 5 "A faithful witness will not lie: but a false witness will utter lies." Witnesses always have a message of some sort which they are obligated to deliver without augmentation or reduction. The difference in a faithful and a false witness lies in what he does with his message. An unprincipled man will use his office for his own purposes without regard to whether his message is faithfully delivered or not nor benefits those he was sent to or not. God's view of liars (*The Original Liars that will not make Heaven*) is seen in Revelation 21:8, 27; and 22:15. For a faithful witness, one must choose a man who his life portrait or he who lives in the truth in private, and then it will be a way of life to him physically.

God is under no obligation to reveal truth to any unless they come as humble and submissive seekers. The scorner and unfaithful witness are one with an arrogant attitude toward much spiritual truth, and he is the one who seeks to pick and choose which truth he wants, according to as it is profitable to his pride, or position. The reason why some people seek wisdom and do not find it is because they do not seek it from a right principle," - That is, they seek it only for the sake of pride, or advancement, but never when it is for the glory of God, that which makes learning easy.

v. 7 "Go from the presence of a foolish man, when thou perceive not in him the lips of knowledge." Removal from the presence of a foolish person has several purposes: To prevent him from infecting you with his foolishness. Many people absorb foolishness from fools simply because they associate with them regularly. This involves the Biblical doctrine of separation. Since all the counsel and teaching in the world will not change his mind.

The wisdom of the prudent is to understand his way: but the folly of fools is deceit." The wise man will apply his wisdom to understand and direct his own way so that it will be acceptable to the Lord; but the unwise person will busy himself about other people's matters, deceiving himself into thinking that he has been appointed a judge and corrector of other people's faults. Though; fools mock at the presence of sin by denying it, the power of sin by limiting it, the penalty of sin, by doubting it, and the provisions for sin, by rejecting it.

v. 10 "The heart knoweth his own bitterness; and a stranger doth do not intermeddle with his joy." There was a saying in according to American Indians proverb: "Do not criticize an Indian man until you have walked two miles in his moccasins." No one can appreciate nor understand one suffering like the individual himself, 1 Cor. 2:11; Gal. 6:5. Though wicked men may have great mansions, and possess much that appears permanent, yet it shall all be overthrown and he shall lose all; and though the righteous have but a frail tent, and seem to be so very temporary in his abode, yet, by the blessing of the Lord, which the wicked have not, he shall grow, develop and multiply.

A general principle, but may be applied in many circumstances; what is right in our own eyes is not to be the standard, Deut. 12:8, for this leads inevitably, because of sin, man never thinks as God does, Isa. 55:8-9, and so he cannot reason out spiritual truth, but what seems to him to be right as per works for salvation, which indeed a reality of spiritual death. Spiritual truth is a mystery; i.e., something not found out by human reason, but divinely revealed to man by God. v. 13 "Even in laughter the heart is sorrowful, and the end of that merriment is heaviness

"The backslider in heart shall be filled with his own ways: and a good man shall be satisfied from himself." All backsliding is not open and obvious. Indeed, backsliding is always first done in the heart before it is ever manifested outwardly, and, for that matter, may never appear outwardly, but it is known to God Who looks upon the heart, 1Samuel 16:7. Therefore, though a person's backsliding may never come open, yet God may bring his sinful ways upon him even while he appears to be holy and just. This was what Job's friends assumed;

was true of him, but in his case, God was simply testing and proving his righteousness.

Technically speaking, none but a saved person can backslide, for the unsaved have nothing to slide back from, but the word is commonly used for turning aside from truth and right practices. "Backsliding" is never used in the N.T., but only of Israel. Saved people are maintained in a continual state of acceptance by the intercession of Christ, Eph. 1:6; Heb. 10:14.

To believe everything that one is told is not an act of faith: it is gullibility. God's Word alone is to be believed wholly and without questions, yet even this, we are commanded, like the Bereans to searched and rightly interpreted and discerned whatsoever word we are receiving in the Name of the Lord. If God, who is infallible, expects this of us, how much more must we be prudent in our acceptance of the words of sinful man? As a wise man, we should reverence God and fear in transgressing His Word. Sin, above all else, should be feared, for it is the deadliest thing of all. Only a fool does not fear it. Hot-tempered people almost always get themselves into trouble and make fools of themselves by too quickly responding in anger to a supposed offense. All anger is not sinful, but one must be careful not to sin through unrighteous anger Eph. 4:26 and those who refuse instruction set themselves up for problems, for all problems come either from ignorance of, or rebellion against the Word of God. To obey is to be blessed, since the Word always leads people into right paths, and so into the way of blessings. Evil will always bow before the good; and the wicked at the gates of the righteous." Of course, this is not often literal in the present evil world, where wicked men often persecute the righteous, but this is God's plan, and shall be fulfilled in due time, for the "meek shall inherit the earth," one of the most frequent promises in the bible, (Ps. 25:12-13; 37:9; 11, 22, 29, 34; Isa. 45:3; 57:13; 60:21; 65:9; Matthew 5:5; Rev. 21:1, 7).

Man generally cares for nothing except those who can benefit him. Whatever his pretense may be, the average person loves things more than people, and so he doesn't want to involve himself in anything that will cost him personally, but if something can be turned to a profit, he may has deep convictions about getting involved in it. "Most are swallow-friends that are gone in winter.

Respect of persons, simply because of their riches or lack of it, is a sin, James 2:1-9. Neighbors are to be loved as we love ourselves, Mark 12:31, not less, not more. God made them the same as the rich, and to despise the poor is to despise God's handiwork. Our Lord set the example by ministering to the poor most of all time, and we are to have the same faith that He had. To do good to the rich is often to seek to put him under obligation, which he may or may not honor; but God has promised to repay that which is done for the poor, and He will honor His commitments, Luke 14:12-14.

There are some evil individuals who may not have the courage to do evil, but they will devise it, and will encourage others to do it: these also err, just as those who actually do the evil, and they are to be punished as certainly as the actual doers, perhaps more so, for their very fear to do the evil shows their knowledge of right and wrong, and so their devising evil for others to do is a sin against light, and encouraging others to sin. Mercy is what all sinners need, and truth is the avenue to that mercy. Labor may be the result of the curse, Gen. 3:17-19, but it still has a profit in it for man.

The profit is not always immediately discernible, for what seems utterly unprofitable, will teaches patience, human inability and trust in God. But those who talk most often do the least, and talk without labor produces only poverty and even in religious exercises, too many words can be sinful, Eccl. 5:1-7. Perhaps; the hardest thing for any of us to learn is to control that wild beast, the tongue. It cannot be tamed, James 3:8, but it can be caged and controlled. That's what the teeth are there for.

There was wisdom as a crown of glory to seekers; in 14:18, the prudent are crowned with knowledge; and riches are added as a crown to those who seek first for divine wisdom and knowledge. This was the very order that came to Solomon, 1 Kings 3:5-13. Unless there is first wisdom given to one so that he will know how to wisely use what he has, his very riches can be a curse or sin to him. Whatever the sin may be, it has an impetuous action upon those who commit it—destruction'. A true witness by his faithful testimony delivers the innocent from those wrong-doing he is accused of; that may be slandered by evil men for their own profit. The faithful witness will always tell the truth, whatever the circumstances may be; whoever speaks a lie manifests his own bad character.

Why do men lie? Generally: 1 Out of fear of the consequences of telling the truth, out of a desire for some sort of gain, which they think will not come to them except they lie we have the faithful and true witness, a title given to Christ, Revelation. 3:14 - a description of His work. He delivers souls by telling them the truth about themselves, sin, God, salvation, etc. Satan, on the other hand, is the great arch-liar, John 8:44, and the original false witness, Gen. 3:1and 3-4.

We do not need to fear Satan; we should and only fear Jehovah Elohim. "Fear" here means a reverential fear, which only the saved are capable of having, and this reverence in the Lord results in confidence in the Lord, that He will take care of and keep secure what we commit to Him, 2 Tim. 1:12. The Lord's children always have a place of refuge, for the Lord is their refuge, Deut. 33:27; Ps. 46:1. This is what promotes boldness in the believer, Heb. 4:14-16; 12:5-6.

The truly wise person recognizes that the will of the Lord is the law of his life and that it will lead him to life eternal, and so he will depart from those things which would ensnare him to sin, which leads to death. This fear involves trust, and promotes confidence, but not presumption – (it does not matter, God understand that is not easy and or; misquoting God's grace), which moves upon a lack of fear.

Some rulers are so interested in increasing the national wealth that no care is taken of the nation's greatest natural resources—its youth. A wise ruler, who keeps his nation out of devastating wars, will have many people, but he who gets his nation embroiled in wars will kill off the young men of the nation until it may eventually take away even the king's son. It is very bad when an ordinary person loves possessions or calls it; materials, properties, and money more than people, but it is very much worse when the ruler feels this way, he will be a curse to his nation. Just like an angry man, for there are so many unseen factors that the hot-tempered never considers, but which have an important bearing on a matter. We need to be God-like in longsuffering. He, who is short-tempered, is not only foolish, but he even exalts folly. Lack of restraint upon one's temper will soon earn one a reputation which will do no good to him. A bad spirit in a person will often disrupt his physical health – cause tension, headache, upset stomachs, ulcers, sometimes even heart attacks. Anger, envy, bitterness, etc., is each its own punishment, but a spiritually healthy spirit promotes a physically healthy body.

v. 31, as mention above "He that oppressed the poor reproached his Maker: but he that honored him hath mercy on the poor." God both made the poor, and it is because of the lack of His blessing that one remains poor, to oppress someone simply because of his poverty is to assume that the poor is God's enemy and that one is justified by mistreating them. Many people forget that this world is now in Satan's hands, and is used by him to reward his people, Luke 4:5-6.

A poor man is more apt to be a man of God than a rich man. On the other hand, the righteous has a confidence that a glorious heaven awaits him and the wicked will die in his wickedness, and since no sin can stand in the presence of the holy God, the wicked shall be driven away from the presence of God into Satan domain, the refuse dump for the spiritually worthless. "This principle is operative in all realms of life. The dead are separated from the living—Refuse is separated from the things of value "Those who refuse life in God become 'refuse' in character sooner or later, and with the look and the nature of things they must be removed to a place apart, Luke 3:17. To be wise is of a great value and it must be in the heart in order to move one to right living any merely outward or even mental wisdom is of little practical value.

A sinful nature cannot long be hidden, for, like cancer, it will eventually break out into the open with other symptoms. The fruit is always the proof of the plant. God honors righteousness wherever it is found and He causes it to exalt the nation that practices it.

A righteous nation is one that keeps the truth, Isa. 26:2 and where truth is not kept, there will be no real righteousness. Perhaps this is why our nation is falling away from its former greatness: it has forsaken the truth in its schools, law-making bodies, the judicial system, etc. It is natural and Wisdom expedient for a king to reward the wise and good servants, for this will promote the stability of his kingdom, and as this is a recognized fact in earthly kingdoms, so in God's greater kingdom, righteous nations, being God's servants will be blessed, but rebellious nations will be punished, Matthew 13:41-43

IN REALITY - IF ONE PRACTICES THE ENTIRE NUGGET
OF WISDOM IN THIS BOOK OF PROVERBS, HE WOULD
ELIMINATE MANY TROUBLES FROM HIS OR HER LIFE.

CHAPTER FIFTEEN

SUMMARY

Proverbs 15:1-14

A soft answer turned away wrath: but grievous words stir up anger. Nothing so appeases anger in a person like presenting a quiet, unresisting answer. But a strong word only causes an angry man to feel that he must further defend his position. "Stir up" is literally "make to ascend" and pictures anger, like a fire, being fanned into an even greater fire. Soft words, like oil on a wound, have a soothing effect. This does not mean that we can never disagree with an opponent, for often truth demands that we do, but we are simply to use words that do not uselessly antagonize him, for if we do this, we lose all opportunity to declare truth to him, for he closes his mind to all we say. Also is the truth that a man is known by his speech, and this also teaches that one may have knowledge, but misuse it. "Think twice before you speak once" is good counsel, for "While the word is unspoken you are master of it, but when once it is spoken, it is master of you," [Author unknown].

V. 3 "The eyes of the Lord are in every place, beholding the evil and the good." This refers to Jehovah Elohim as the omniscience (all-knowing

God) for "eyes" are suggestive of knowledge, since so much of our knowledge is gained through the eyes—reading, observing, etc. Many texts speak of this, Job 34:21; Ps. 94:9-11; John 2:24-25; Heb. 4:12-13. The eyes of the Lord are apparently like a great TV camera, for they not only observe all things both in Heaven, Earth and deep of the Sea but also record all to be played before each one at the judgment Day Revelation 20:12.

A healthy tongue is a tree of life in that it is the instrument of a witness, leading the erring back into the way that leads to the tree of life. Wisdom is the tree of life, Prov. 3:18, and wisdom comes to us by the teaching of someone who has already received wisdom. A godly parent that have received grace from Wisdom should be heeded and obeyed: Because God has given them authority over their children, generally have from twenty to forty years more experience in life than their children and they are generally better educated than their children, however, the children may think otherwise. Yet; godly parent generally has only the children's best interests in mind, while the children are often selfishly motivated in their desires. No one has to prove a fool to be a fool: he will prove himself to be so when he despises discipline and reproof.

To be born and reared in a godly home is to have a foretaste of the new earth. Those born in a home where righteousness is the chief characteristic are rich, though they may not possess anything of this world's goods, but those who are rich without being righteous shall have only trouble for the increase of their riches. God can easily make riches to become a curse to those who possess them. Godliness with contentment with what one has is a great gain, 1 Tim. 6:6-8, 17-19). To make use of our lips for the uplifting of our friends is godly; Jesus taught several parables in which the Word of God is likened to seed which is sown by the faithful teaching and preaching of it, Matthew 13:3.

It is blasphemy when a man uses his lips against the purpose for which they were created; of which dishonor and degrade God and His truth. The best efforts of a religious man are still hateful in God's sight because they spring from a heart still in rebellion against the Lord. This is why human works can never avail for salvation, though they may be done sacrificially;

they are "wicked works" because of their source, because they are done as a substitute for, and in contempt of, the work of Christ, being an evidence that one thinks he can serve God acceptably in his own wisdom and strength, and for other reasons. In nothing can the way of a unsaved man (Arthropods) please God: it takes a believing heart to please God, Heb. 11:6. "Way" of course, has to do with the daily walk and behavior.

A man's religious exercises may be hypocritical and his daily walk might not be a reflection of his heart's real condition, but his thoughts will reflect his heart, and God knows the hearts of all men. Those who are really saved will have an internal drive to follow after righteousness, for the righteous heart of the saved will pursue and seek to attain to greater righteousness in the Lord Jesus Christ.

Sin always has both a hardening and a blinding effect upon the sinner, and the more conviction he feels, the more hardened he becomes. It is like the tempering of metal: the more it is heated and pounded, the harder it becomes. Only the grace of God can break this vicious spiritual circle and enable one to repent and believe, Acts 11:17. God sees through all the hearts of the children of men." "Satan domain and destruction are before Him "Hell" here is Sheol, which is much more than equivalent to the Greek Hades which is the unseen world and "Destruction" is the Hebrew Abaddon, Rev. 9:11. "That destroyer, though he deceives us, cannot evade or elude the divine cognizance. If Jehovah sees through the depths and wiles of Satan himself, how much more can He search men's hearts, yet; God sees a man in their real character in the heart and will deal with them as they justly deserve. But the heart is deceitful above all things and desperately wicked, Jer. 17:9, a scorner deceiving even itself into thinking that it can be sinning with impunity. The whole problem with the scorner is that he is too proud to admit that he is ignorant and sinful, and he hates anyone who speaks so as to reveal this to him. He is sinfully self-satisfied in his present condition. Thus sin ever operates: it hardens one against the remedy for it and so increases sin by denying the existence of sin, hating the one who reveals it, and so not only continues in the original sin but sins against the knowledge of one's sinfulness and need to repent. It is a sin against light and Divine Spirit. When the heart is right with the Lord, and He is giving regular evidence of His favor, it is easy to have a cheerful countenance. However, the Lord has never promised an unbroken series of joys in his life: conversely, we are promised tribulation and persecution in this world, John 16:33; Acts 14:22; Rom. 8:17; II Tim. 3:12. However, blessed by our God, He has promised that we can glory even in tribulation, Rom. 5:3; 12:12; 2 Cor. 4:17-18. On the other hand, the continual sorrow of heart destroys the will to live, as doctors so often have found in patients who had sorrow of heart.

The heart, like water, seeks its own level; the renewed heart, having come to know the Lord, hunger after further knowledge of Him, but the unsaved heart, being yet dominated by sin, feeds on the things of sin. One generally manifests the condition of his heart by his attitude toward Divine truth: it is one of the laws of the kingdom of God that those who hunger and thirst after righteousness will be filled, Matthew 5:6, which is, characteristic of the one who has spiritual understanding.

Proverbs 15:15 – 33

"All the days of the afflicted are evil: but he that is of a merry heart hath a continual feast." It is sometimes the lot even of those who are genuinely saved to be afflicted most of their days on earth; we do not always understand why God chooses to allow some to suffer, but when it is for His glory, they will be abundantly rewarded. We should have sympathy for any who are suffering, not self-righteously to set ourselves up as censors and judges of them, for we know not all the facts. But he who is merry of heart will be in continual rejoicing and every day will seem like one of Israel's national holidays, of which there were much joy and rejoicing, dancing and feasting. The "fear of the Lord," which involves salvation, is the supreme treasure, for if one only has "little" of this world's goods with it, he is still supremely rich in that he is an heir of the world that is to come. Many, while possessing great riches, are not rich toward God, Luke 12:21

V. 17 "Better is a dinner of herbs where love is, than a stalled ox and hatred therewith." "Dinner of herbs" refers to a restricted amount of food, even a poor meal is a feast if there is love there, but even the most sumptuous meal without the fear of the Lord is no profit, Luke 16:19, 22-23. The main trouble with people today is that they do not keep things in the proper perspective: they give much care to the body which is to perish after only seventy years or so, but they totally ignore the soul which must eternally exist somewhere either in Heaven or Satan domain. " A "wrathful man" is one who is full of hatred and anger, a frustrated, hateful person, and such will continually be the source of strife, stirring it up even where a perfect harmony existed before.

We all have to be careful that we do not take out our anger and frustrations on those who are not the cause of them, for life is such that there will always be things to anger and frustrate us, and if we do not have the love of God pervading and sweetening our hearts and lives, we will go about with a continual chip on our shoulders. Slowness to anger is the Christian way, James 1:19. Hasty words are almost always unwise. v. 19 "The way of the slothful man is as a hedge of thorns: but the way of the righteous is made plain." Anciently fields were fenced with hedges of thorns, which not only were prickly to the touch but which also were inhabited oftentimes by snakes, Eccl. 10:8), the slothful man sees all sorts of difficulties and dangers to the work that he ought to do, for he looks for excuses not to labor.

The way of the righteous, however, shall be made an elevated, even walkway that is easy and safe. God makes all things work together for good to His righteous ones, for He delights to do good for them, and has determined to do so for them. See Proverbs 20:4 and 22:13 for other excuses that the slothful man makes for not performing his work.

The Biblical command is not merely to obey parents, which might be done scornfully and hatefully, but rather is to honor them, which requires respectful obedience to parents. "A wicked man sins, not only without regret but with delight." A saved person often falls into sin, but unless he is terribly backslidden, sin will bother him. What kind of a person would joy in folly? Surely not one who knows not the way of the Lord, nor has received the Wisdom of God.

By way of contrast, a man of spiritual understanding will live a life of uprightness. The man was originally created upright in behavior, but he has sought out many sinful inventions, Eccl. 7:29. Salvation enables man to and this comes about by knowing the Lord as Savior and Master.

When anyone makes a rash decision without properly considering godly counsel, he will have occasion to repent of his haste. "Counsel" is more commonly rendered "secret" or "secret counsel," and so seems to refer to one's inward counsel before making any decision. And it is generally wise to seek the counsel of several others who are qualified to give counsel in the particular matter to be decided. Perhaps there is here also a reference to the folly of the scorner.

In verse 12, who will not take any counsel from anyone? Even the Almighty God took counsel between the People of the Trinity before the great purposes were set in motion, Jeremiah 23:18; Gen. 1:26; Psalm. 33:8-11. Of course, counselors should not be multiplied simply for numbers' sake, but rather they should be chosen for their wisdom and spirituality. It is far better not to be rash in a word in other to avoid unnecessary pull and push.

How easy it is to speak without considering well the consequences of that word, yet how far-reaching and sad may be the results of a thoughtless word. Countless reputations and lives have been destroyed in this way. Let us always diligently consider the effects of our speech before we speak, and then not speak if there be any question about its appropriateness. Many people expect to get to heaven without being, thinking or acting heavenly, but this is one of the devil's deceptions. Salvation is not only an instantaneous event, but it is also a way of life which continually tends upward morally and spiritually, (Col. 3:1-2).

The proud seems to act out his pride, of which tend to be an abomination to the Lord, Prov. 16:5, for it is not a part of the way of life that is heavenly but is rather that form of life which leads to Satanic domain. "The proud, by oppression, build a strong 'house,' or family, which they are confident will never be overthrown, but the widow (Hebrew, Almanac, to be dumb, or powerless against adversaries) seems to the proud 'a prey' that can offer no resistance.

God will destroy the seemingly strong 'house' of the proud, and will protect the border' of the widow. v. 26 "The thoughts of the wicked are an abomination to the Lord: but the words of the pure are pleasant words." "As the thoughts are bad or good, so the words are abomination or pleasantness before the Lord. It is a vain excuse for bad words to say, 'I meant no harm, men may hide their wicked thoughts from men, but God, who knows the thoughts of men, sees all, and hates even the inward thoughts, though no wicked acts may be done.

Hence, one who outwardly appears righteous may actually be hated by the Lord because He sees the true condition of the heart. To some people material security is a god, which is why covetousness is termed idolatry, Col. 3:5 and "Gifts" refer to bribes, which always tend to pervert justice in those receiving them, Ex. 23:8. The greedy man's philosophy, however, is "get all you can from anyone you can in any way you can and save as much of it as you can without considering the consequence that follows which is always a curse to the individual, and to his household, for he generally conforms all things to his pursuit of material things, and so, often ignores the feelings and needs of his family; this is wickedness.

Rashness in speech is always a great evil, Eccl. 5:1-7. Some matters require much thought before an answer is given, and rash speech is often dangerous. As the parallel statement suggests, God is far from hearing the prayer of the wicked, but He is always near and hears the prayer of His own, and actually delights in it, Prov. 15:18; Ps. 34:15-16. What a horrible situation? If God refuses to hear the prayer of the wicked, how then can he be saved? Of course, this refers either to those who have continually rejected the Lord when He called them, Proverbs 1:24-33, or to the ones who pray for other things, while rejecting the Lord's salvation and headship.

However, our eyes are the avenues through which truth enters into the heart, and this causes rejoicing and or; the good news of any sort, especially the gospel, blesses the whole man, giving him hope, and so, causing good bodily health. It is now well known that a hopeless attitude works against one's recovery of health.

There are some reproofs which are not unto life, especially if someone is a victim of ridicule and persecution, but consolation and comfort derived from truth can be found among the spiritually wise, for the rebel against God never has an ear capable of understanding spiritual truth. There must be a willingness to obey before there can be a knowledge of the truth, John

7:17; One of the most common phrases in the N.T. is "He that hath an ear to hear, let him hear ..." It appears sixteen times and implies that not everyone is capable of hearing the spiritual truth, Prov. 28:27; Rom. 11:8.

Rebellion against known truth tends to further deaden one's ability to hear. This takes up the thought of the last verse and carries it on. Rebellion against instruction may please the pride, but it is a sin against the soul. It is the trading of things of eternal value for worthless momentary pleasures for the body. To hear the reproofs of the Scriptures is to gain more spiritual knowledge. Throughout Proverbs there is continual stress laid upon hearing and receiving truth and it is this discipline of wisdom which promotes the fear of the Lord, and a fear of the Lord will be manifested by submission to this discipline of the Word, for this is the key to all good things.

WE SHOULD LIVE OUR LIVES AS THOUGH
CHRIST IS COMING TODAY

CHAPTER SIXTEEN

SUMMARY

Proverbs 16:1 - 24

The preparations of the heart in man and the answer of the tongue are from the Lord. "Preparations" means to dispose or to set in order, Man may imagine many things in his heart, but if there are any right and orderly thoughts, they must be traced to the Lord's workings, because nothing is as characteristic of man as his pride and self-righteousness. We all tend to think of ourselves as the standard by which all others should be judged. This is but one of the many pieces of evidence of the total depravity of the human mind and heart, and the idolatrous self-worship of the heart. God weighs and ponders man's spirit and heart, Proverbs 21:2, and He judges by the truth. God's judgment alone is perfect and just.

Man's works are never in themselves pure, Isa. 64:6, and so they are never profitable, Isa. 57:12, but if we commit ourselves and our deficiencies to the Lord, He will work in our works that are acceptable, Isa. 26:12; Phil. 2:13, for He will work the righteousness of Christ in us, Rom. 4:1-5, and this is the only kind of works which finds a perfect acceptance with God, and that will establish us in peace, Rom. 5:1; Isa. 26:3-4.

There can never be an established peace of mind in him who trusts his own works, for he is always conscious of the shortcoming of his best works. God is the great first cause of all things—the original creator of all alike. However, it may at times seem that God has lost control, and however wicked men may even disclaim God's control over them, it is nonetheless true that God has never surrendered His control for even a moment.

LIFE APPLICATION:

I remember an article of some sects that expresses their belief about God: To the Mormon they said God is weak, to the Occult they said God is wicked, that He always allow His children to suffer and that in their own secret coven nobody dare maltreat their follower without dealing terribly with such one and the Buddhists and New-Age Movement threw the question back to Servant of God that interview with them and they said 'is there God?'

All these evil statements and portraits happen just because Jehovah Elohim, Almighty God is full of Eternal love and patient, even evil things, are still by God's permissive, if not His determinative decree. Wicked men do not exist just because God cannot control them, but He permits them to exist, and brings His own good and glory to pass in spite of them, and sometimes through them, as He did at the crucifixion of Christ, the greatest good that God ever did. "God is the last end.

All is of Him and from Him, and therefore all is to Him and for Him. Pride cannot often be seen by man, for it has its residence in the heart. It may be manifest by actions, but often it is not. However, God sees it in the heart and hates it, for pride is principally that which causes a man to reject God, Ps. 10:4, since it always endeavors to exalt self to an underserved position.

Pride was the original sin of the universe, being the sin of Satan, 1Timothy 3:6; Isa. 14:12-15. In his pride, man has raised up many unholy alliances which he fancied that none could call him to account for his evil, but God decrees otherwise. Nothing can prevent the judgment and condemnation of evil men but the blood of the Lord Jesus Christ applied to the individual heart. "The guilt of sin is taken away from us—the mercy and truth of God in Jesus Christ the Mediator, and not by the legal sacrifices, Micah 6:7-8.

The power of sin is broken in us. This does not mean that by our practice of mercy and truth iniquity is purged, for this would be to make us our own savior, but it refers to the mercy and truth in Christ who died to save men, John 1:14, 17; Titus 3:4-7.

The outward departure of men from evil is only made possible by an inwrought "fear of the Lord" which is the accompaniment of the new birth, and is one of the manifestations of the "new creature." Unchanged men do not fear God, Ps. 55:19, and so they do not depart from evil.

God has the hearts of all men in His hand, from the mightiest to the least, Prov. 21:1, and He is able to sway the heart any way He pleases, He is able to turn enemies into friends. How often has God given men favor in the eyes of those who might easily have hated them, Gen. 31:24, 29; 33: 1-4, 39:21). By the same token, God can stir up animosities against a person who is not in His favor because of sin, 1 Kings 11:14; 1 Chron. 5:26; 2 Chron. 21:16. Thus, the key to getting along with man is to be in the will of the Lord. He then will take care of any problems that arise because of man's hatred of us. If one has the Lord's righteousness, it matters little what else he may not have, for as soon as this short life is over he goes to eternal riches with the Lord. But to possess great wealth without righteousness is to only to generate a taste for luxury which shall be eternally unsatisfied even after death, yet; many are daily selling their souls for the revenues of earth and to Satan deceptions.

We all need to daily pray the prayer of 1 Thessalonians 3:11. It is natural for a man to proudly think that he can direct his own way, but it is spiritual for one to confess his own insufficiency, and to submit to God's direction, 2 Cor. 3:4-6. What direction does the Lord's direction lead? He must have divine direction if he is to fulfill the divine purpose. Every ruler ought to see the importance of his position and so pray that he may speak as an oracle of God. This is the divine ideal for all who are in authority; this does not mean that rulers always speak the Lord's truth or that they never make mistakes in judgment. The king and leaders' observance of justice in the civil of commerce between man and man is likewise a divine appointment," Deut. 25:13-15. Behold, then, that God takes an interest even in commerce, that it should be honest. But for many people, too much of gain is their supreme god, and they will use every unscrupulous means to attain it, this is idolatry.

"It is an abomination to kings to commit wickedness: for the throne is established by righteousness."

He that makes conscience of using his power aright shall find that to be the best security of his government and it will obtain the blessing of God, a basis to the throne and a strong guard about it. It is a fact obvious to all, that people tend to follow the example of national leaders, so that a king who sins, not only sins as a private person, but also in his official position, and his sin is greater in evil because of his influence on the people 2 Samuel 24:10-17.

Every ruler has to contend with flattering parasites who desire to favor themselves with the king for the sake of power and position so that to find one who speaks honestly is sometimes a rare thing. But if a king is what he should be, he will not only be righteous himself, v. 12, but he will surround himself with aides and subordinates who are likewise righteous. Sometimes good kings have lost their kingdoms because they were careless about those whom they placed in office under them, and so the kingdom was corrupted in spite of the king's own personal integrity. Kings today are, for the most part, mere figureheads and do not have the absolute arbitrary power of life and death that all kings once had. It was not at all uncommon in ancient times for men to lose their lives at a whim from the king, so that in every sense, it was wisdom to pacify the king's wrath, lest one lose his head. Solomon spoke from actual experience, for him himself had sentenced men to death, 1 Kings 2:22-25. Especially in ancient times, and even today in some countries, the ruler had to always be on guard against those who would try to overthrow and supplant him.

As the king's anger often resulted in death, so his favor tended toward life. Psalm 30:5 has special bearing on this matter, as regard the King of Kings, for unless one has God's favor (grace) he is hopelessly shut out from all good, and is under the wrath of God. Faith is the evidence that one is in God's grace, (John 3:36). Grace is more valuable than gold. Grace is the gift of God's peculiar favor; gold only of common providence." Gold can purchase many things, but those things which are of most value cannot be purchased by gold, but they can be obtained by wisdom. If a person has only gold, there are many things he cannot obtain it, but if he has wisdom, he can obtain all things, including gold. It is sad; however, how many people make an idol out of wealth.

V. 17 "The highway of the upright is to depart from evil: he that kept his way preserved his soul." A highway is the way of common travel, and is generally the best way of travel, being compared with the mere byways and paths. The way of unrighteousness may appear broad and easy, Matthew 7:13-14. The greatest sins in the world always start with just one small step out of the way of truth and holiness. Hence, if we guard our way from that first false step, we preserve our souls.

Pride attempts to exalt itself, but it always leads to destruction—a fitting reward, which is why it is never a profitable thing to anyone. A humble attitude and Keeping company with those who are humble is a great displaying of wisdom rather than with those who are proud. Never forget it: our associates influence us more than any of us realize. To associate with the lowly is to be more apt to be in fellowship with the Lord's people than if we try to be social climbers and associate with the upper-crust, 1 Cor. 1:26-29. Even worldly wealth means nothing if it is gained in improper ways or by association with worldly people, who corrupt us in the process. Prudence in business may cause men to respect a person, but only by trusting in the Lord will men find true happiness both here and hereafter.

There are many intellectually smart men who are called intelligent by the world, but who are actually fools in God's sight. The last part of this verse suggests that as the wise in heart faithfully present the sweet richness of the Word to others, they will increase their own learning, as well as instruct others.

Those who have been saved have the ability to tell others of their experience and so to lead them to a saving knowledge of Christ. Too often Christians do not witness to others because they have erroneously assumed that it takes a degree of theology to do so. Nothing could be further from the truth. See Mark 5:18-20. As per: Experience, Explanation, Evangelization and which doubtless resulted in Exaltation of the Lord. But the unsaved person's teaching of others only leads to the deceiving of them as well. Wisdom in the heart is the main matter, the lips are only the mechanical ways which form the words, but the words are the expression of the thoughts of the heart. On the other hand, evil words hurt the speaker more than the one against whom they are directed, for bitter words show a bitter heart, and this poisons the whole person, body, mind and spirit.

Anciently, even as now, honey was a medicinal, as well as a pleasant food, and so also are words well spoken. Sometimes we must force ourselves to speak pleasantly when we would rather lash out with angry words, but it is always better to speak soft words, for we never have to repent of them, but we often do of bitter words.

v. 25 - "There is a way that seems right unto a man, but the end thereof is the ways of death." This was similar to Proverbs 14:12. God has repeated this truth to show its certainty, Gen. 41:32. Carnal reason instead of submission to God has damned as many souls as any other single sin. Following what "seems right" shows self-sufficiency on man's part, 2 Samuel 24:10-17. Man does not think as God thinks, Isa. 55:7-8, and so he must unquestioningly submit to God's Word in order to do what is right. The same notion denotes when a man is trusting in the self-efforts for salvation. Physical labor is man's appointed lot, and is generally necessary to life, (Gen. 3:17-19). It was ordained because of the curse.

However, labor for spiritual life is not only not commended, it is forbidden, and the attempt to earn eternal life by human effort is always fatal, for it is under God's curse, Gal. 3:10, for it takes the presumptuous ground that sinful man can put the Holy God under obligation to save him by his works: it is a denial of God's declaration that salvation is by grace, Rom. 4:4-5, 16. v. 27 "An ungodly man dig up evil: and in his lips there is as a burning fire." In the film of His Pilgrim's Progress by John Bunyan, he pictured this kind of man as "unsanctified Simple." This type of person, if he cannot find something to blow up to do evil by suspicious and insinuation, he will lie about another thing just to appear more righteous in other to deceives a righteous pilgrim out of the right path.

How large a lie or even a suspicion does take to destroy a reputation? A man's very use of falsehoods against a fellow showing his wicked character, Rev. 22:15.

There is no relationship so holy or so close that wicked people will not attempt to disrupt it by sowing strife and whispering lie in the first one and then the others' ears. Suspicions, wrong accusations, and outright lies are the seeds that generate strife, and these are what the wicked person sows. Why would anyone deliberately try to cause strife: Some, because they do not have the capacity or the desire to love others, seem to be antagonized by those who do love one another, and so they try to disrupt the relationship? Some are jealous of others' happiness, such are like the devil.

The violent man, when violence is not likely to succeed, resorts to enticement, and stitches the fox's skin to the lion's skin, in order to effect his violent purpose of destroying 'his neighbor' Ps. 10:4-10. It is strange, but sinners are never content to sit alone: they always want to entice others into sin with them. Sin is a sin if one commits it or if one million commit it and God's Word determines what sin is.

Instead of the wicked men meditating on spiritual things, he meditates on sinful things, planning on how to accomplish the evil of his heart until he has thought it out, then he gives the command to his subordinates and associates to accomplish it. A good description of such is that given in Genesis 6:5. This describes the total depravity of all men by nature, and only the restraints human right law imposed by society, circumstances and the restraining grace of God keep many from going to these lengths.

The gray head is a crown of glory if it is found in the way of righteousness." This refers to gray-headedness, which is to be honored, Lev. 19:32, for it represent acquired wisdom and experience which the young generally do not have. There are exceptions, for not all gray-haired men are wise or experienced, and some youths are. Gray hair is a crown of glory only if it represents wisdom and experience in the way of righteousness. Many gray-haired people are only wise to do evil and experienced only in sin and rebellion, Jer. 4:22. To them, their hoary locks will only be a badge of shame in the Day of Judgment. The Lord's righteousness, not man's ideas of righteousness, not the mores of society will be the absolute and unvarying standard on the Day of Judgment. (See the Life application above about my old aunt and aunt prophet).

Those that control their anger and rule their spirit in righteousness are mightier and the later revelations show that the way to rule one's spirit is to have it in total subjection to God's Spirit who leads into all truth both in doctrine and in practice.

Many things that we read of in Scripture seem at first glance to be mere accidents, but are later revealed to be the outworking of God's providence. This last verse of this chapter shows that even insignificant matter as per casting the lot into the lap was controlled by the Lord. Since the belief of this fact, People anciently often decided matters by casting the lot, sometimes even at the Lord's command, Lev. 16:8-10; Num. 26:55-56; Joshua 7:14-18; 1 Sam. 10:19-21; Neh. 10:34; Esther 3:7; Jonah 1:7; Matthew 27:36; Acts 1:26. "Lot is a mutual agreement to determine an uncertain event, no other ways determinable, by an appeal to the providence of God, on casting or throwing something.

WHATEVER MAKES MEN GOOD CHRISTIANS
MAKES THEM GOOD CITIZEN

CHAPTER SEVENTEEN

SUMMARY

Proverbs 17:1 - 28

Better is a dry morsel and quietness therewith than a house full of sacrifices with strife. Bread, the staple food in ancient times, was eaten with butter, honey or a vinegary dip. A dry morsel would be a bit of bread without anything to go with it. The best beasts were used to sacrifice, yet even the dry crust of bread would be better in a house where there were peace and harmony than the choicest food with constant wrangling. Who can enjoy food if the stomach is upset because of an inharmonious home? The inharmonious home may also be caused by a son who lives shamefully.

A wise and godly servant was sometimes given authority over the minor children. This imagery is at the base of Galatians 3:23-25. It was not uncommon for men to cause faithful servants to inherit with the true sons. Sometimes the servant acted more like a son than the real son did, so far as honor and respect were concerned, and so was given the place and honor of a son. As crucibles were used both to prove and to purify metals, so the Lord also often puts people in the crucible of trial both to prove and to improve them. Fire will destroy some things, like wood, hay, and stubble, but it only purifies such things as gold, silver and precious stones, 1 Cor. 3:12-15.

We are tested as to our works, and the defective are burned up but the good is only purified. When trials come upon us, let us not grumble and complain: let us examine ourselves as to whether: this is a chastisement for sin, for purification of some fault, or preparation for some great blessing and or opportunity to glorify God by our patient endurance of sufferings. v. 4 "A wicked doer gives heed to false lips, and a liar gives ear to a naughty tongue." Sin in action appeals to sin in the heart, and wicked men find it easy to heed other wicked men.

The Bible gives special emphasis to liars, showing their satanic character, John 8:44; 1 John 1:10; 2:4, 22; 5:10; Rev. 21:8, 27; 22:15. v. 5 "Whoso mocked the poor reproached his Maker: and he that is glad at calamities shall not be unpunished." To ridicule a work is to ridicule the workman who made it, and so this reflects upon God. To mock those who are suffering calamity manifests a proud, self-righteous spirit on our part as if the same could not happen to us. We must all remember that if not for God's grace and mercy, we could all be in much worse state than we are, and if we tolerate pride in ourselves, we may fall, Prov. 16:5, 18. "Those who trample upon the poor, who ridicule their wants, reproach their Maker, who owns them, and takes care of them, and can, when he pleases, reduce us to that condition

v. 6 "Children's children are the crown of old men, and the glory of children are their fathers." This shows that fathers, children, and grandchildren should constitute a mutual admiration society. It is natural for people to rejoice in their offspring, and for children to admire their parents. When either one does not live so as to deserve the love and admiration of the other, it is a sad matter. Worthless children may make parents wish they had never lived, for they feel their lives were pointless. By the same token, children of worthless parents, having no heritage to look back upon and admire, often feel inferior and have no high standard of life to strive for. v. 7. A fool, in Solomon's proverbs, signifies a wicked man, whom excellent speech does not become because his conversation gives the lie to his excellent speech. Many people talk religion and morality very well, but they are strangers to the practice of it, and so they are hypocrites to all who know their lives. Just as excellent speech is unbecoming but lying lips are more characteristic to the wicked, so excellent speech is becoming to a prince, but lying lips are not. A prince, because of his position, is to lead an exemplary life before his people. There was a biblical injunction that he would not take a bribe in other to turn away justice. People often use gifts to bribe others.

The purpose behind a gift determines whether it is right or wrong Prov. 18:16; Gen. 32:20; and Abigail's to David 1 Sam. 25:27. It is both an act of love and the promotion of love to cover a transgression. There are times when to cover a sin would be wrong, as when it is a public sin and brings reproach against the Lord and His church, as in 1 Corinthians 5. This does not mean that acts of love serve as atonement for our sins before God, but they do prevent hard feelings toward those who have sinned against us. The gossip-monger, however, may ruin the best of friendships.

A person actually reveals what he is in the heart by his response to a justified reproof: the wise person accepts it and appreciates it, but the fool resents it and rebels against it. Peter took Paul's reproof of him well, Gal. 2:11-14. 2 Pet. 3:15-16. The fool, because of his naturally rebellious nature, is generally only hardened by reproofs and punishments, and he generally hates those who reprove him, Prov. 9:8; 15:12, but better to be reproved of rebellion act by man than to have to face God unrepentant, rebellion is an evidences of an evil heart, for the Christian is commanded to submit to government, Rom. 13:1-7, to one another and to God, 1 Pet. 5:5-7, and we are not even to resist evil that is directed against us personally, Matthew 5:39-42, for God, often sends men to execute judgment upon rebellious men, and certainly angels shall do the same at the end of the age, Matthew 13:39-40.

v.12 "Let a bear robbed of her whelps meet a man, rather than a fool in his folly." She-bear, robbed of her cubs, will attack the first creature that crosses her path; so a fool in his sin will rage against the first person he meets without regard to his innocence or guilt in the matter. Sin robs men of reasoning power. Anger is temporary madness and often sin causes sinners to act rashly, adding sin to sin. To render good for good is human: to render evil for evil is brutish, but to render evil for good is devilish. Only God and those lead by Him render good for evil. God's command is for His people to overcome evil with good, Rom. 12:21. He who renders evil for good shall have as his reward, not only evil upon himself; but on his house as well, for generally, an evil man's household are partakers of his evil nature and follows his lead. One hot word begets another, and so on. The Bible is very plain-spoken and often uses body parts and functions to illustrate spiritual truth. In either case, the truth is plain: strife is easier started than stopped. "It is easier to abstain from a contest than to withdraw from it." The whole purpose of government is to punish evil and to reward good, and so to encourage right living, Rom. 13:1-4; 1 Tim. 1:8-10.

Therefore, to justify the wicked or to condemn the righteous is to tend to the overthrow of all government by the encouraging of evil and the discouraging of good acts. For any person, but especially for a ruler, to justify the wicked is to show one's heart to be really wicked, God cannot but hate all wickedness, and in anyone, it is found. He will not align Himself with sinners: sinners must align themselves with Him.

v. 16. It is the practice of many to go to college, not to learn, but only to get a degree, while one continues to hold on to his original preconceptions and prejudices. The difference in a fool and a wise man is that a fool forms his ideas, and then studies for facts to substantiate them, while the wise man studies to learn the truth, bringing all his ideas to the touchstone by asking himself, "Is it in harmony with the truth?"

v. 17. Someone has wisely said that "A friend is someone who knows all about you and still loves you." Adversity is the test which proves who real friends are: false friends will not want to get involved when it costs effort, money or a stand against the popular practice, though; not as a fool. Like in this very verse 18, compared with previous verse as per assisting a friend in time of need, still need one to take caution. To become surety "in the presence" of one, especially if he is unscrupulous, is to encourage his negligence, for he knows that after a time of being unable to collect from him, the creditor will go after the surety and collect from him and this was the beginning of strife. Thank God we have a Surety who delights to make up what is deficient for us, Heb. 7:22. Do we love Him enough for this to honor Him above all things? Strife is one of the words of the flesh, Gal. 5:20, and is often condemned Rom. 13:13; 2 Cor. 12:20; Phil. 2:3; James 3:14-16. In strife, both can be wrong, but both cannot be right. This may have reference to the previous verse, for strife arises from a proud and perverse heart.

The tongue is always the index to the heart. A Perverse heart is a double heart, Ps. 12:2, a deep heart, Ps. 64:6 and a deceived heart, Isa. 44:20. Under these circumstances, naturally there can be no permanent good. "Perverse" means turning or changing as the circumstances may be, and so it refers to the double-tongue person who tells one story to one and a different one to another.

There is generally joy at the birth of a child, but sometimes twenty years later, there is great sorrow that such a child was born, for he grows up to be a wicked man. When the father finds afterward that what he had regarded as a joy is but a 'sorrow,' when the son betrays and display his foolishness. It is a true saying that a cheerful outlook prevents sickness, and it promotes healing when sicknesses demand taking medicine. It generally promotes longevity, but "hope deferred" time after time "makes the heart sick," Prov. 13:12, crushes the spirit and tends to early death, for no one lives long unless he has the will to live, and this requires some kind of hope. Hope always deals with the future and with the unseen, Rom. 8:24-25. Those that lack hope live in despair.

There is a "God-shaped vacuum" in the heart of every lost and a depressed person, and it is this attempt to fill the vacuum that drives many to drink, drugs, fleshly pleasures, to the pursuit of power, possessions, etc. But only Divine Wisdom, i.e., Christ Himself, can satisfy this longing, and He is to be found, not at the ends of the earth, but as near as the believing heart, Rom. 10:6-10. Knowledge and understanding do indeed promote cool-headedness and prevent rash words from being spoken in the heat of anger. This harmonizes with verse 28 also. Harsh words, like a spark in an explosive, gaseous atmosphere, are all that is needed to set off troubles that can scarcely be control. Excessive talking is almost always the evidence of a fool, while restraint of the lips marks a wise man. A fool may temporarily refrain from talking, and he will be counted wise until he dispels that illusion by opening his mouth. It must be remembered that we cannot listen, and so cannot learn, while we are talking.

THE FEWER THE WORDS, THE BETTER THE PRAYER

CHAPTER EIGHTEEN

SUMMARY

Proverbs 18:1

The contrast between the Wise and the Fool continue with this chapter. V. 1. The desire of the fool is not to gain wisdom for the sake of being more righteous and just, but rather is through a proud desire to exalt self by being thought wiser than others, and so. In his own mind, the fool separates himself from others, as being superior to them. All his efforts to gain wisdom with such an attitude is simply an endeavor to glorify himself. " All heresy has more or less originated in the self-conceit which leads men to separate themselves from the congregation of the Lord Ezek. 14:7; Hosea 9:10; Heb. 10:25. Though; not all separation is evil; sometimes circumstances demand it, 2 Cor. 6:14-18. A defective heart reveals its true nature by what it hates as well as by what it loves.

A fool is willing to use wisdom and understanding to further his own proud desires but has no real delight in it simply for its own sake. Most unsaved people have a utilitarian view of religion; i.e., that it is only useful for what you can get out of it, and do not realize that the primary purpose of all real religion is to honor and glorify God. The pursuit of understanding ought to be for the sole purpose of being better fitted to do God's wills. The righteous sometimes take a stand for righteousness and against evil men, because, the wicked hold others in contempt, both as to their person, and as to their rights, but God's law of sowing and reaping has never been repealed, and so they shall reap of their contempt.

The wicked desire wisdom only for the noise that he can make with it, in other to attract attention to himself. He desires it to be only for himself and his use, but the righteous man desires wisdom that he may share it with others, as is suggested by "flowing brook." A brook cannot continually flow unless it has a spring to feed it. This suggests the need for a heart well endowed with heavenly wisdom, for who can teach truth if he has not received it himself. Paul spoke what he knew to be true, 1 Cor. 15:3. How often do people judge by outward appearance, which is condemned by the Lord, Deuteronomy 1:16; Prov. 24:23; John 7:24; 8:15; James 2:1-9. Showing respect of persons in judgment has always been wrong, but rich and influential men often bribe their way out of trouble, but God condemns this and warns of judgment to come. In some areas men have a right to show respect of persons— Even God shows respect of persons in some areas, Gen. 4:4; Ex. 2:25; Lev. 26:9; Ps. 138:6, etc. The phrase "God is no respecter of persons" always refers to a judgment context.

A fool's lips enter into contention, and his mouth called for strokes. These two things often go together—contentiousness and chastisement—for the fool's very contentiousness is to propel punishment since it serves no good purpose but is only done in an attempt to exalt his ego. There is much difference in contending for truth, which involves standing firm in it when others would compromise or contradict it. It is often of the party spirit to divide a church and draw off disciples to the author of the contention.

Very few people realize the destructiveness of the mouth; it destroys truth, reputations, and lives, and even destroys the one who speaks, Matthew 12:36-37, for everyone, must answer for the words of his mouth. From this text, it is clear that in the Day of Judgment there is going to be a playback for all to hear of all that the unsaved has ever said, and God's great audio recorder makes no mistakes, and the only thing that will erase those words is the redeeming blood of Christ. Here is the other side of the matter: not only is a fool's mouth destructive of his own soul, but it also wounds others as well, against whom he speaks. Thus there is a three-fold evil done by the unrestrained mouth: It destroys the speaker, it wounds the one spoken against and It harms the listener, for it creates suspicion, distrust, and dislike in him for the one spoken against.

The bad thing about talebearers is that they are seldom satisfied with the tale they carry, but must continually revise it and add to it, and always they worsen it as they do so; since talebearers are generally also slothful persons. A diligent worker seldom has time to go about spreading rumors. The slothful and the waster are very much alike. Most of the references to the slothful are in Proverbs: 12:24, 27; 15:19; 18:9; 19:15, 24; 21:25; 22:13; 26:14, 14, 15. All that any person has is from the Lord and to be wasteful is to be scornful of His gifts.

v. 10 "The name of the Lord is a strong tower: the righteous runneth into it and is safe." The "name of the Lord" is of frequent occurrence in the Bible, and refers to what the Lord is, as manifested in His names, such as Jehovah-Jireh, "The Lord will provide," Gen. 22:7-14; Jehovah-Tsidkenu, "The Lord our righteousness," Jer. 23:6; 33:16, etc. He is all-sufficient for our shelter and defense, Isa. 26:1. Anciently, towers on city walls were the strongest points of defense and were often the last points taken in battle. Wealth is not really much of a defense, but in the conceit of man it is thought to be, and too many people, wealth is their god, which they trust in rather than in God, 1 Tim. 6:17. The folly of trusting in material things is to be seen in that: They can be taken away by robbery, inflation, etc, secondly, they cannot purchase the most needed things—salvation, peace of mind, life, etc and the owner of them may be taken away from them by death. Trust in God guarantees all of the needed things in life, and he who trusts in God cannot be defrauded of these good things. He who trusts in earthly things does not realize that these are all soon to pass away, 1 John 2:15-17, and those trusted in them will be destitute. While in good health and unthreatened by danger, man is proudly self-sufficient and thinks he is "captain of his soul and master of his fate," and so it is often necessary for him to be humbled by tragedy so that he can see himself as he truly is.

No one is honored by God until he has first humbled himself; note this order in 1 Peter 5:5-6. There is room for but one king, both in heaven and in the human heart, and that one must be God; man must abdicate the throne of his heart before he can be saved and have honor from God. Have you submitted wholly to King Jesus?

v. 13. Too many people want to refute the view of others even before they understand what it is. They self-righteously assume themselves to be the standards of truth, and others to be automatically wrong. Often these try to dominate the conversation so that the others cannot even explain what they mean. To every seeming opponent, we owe by Christian courtesy, a proper understanding of his views before we condemn them. Often apparent disagreements are due more to a difference in terminology than in theology. Pride and self-importance often are at the root of such arguments, and these, being folly, naturally lead to shame. It is the office of the spirit, or mind, to govern the body, but not that of the body to govern the mind: it takes an act of Divine grace to accomplish this. Such is the depravity of the human spirit that so far from voluntarily humbling itself, it will do all in its power to defend it's natural pride and vanity. The man's Heart involves understanding, the emotions, and the will, and there has to be an intensive seeking by all these inner functions before any permanent spiritual knowledge is attained. The ear alone may seek for knowledge through outer information, but there will not be much real knowledge gained unless the heart is in search for it, Prov. 17:16.

v. 16. "A man's gift maketh room for him, and bringeth him before great men." This has to do with the giving of bribes, and it pictures the way of the world, not the way that things ought to be. Herein is another evidence of man's idolatrous worship of material possessions: they are considered of greater value than truth and righteousness, else; gifts would not gain men an entrance where these will not. Because of the innate selfishness of man, most people are always open to any profit they can get, and so bribes are easy ways to gain access to great men. *See how corrupt the world is when men's gifts will do that for them which their merits will not do.*

v. 17 "He that is first in his own cause seemed just; but his neighbor cometh and searcheth him." There are always two sides to every story, and though the first man who tells a matter may make his story sound so very plausible and just, yet the judge must not give sentence until the other party has had opportunity to tell his side and to cross-examine the first party. The man is a notorious twister of facts when trying to establish his own case, and the opponent is equally notorious in trying to demolish the facts and to establish his position, but even the judge can err if he is rash and precipitate in pronouncing judgment before all the facts are considered. Sometimes a gift is employed, (v. 16), to obtain such a decision. To those who believe that the whole disposing of the lot is of the Lord, it is a cessation of all contention, for when the lot is cast, it is assumed that the Lord has spoken and that His will is manifest. Not many people today believe in and use the lot to determine matters since so few actually believe that God takes an active interest in, and directs, the affairs of His people. Most people would believe that the decision of the lot was only an "accident," or blind chance. But even so important a matter as choosing an apostle was done by lot in Acts 1:26. This was a form of voting, yet it still involved the use of lots, and was done in dependence upon God's guidance. Ordinarily, determination and decision by lots should not be resorted to, since the decision can be arrived at in other ways, especially, by the power and genuine gifts of the Divine spirit of God.

v.19 "A brother offended is harder to be won than a strong city: and their contentions are like the bars of a castle." The nearer the relationship is, the harder it is to heal it once it has been disrupted. Because one expects something better from one that is related, so an offence is all the more bitter to the offended one. Sadly sometimes family disputes have been bitterly carried to the grave, with profit to none and hurt to all. This only emphasizes, however, how careful we all ought to be lest we offend. And it must be remembered that there is a closer relationship between spiritual than natural brothers. Christians' duty in this matter is made clear in 1 Corinthians 10:32. v.20 "A man's belly shall be satisfied with the fruit of his mouth; and with the increase of his lips shall he be filled." The "increase" of the lips refers to excessive speaking in which there is always sin, Prov. 10:19. "Each one gets the fruit, whether good or bad, of his words, according as these are good or bad. "The belly is here put for the conscience, as chapter 20:27.

There is the power of life in the right use of words, in that through the preaching of the gospel and witnessing of Jesus Christ, people may be brought to repentance and faith. Not only so, but speaking comforting words to God's people are also a good use of the tongue, and God blesses all right uses of the tongue with rewards. But there are altogether too many people who delight in the misuse of the tongue—criticism, tale-bearing, gossiping, backbiting, lying, cursing, taking God's name in vain, teaching falsehood, etc., and the tragedy of it all is, that few realize that there is both life and death in the spoken word, according to how one uses it. However one uses his tongue, he shall reap of his sowing, Matthew 12:36-37, James 3:6, Roman 14:12.

V. 22. Whoso findeth a wife findeth a good thing and obtaineth favor of the Lord. "Findeth" suggests a search, so that it is not a matter of just marrying the first willing one that comes along. Many insecure persons, afraid that "this is my last chance" marry the first person they can, and these are seldom good marriages. Christians are to marry "only in the Lord," 1 Cor. 7:39, which means: Only to another Christian, only as the Lord directs, for some Christians have personalities that clash, and so, they should not marry and only to those within the same denominational and or Faith and doctrinal groups.

A wife who is a wife indeed—a help, meet for him (appropriate to his needs, filling out what is lacking in him, as the word means) is truly a great gift from the Lord, Prov. 19:14. v. 23 "The poor uses entreaties; but the rich answereth roughly." Poverty generally causes one to feel helpless and in need of others' aid so that the poor must often beg for help. Conversely wealth tends to produce self-sufficiency, and the rich often are rude and unmannerly toward those who are less fortunate. But riches can be taken away overnight, and the rich may become destitute. Good manners are never out of place, nor are bad manners ever justified. Sadly, some people think that having money makes them sort of royalty, with a right to ignore the common courtesies of life. They degrade themselves more than anyone else by their ill manners. "A man that hath friends must show himself friendly: and there is a friend that sticketh closer than a brother." Even the pagans recognized this principle, according to Seneca: "If you wish to be loved, love." Friendship is not a one-way street, nor is it a spectator sport. There may be close friends whose love is greater than blood kin, but the friend that sticketh closer than a brother finds fulfillment in the fullest sense only in Christ. Do we reciprocate Christ's love by serving Him, 1 John 4:19; John 14:15?

A MAN THAT HATH FRIENDS MUST SHOW HIMSELF FRIENDLY AND THERE IS A FRIEND THAT STICKETH CLOSER THAN A BROTHER.

CHAPTER NINETEEN

SUMMARY

Proverbs 19:1 - 9

Better is the poor that walketh in his integrity, than he that is perverse in his lips, and is a fool. Poor people are often looked down upon by the rich, but often the only difference between the two is that the rich man is less scrupulous about how to get riches than the poor man. Anyone can become rich if he is unscrupulous enough. But honorable poverty is better; however, the rich man may boast of his wealth and scorn the poor. The soul of man was created for higher purposes than the earth can provide, but when it is without Divine knowledge, it can never come up to its highest potential. The feet are the means of driving force for the body, and if the body moves about without the intelligent direction of the soul, it will tend only to sin, and to the degradation of the soul, and also, that was the problem of the "fool" because of the lack of divine knowledge in the soul. All of the man's problems stem from his own willful and sinful ways, but how often he tries to blame the Lord for all of the punishment that befalls him, and he frets against the Lord's restraints. How can anyone read the Bible and not see that all of God's desires are for man's good, and that good only fails to come to man because he sins against God's will, and so against his own good.

The perversion of the way of the foolish man is parallel with the soul being without knowledge. Though the poor man may walk in his integrity, (v. 1), yet the foolish man, because of his perverted way, (v. 3), is separated from the poor as well as fretting against the Lord. He finds it hard to get along with everyone. Such men are described in 1 Thessalonians 2:14-15. Too many people judge others according to how much they can get out of them, and the poor man, though he may be godly and so, that which very profitable to him spiritually, they scorn. The friendship that is based on one's wealth or dislikes occasioned by one's poverty is neither one to be esteemed as a matter of any account. They are all fool's practice. Men may deceive men, and their lies may never be detected in this life, or they may be passed over, but they shall not escape, for there is a judgment at which all liars shall be condemned, Rev. 21:8. Lying always increases, for each lie needs another to support it until it becomes a habit, and truth is hard to even recognize. "False witness" has to do with public and official falsehoods, while "lies" has more to do with private misrepresentations. See God's view of lies in Jeremiah 9:3-6. Another side of lies is a tendency to the natural selfishness and greed of men, for they will do almost anything and pretend almost anything in order to get material things. This contrasts with the integrity of the poor but godly man in verse 1. Since Satan is the prince of this world, John 12:31, and has control over it to give it to whomever he pleases, (Luke 4:5-7), little wonder that he is able to buy and sell men so easily because of material things, for many sell their souls for these passing things, 1 John 2:17. The act of pursuing the earthly thing than God Almighty made many people outrun their divine purpose on earth.

The poor man's brethren think he will be a disgrace and injury to themselves. The essence of this is that generally speaking, people want nothing to do with anyone who might need help from them. And though the poor might call out after those able to help them, his words are unheard; they hear not his entreaties. It is sad how many are concerned for the body, but has no concern for the soul; here is where true profit is found, not in material gain, but in spiritual wisdom. To find and keep wisdom is to do good to one's own soul, for wisdom leads one into earthly and temporal good, as well as into heavenly and eternal good. Salvation, sanctification and comfort all come through the wisdom and knowledge of the Lord, it is easy to see its importance, and why the devil fights this knowledge so hard. v. 9 "A false witness shall not be unpunished, and he that speaketh lies shall perish v 5. "Not be unpunished" means shall certainly be punished. "Perish" has to do with spiritual destruction, for many habitual liars are never unpunished in this life for their lies, Revelation 21:27; 22:14-15

Proverbs 19:10 - 29

Delight is not seemly for a fool; much less for a servant to have rule over princes. "Recreation and pleasure are seemly for a wise man, as a temporary relaxation; but a 'rod' of correction is what is most seemly for a fool (chapters 10:13; 26:3). Though it is common for all kinds of people, but unsaved people especially, to seek for pleasures, yet of all people it is most out of place for the unsaved to have delight, since they are living a Christless eternity: Just as it unseemly for slaves to rule over those nobly born, or elevated to high office. Hastiness of spirit is the easiest way to make a fool of one's self and to speak and act rashly. Many of the murders that are committed are traceable to a rash and uncontrolled anger. Ability to conquer one's anger is not a mark of cowardice or weakness, as the world counts it. To practice this character quality is to be like God, who both defers His anger through His long-suffering, and passes over transgressions through His grace. v. 12, the king's wrath is as the roaring of a lion; but his favor is as dew upon the grass." Kings and other rulers are not ordinary persons, and cannot be treated as such. This was even true in the days when rulers exercised the arbitrary power of life and death. Hence, his favor was to be sought and his frown to be dreaded and it was wisdom to act in accord with the king's wishes. Since Christ the King of kings has the power, not of life and death alone, but also of heaven and Satan, how much more so is it wisdom to submit wholly to Him?

A foolish child is not a desirable continuation for a parent but makes a parent wonder if his life has counted for anything worthwhile. In like manner, a contentious wife makes for a miserable home. One may inherit from one's parents a fine home and riches, but not so a prudent wife: she is a gift from the Lord. Even in the days when parents arranged marriages, none could know for sure how a woman would turn out to a wife. It is still so today. Some men fall in love with a girl's dimples and then make the mistake of marrying the whole girl. What kind of a wife a person has will determine to a great extent what kind of a home-life he has, and so, choosing a godly, prudent wife is very important. Ever since the fall of man in Eden, his decreed lot has been labor for his daily food, and many and various have been his attempt to circumvent this curse. All cheating, fraud, robbery, etc., have been for this reason. It is true that "an idle mind is the devil's workshop," and so it is wise to stay busy, both for the sake of earning one's daily food, and also to keep out of mischief. God doesn't believe in welfare for the lazy person, 2 Thess. 3:10-12.

Many people, in seeking to do only what pleases them, and to have their own way, actually destroy themselves, for sin is like cancer in the body— fatal unless stopped, and only grace of Divine God can do that. No commandment of the Lord is hurtful to man: indeed, each tends to life and good, and every harm that comes to a man comes because someone has violated one of the Lord's commandments. "If we keep God's word, God's word will keep us from everything really hurtful," Lord will not remain in debt to anyone: He abundantly repays all that anyone does to His people, even to the rewarding of the smallest and most insignificant of deeds, Mark 9:41. Clearly then no one can lose by doing well to the poor, if he does it in the right spirit and What is given to the poor, or done for them, God will place it to account as lent to him, lent upon interest (so the word signifies); he takes it kindly, as if it were done to himself,—because we multiply by dividing.

Parents, who allow children to get by with things while small, harden them in evil until it is impossible to discipline them. If a child's will is not broken to submission to authority by the age of five or six, he will never be. Because there is a time when a child passes beyond hope, and if he is not chastened before then and taught submission to the authority he will eventually come under the sword of civil justice and then under the sword of divine justice, for which there is no remedy.

Those who get their way in childhood by throwing bad temper will grow up to be men of great anger every time their will is opposed, and these will be in continual trouble with the law. Parents who have let their children get away with mischief in childhood are often made paupers trying to pay their way out of cramps when they become adults. Proverbs 23:13-14 deals with this even more fully, and shows the absolute necessity of stern discipline on children if they would be delivered from Satan domain. Discipline must begin in the life of a young child early enough: because in the teenage is too late. "Hear counsel, and receive instruction, that thou may be wise in thy latter end." "Hear" has to do with the ear, but "receive" refers to the heart's response to the truth, and only as instruction sinks down into the heart will one be truly wise. Shallow learning has little effect upon one's life either at the present time or later in life. Only good and godly instruction absorbed in the heart profits one. Many people, in their pride, refuse to be taught while in their youth, and they think that their delinquency habit is no matter, but those very things go to extreme lengths in their old age and cause them to become extremely obsessed. Wisdom and righteousness in old age are dependent wholly on right teaching and practices on one's youth. The enrichments of elderhood lies in the proper and early foundation—that is; as you lay your bed your lie on it.

v. 21 "There are many devices in a man's heart: nevertheless the counsel of the Lord that shall stand." Man's cunning and evil is well-known, Eccl. 7:29, but it is not enough to devise many things in one's heart, even if all those things are of a religious nature. What one has in the heart must be the counsel of the Lord, (v. 20), for this alone will stand on the day of testing Isa. 46:9-11; Eph. 1:11, and unless the way of man harmonize with the eternal purpose and counsel of the Lord it would be like praying amiss, It is the worst kind of folly to resist God's perfect will and counsel for one's own imperfect counsel. The desire of a man is his kindness: and a poor man is better than a liar." Kindness acts by a person make him a desirable person to have around, and even if he is poor and has not the means to do well, he is still a better person to have around than the man who professes to be concerned, but who never does anything to support the needy. Poor men can also lie, but they are not as likely to do so when approached for help as the rich man who is covetous. Three blessings result from the fear of the Lord namely, Life, Satisfaction, and Deliverance. The fear of the

Lord tends to life in those that fearing Him and they will not anger Him by sinning. And in as much as the fear of the Lord restrains sin, it also restrains the evil that follows sin.

v. 24 "A slothful man hide his hand in his bosom, and will not so much as bring it to his mouth again." Perhaps putting the hands under the clothing on cold days is to warm them, and refusing to take them out is definitely not to earn one's daily food, hence, this is how much man-comfort can rule his lives. So many people today refuse to work on their jobs, and only want to draw their pay for loafing; many people would rather starve than do honest work. v. 25 "Smite a scorner and the simple will beware: and reprove one that hath understanding, and he will understand knowledge." When sin is left unpunished, it emboldens others to commit it also. Those who have understanding will prove it by taking reproof and profiting from it. Only a scorner hates reproof, (9:8). v. 26 "He that wastes his father, and chased away his mother, is a son that causes shame, and bringeth reproach." "Wastes," i.e., his father's substance, as the prodigal son did, (Luke 15:11f. "Chases away" by making her feel uncomfortable and even unwelcome in his presence. v. 27 "Cease, my son, to hear the instruction that causes to err from the words of knowledge." Many who will not be taught by words of truth, will readily listen to instruction on how to pervert the truth, they do these to escape the penalty of sin, and to deaden the conscience. False teachers teach much, but it is always contrary to truth, and tends to folly, for it deceives further those who are already in rebellion against truth. Better not listen to any teaching and be in ignorance, than to listen to that which causes one to err from the truth.

An ungodly witness is a false witness who cares nothing for right judgment but is willing to pervert justice for personal gain. The way of Truth is always controversial to the lost and ungodly witnesses; some people will even swear to anything if there is an advantage to be gained. They think of truth as only valuable if it can be used for personal advantage. By their ungodly attitudes, they fill themselves with sin, and shall be dealt with accordingly. Judgments are prepared for scorners and stripes for the back of fools." They scorned to practice right judgment, perverting it with false witnesses, (v. 28), and so righteous judgment must fall on them, for that is God's law of sowing and reaping. God has declared that all sin must and will be punished; if not in one's Substitute, and then it must be punished in one personally. Those who suffer the punishment of Satan domain, do so because they willingly chose this in preference to the Lord's deliverance, which He offers to all who repent and trust him.

LIFE IS AN ADVENTURE IN FORGIVENESS – THE FRUITS AND GIFTING OF THE HOLY SPIRIT GOES TOGETHER

CHAPTER TWENTY

SUMMARY

Proverbs 20:1

Wine is a mocker, strong drink is raging, and whosoever is deceived thereby is not wise. A sane, sensible man when sober loses all restraint when liquor is received into his system, and his mind does not function properly, for all alcoholic beverages are poisons which destroy the brain cells. Wise men will shun all forms of liquor for the poison that they are.

The fear of a king is as the roaring of a lion: whoso provoke him to anger sinned against his own soul. In the ancient time, kings had absolute power there are illustrations of this from Solomon's own life, 1 Kings 2:23-25. No sane person would challenge a wild lion when he had no way of defending himself; so likewise was it folly to provoke the one man in the nation who had the absolute power of life and death. Pride would insist on one holding on to one's position to the bitter end, and the fool would continue to meddle and stir up more strife when others would cease. Christians are called to peace, 1 Cor. 7:15. "The sluggard will not plow by reason of the cold; therefore shall he beg in the harvest, and have nothing." The Hebrew word sluggard is rendered "slothful" (8 times) and it also is found only in Proverbs. It refers to a lazy man. The words rendered "cold" are rendered "winter." There are always excuses enough where there is no inclination to do honest work, and small difficulties are easily magnified into reasons to indulge the fleshly desire for ease. And just as many are careless about the needs of the body, so even more; are careless about the needs of the soul.

v. 5 - 6 Counsel in the heart of man is like deep water: but a man of understanding will draw it out. So far in Proverbs we have seen: The counsel of the rebellious, Prov. 1:25, 30, the counsel of the Lord, Prov. 8:24; 19:20-21; 21:30 and counsel of the wise men, Prov. 12:15. It is in this third class that verses 5, 18 and 27:9 falls. But while the fool is always ready to give counsel—even when it is unsought— the wise man may be reserved about giving counsel, so that one must draw it out, as refreshing water is drawn from a deep well. That counsel which is deepest in the heart, like water from the deepest well, is often the best of all. Most men will proclaim everyone his own goodness: but a faithful man who can find?" (Luke 18:9-11). The man is by nature an egotist who thinks more highly of himself than he has reason to do, and most of man's "charity" is done for self-glory. Tragically, even among the genuinely saved, our motives for our religious and charitable exercises are often suspected, as the egotist who is attempting to promote himself in the eyes of others. A truly faithful man will not have to praise himself, (27:2). It is the perverted belief of our day that integrity is good but impractical, and that one must lay it aside in order to profit. Many use their children as excuses for their dishonest dealings, but such becomes a curse to one's children, Prov. 3:33, for God cannot bless the house of the wicked because they generally follow the evil examples that the parents set before them. The just man not only does well to those with whom he deals justly, but he sets an example of righteousness before his children that powerfully influence them, as well as bringing them blessings.

v. 8 "A king that sitteth in the throne of judgment scattered away all evil with his eyes." God requires kings to rule justly in the fear of God, 2 Sam. 23:3, and that ruler who is known by his righteous judgments will not want to be faced by any evil man, and so he will indeed scatter away all evil. This will be especially true if he personally inspects many things in his realm, instead of leaving it all to his deputies. Often righteous kings have fallen because they had unrighteous subordinates who were trusted to administer the justice of the kingdom. More especially does Christ the King of kings hates evil, Ps. 5:5; Hab. 1:13, all Bible saints lamented their great sinfulness, knowing that they inherit a sinful nature from their parents, Job 15:14; 25:4. Not only is a man a liar if he denies that he has never sinned, but even the Christian lies and deceives himself if he thinks he is sinless after the new birth, 1 John 1:8, 10. This does not mean that the saint is yet under condemnation, for the blood of the Savior is an efficient and eternal cleanser from all kind of iniquity, 1 John 1:7

v. 10 – 12. "Divers weights, and divers' measures, both of them are alike abominations to the Lord." means having two different weights and measures, a smaller one when that would be advantageous, and a greater one when that would be profitable. We see here that God is concerned for righteousness even in the realm of economics. By "weights" and "measures" are included all sorts of fraudulent business practices. V. 11 what the child is, so he will be when he grows to adulthood. Thus, a proud, rebellious or mischievous child will grow up to be the same sort of an adult. In like manner, a well-behaved child will generally grow up to be a well-behaved adult. Many, who have good hearing and eyesight, are nevertheless spiritually blind and deaf to the gospel. Isaiah 6:9-10 is quoted in John 12:37-40 in proof of this. Spiritual truth is discernable only by the aid of the Holy Spirit who is the author of it, (1 Cor. 2:14-16). The "hearing ear and the seeing eye" are those faculties which are enabled to discern the truth. These are the learning senses, yet man does not have the spiritual capacity to learn the things of God apart from the Lord's illumination.

V 13 - 17 "Love not sleep, lest thou come to poverty; open thine eyes and thou shall be satisfied with bread." Sleep is a necessity, but excessive sleep—sleep merely to avoid facing the responsibilities and problems of life—leads to poverty. "Wake up and go to work" is the teaching of this Proverbs 20: Many people are poor, not due to bad luck, but simply because of laziness.

It is naught, it is naught, saith the buyer; but when he is gone his way, then he boasted." Making the goods and product of another look worthless for our own advantages is not of wisdom practice, in fact, this is a lie. Many business entities and organization also practice this to an excessive degree in the name of marketing and or business strategy. There is nothing wrong in trying to support and developed our businesses, provided we do not resort to lies in doing so.

There are gold and a multitude of rubies: but the lips of knowledge are a precious jewel." Alas, how few realize the discrepancy between the value of mere material wealth and the value of truth. While men avidly pursue material wealth, which can be taken away from them overnight, and from which they must be parted at death, they almost totally ignore spiritual knowledge which can never be taken away. O how Satan has blinded the human heart to true riches. "Lips" suggest not just theoretical knowledge in the head, but the teaching of this true knowledge to others. There are dangers of becoming a surety for one known to be dependable.

A "strange woman" is generally an immoral woman, who often obtains promised from men during their unholy passion that causes them loss afterward. So did Judah with Tamar when he supposed she was a prostitute, Gen. 38:12-26. One should never pledge nor promise anything for use as a surety that he is not willing to lose, for this is often what happens to sureties. Many make a living getting others to stand for them with their good then leaving them to pay the creditor. Satan often convinces people that anything that is forbidden, or that is obtained in forbidden ways, is more enjoyable, Prov. 9:17, which only reveals the natural corruption of the human heart that it could be so easily convinced to do evil. Little things are as painful as a broken tooth that results from biting unexpected stone in food.

Every purpose is established by counsel: and with good advice make war." Luke 14:31-32. Impulsive actions are perilous actions, for much thought and counsel is necessary for every major move that one makes. Especially would this be true where the safety and security of the nation are concerned? It is good to seek counsel with wise men, Prov. 11:14; 15:22, but best of all is to seek for, and follow the counsel of the Lord, which is already established and can never be overthrown, Prov. 19:21; 21:30. Counsel for war is again mentioned in Proverbs 24:6. While war for gains sake is wrong, war is sometimes necessary to protect a nation's rights, and God even at times commands a nation to go to war. Here He commands war to be made only for good and just reasons and with good advice as to how it is done Judge 4:4-8.

"He that goeth about as a talebearer reveals secrets: therefore meddle not with him that flattered with his lips." The talebearer not only reveals secrets by telling all that he knows, but he generally tells more than he knows, for he embellishes the rumors with added juicy gossip. Talebearers are unprincipled people who are small in their own eyes, and can only feel self-important by bearing tales about others. They flatter others that they may draw out from them secrets. They may pose as helpful counselors, (v. 18), in order to elicit secrets from those who do not know their evil ways. Better to have nothing to do with the person who talks about others: he will do the same for you.

"Whoso curseth his father or his mother, his lamp shall be put out in obscure darkness." One of God's ten basic laws is that parents are to be honored, (Ex. 20:12). God makes no conditions to his law, such as: "If they deserve it," "if they please you," etc. It is an absolute command, for the parent stands in the place of God to the child until he is old enough to understand the idea of God.

A child's idea of God will depend on to a great extent upon parental example and teaching. To dishonor parents is to cut short one's life, (Eph. 6:1-3). "Lamp often refers to life, (Prov. 13:9). But here "obscure darkness" may refer to Satan domain itself, for it sounds much like the "mist of darkness" (2 Pet. 2:17), and the "blackness of darkness," (Jude 13) which describe hell.

"An inheritance may be gotten hastily at the beginning, but the end thereof shall not be blessed." Sometimes people are so anxious for riches, that they have no sense of right and wrong as to how they obtain them, and may, like the prodigal son, (Luke 15:11), beg for the inheritance before it is due him. Worse still are those who actually cheat parents in order to be rich. It is not enough to have riches; for it to profit, it must have the blessings of God on it, which it cannot have if it is gotten in the wrong way.

"Say not thou, I will recompense evil, but wait on the Lord, and he shall save thee." If we try to pay evil with someone who has done evil, is like stepping down to his level. Judgment and punishment of evil are God's work alone, and He alone has the wisdom to deal justly with all parties Romans 12:17-19, 1Thessalonians 1:5-8, Deuteronomy 32:35, 41.

"Divers weights are an abomination unto the Lord, and a false balance is not good." Similar to v. 10; what God hates? He makes unprofitable to those who delight in it. The false balance is not good for the one cheated by it, but it is even more so not good for the one cheating with it, for while the one cheated loses only material things, the one cheating comes under God's curse, and may lose his soul. Many sell souls for gain.

"Man's goings is of the Lord; how can a man then understand his own way?" The first "man" means "a mighty man," while the second means man in general. If even the mighty are directed of the Lord, how can the ordinary man even understand his own way, much less direct it? "We have a constant dependence upon God. However it may not look like it, God is still in control of all things: He only permits evil insofar as it will glorify Him, and all other evil He restrains, (Ps. 76:10).

For a man to be on the winning side, and where blessings are, he must submit himself to the Lord's will to be willingly directed by Him. It is a snare to the man who devoured that which is holy, and after vows to make an inquiry." To "devour" is to appropriate to one's own use. Holy things are holy only because they are devoted to the Lord. Some people rashly vow without considering the cost of such a vow, and then later change their minds, Ecclesiastes 5:1-7 deals with this. What is devoted to the Lord belongs to Him, and cannot be reclaimed by a man without it becoming a snare to him. Worship ought at all times to be a serious thing, never done rashly or thought he can make inquiries about how to get out of the vow, because God honor vow and take it seriously, Job 22:27 Psalms 50:14, Psalms 56:12 and Psalms 61:8

A wise king scattered the wicked, and brings the wheel over them; Similar to verse 8. The wheel of the threshing instrument which crushed out the grain was sometimes used to punish people or punishment was likened to being threshed, (2 Kings 13:7; Ps. 83:13; Isa. 25:10; 28:27; 41:15; Amos 1:3). Even David used some harsh methods of punishment, (2 Sam. 12:31). Swift, speedy justice for all crimes would reduce crime greatly in our nation. Lack of enforcement and delay of punishment encourage crime.

The spirit of man is the candle of the Lord, searching all the inward parts of the belly. It is man's spiritual nature which must deal with spiritual things, but apart from regeneration, man's candle is unlit, and his conscience, not being rightly taught, cannot lead him rightly.

A life without Christ cannot be hidden in Jehovah and fills with His divine Spirit. It takes an enlivened spirit and an enlightened conscience for all of the man's inward thoughts and motives to be rightly judged and directed. All true worship must be spiritual to be accepted, John 4:23-24. Mere ritualism is a satanic substitute for true worship.

There is a tendency on the part of rulers to think that they are not subject to truth, nor that they need mercy themselves, but God's law is: mercy only for the merciful, 2 Sam. 22:26. Truth, because it tends to the good of the people, also tends to establish the rule of the king who practices it. Some rulers tend to be merciless, which is why their governments are so much less stable than in those nations where Christianity has borne the fruit of mercy.

The glory of young men is their strength: and the beauty of old men is the gray head. Neither can despise the other, for both of these qualities are needful in civil and in religious life. The vigor of youth and the wisdom of age work together for good. Sometimes Satan plays these against each other to disrupt the harmony of a church. In both cases, these qualities need to be cultivated. Apparently, John had this text in mind when he wrote 1 John 2: 12-14.

The blueness of a wound cleanses away evil; so do stripe the inward parts of the belly. Chastisement which does not leave marks does little good. Some chastisement of children is so light it does nothing more than make them mad: this does nothing toward putting fear into them. To do any good, chastisement must make one realize that it is costly to do evil. Most present crime increase stems from too easy punishments for crimes. If the old whipping post were reinstated and vigorously and immediately exercised, crime would be greatly reduced. Crime begins in the heart, and so fear must be put there also.

TO BE LIKE CHRIST IS TO BE A CHRISTIAN – A CHRISTIAN WITHOUT CHRIST, IS A NOTHING

CHAPTER TWENTY-ONE

SUMMARY

Proverbs 21: 1- 31

Anciently; kings were not mere figureheads of authority as they are today, but they held the absolute power of life and death, Prov. 16:14-15, in their realm. But this verse shows that God exercises an even greater power, being able to, and actually exercising, the power to turn even the heart according to His will, as in Ezra 1:1-4 and Revelation 17:17. Mere human power can generally force a man to comply outwardly with rules, but the heart might continue in rebellion against them. But God's power changes even the heart. For other declarations of God's power, see Psalms 103:19; 110:3; 115:3; Matthew 28:18 and Ephesians 1:11.

The tendency to self-justification and rebellion are always dangerous and unprofitable because, while we too often judge by our outward actions and ignore our inward motives, God looks upon the heart and judges the real thoughts and motivations for the deeds. To do justice and judgment is more acceptable to the Lord than sacrifice. The rituals think that God, like himself, looks solely upon the outward performance of the worship and is pleased with it, but such is not the case. Sacrifices were of divine institution, and were acceptable to God if they were offered in faith and with repentance, otherwise not, Isa. 1:11, etc.

A high look, and a proud heart, and the plowing of the wicked is a sin." These are abominations to the Lord, Prov. 6:17, for they are all sins, and while man may commit these with apparent impunity, yet there is coming a day of judgment, Isa. 2:11-12. God's Word determines what is a sin, not calamities befalling men, and those who disbelieve the word and continue in sin only harden themselves more and more and treasure up unto themselves wrath against the day of wrath, Rom. 2:5-6. "Plowing" is a preparation for sowing which suggests that the wicked man's preparations for evil doing are also a sin.

The thoughts of the diligent tend only to plenteousness; but of every one that is hasty only to want." The old human proverb that "haste makes waste" is true. It is an act of wisdom to think a matter through thoroughly before acting upon it, for rashness seldom works out for good, but is often costly. The Christian is indeed to "run" the race, yet it is to be done, not rashly, but with patience, (Heb. 12:1). We are to seek for glory, honor, and immortality "by patient continuance in well doing," (Rom. 2:7). But our thoughts must be on heavenly things for it to tend to our profit; worldly thoughts produce no good.

The getting of treasures by a lying tongue is a vanity tossed to and fro of them that seek death." Some people are so hasty to gain material wealth, (v. 5), that they are unscrupulous as to how they do so, and so they resort to misrepresentation and fraud in business. But so far from this getting them treasures, it only brings death to them. "Vanity" means a vapor and so it suggests the emptiness of ill-gotten gain, and so there is not the satisfaction expected in that which is not gotten by honest and honorable means. They probably do not realize that they are seeking death, but this shall be their end. The most painful things in their wicked acts was that of innocent souls they inflicted with pain and distress, may the good God continually save us from foolishness and wickedness of men.

The robbery of the wicked shall destroy them; because they refuse to do judgment." Robbery is not someone stealing from the wicked, but rather the wicked stealing from others. He who is robbed loses only material things, but he who does the robbing loses spiritual things, yea, even his soul in many instances. "Judgment" here is in the sense of justice. Too many judges only by the scale of how much they will be profited?" and so they pervert justice, and are often guilty of out-and-out robbery. But their covetousness hurts themselves more than anyone else, for it destroys them spiritually, morally and sometimes even physically, but as for the pure his work is right.

What one does is a test of what he really is. "Froward" is a different word than usual, here meaning crooked or perverse. The wicked man is always an opportunist, unscrupulously using circumstances only for personal gain. The pure do what is right without regard to personal loss or gain.

It is better to dwell in a corner of the housetop, than with a brawling woman in a wide house, Vs. 19; 25:24; 27:15. Housetop could be places of retreat for meditation and prayer Acts 10:9, and would offer some shelter from the sun during the day and shelter from the wind at night, but would not be an ideal abode. Yet even this would be better than living in the finest mansion with a contentious woman.

No one, man or woman, has ever been helped to a better condition by nagging and bickering. Criticism springs from a self-righteous spirit. The root of evil is shown to be in the soul. What a tragedy that the noblest part of man is so perverted from its original design as to delight in sin. This is why a total conversion is necessary before one can fulfill the purpose for his existence. Indwelling sin is also the reason for man's innate selfishness, which causes even his neighbor to find no favor with him when the neighbor's need conflicts with his own selfishness. God's requirement is that we love our neighbor as ourselves, Mark 12:31.

If our neighbor does not find favor in our eyes, then we have not measured up to the law of love, and so we are sinners in God's sight.

When the scorner is punished, the simple is made wise: and when the wise is instructed, he receiveth knowledge. Prov. 19:25. Simple minded people are encouraged to do evil when they see others getting away with it, and so immediate, appropriate punishment must be carried out to evil doing. No law discourage crime if it is not enforced, and even delaying the execution for months and years takes away the fear of it. Immediate punishment does put off crime, though this is not the primary reason for it. It is: For justice's sake: Lev. 24:17-21; to cleanse the land of blood-guiltiness, Num. 35:30-34; to prevent others, Deut. 22:21-24; 24:7. Wise men receive instruction, but fools must be restrained by fear. Hence immediate punishment for evil is necessary.

The house of the wicked, though it may appear flourishing, is not secure, for God will eventually overthrow it, and so the righteous man does well to wisely consider that riches, honor and fame matter little if one's house is to be destroyed because it is wicked. Though God suffers long with evil, He must sooner or later deal with it in judgment. Sin must be punished. He, who shows no mercy, shall be shown no mercy. Jesus taught a parable to illustrate this, Matthew 18:23-35. Jesus teaching is that what you wish to be done to you, you are to do to others, Luke 6:31.

This is the "Golden Rule." A gift in secret pacified anger: and a reward in the bosom strong wrath. As strong as is the passion of anger, it is sometimes in order to use a gift to pacify anger if no injustice is done thereby. But here, "in secret" implies that guilt is felt over this, and so it must be a bribe to pervert justice that is meant, as in Proverbs 17:23.

In every age and country, bribery is practiced by unscrupulous persons to achieve their own ends, but there is a judgment to come at which every perversion of justice will be revealed and punished. Righteous people do not delight in bribes, but rather they delight to do justly in all their dealings. A bribe is a tacit confession that one either does not think his case will stand to be judged rightly or else that the judge is not just and so will not bring in a favorable verdict unless bribed. Only those with faith in the Lord believe that justice will finally be done, and so that one can safely and profitably practice the truth.

The wicked have no faith in the prevalence of truth, and their unbelief will be their destruction. The law is only a terror to evil, Rom. 13:3-4. The truth will surely prevail in this present world and eternally.

The man that wandered out of the way of understanding shall remain in the congregation of the dead." That he wanders shows that he is not physically dead, but that he remains in the congregation of the dead suggests that he is spiritually dead. The language here sounds very much like that of Jude 11-12 and 2 Peter 2:20-22, which speaks of religious people who have known the truth, but have not submitted to it, except outwardly, and so are not truly saved.

He that loves pleasure shall be a poor man; he that loves wine and oil shall not be rich." Nowhere else is "pleasure" so rendered: more commonly it is rendered "gladness" or "rejoicing." Taking the two phrases together we see that the one who gives himself over to the enjoyment of life through fake luxuries is doomed. This deals with one's attitude and outlook, for the Lord, has given to His people "all things richly to enjoy," 1 Tim. 6:17, but at the same time, He has warned us to "love not the world, neither the things that are in the world," 1 John 2:15, for these easily become snares to us. One shall never be rich either spiritually or materially who never practices self-denial.

The wicked shall be a ransom for the righteous, and the transgressor for the upright." "The righteous are saved from impending destruction and the wicked come in their room Prov. 11:8. "Ransom" here means a covering: one is ransomed from death because his sins have been covered by the blood of Christ. A ransom was also a substitute for another; this is doubtless the sense here, for the wicked, by this willful refusal to submit to the Lord and His divine Word, goes on in the way of sin until he comes finally to perdition, from which the righteous has been delivered. For Christ has suffered for as many that comes under His Divine atonement. It is better to dwell in the wilderness, than with a contentious and angry woman." v. 9. A house, though it is a grand mansion, is not a home unless there is love there, but the noblest palace is a house of horrors if the people therein fuss and argue all the time. There is a treasure to be desired and oil in the dwelling of the wise: but a foolish man spends it up." "Treasure" is literally "that which is laid up," and oil was one of the staples in ancient times, so that the thought here is that the wise person keeps a stock of necessary food on hand in his dwelling at all times so that he has a supply for emergencies, but the foolish person spends all that he has until he runs short even of daily food. Unfortunately, how many people today spend every Kobo they earn on unnecessary luxuries and live almost hand to mouth? While one should not make an idol of the storeroom, yet it is wise to maintain a supply of extra food when God blesses with abundance. Convenience stores have gotten most people out of the habit of living from drought.

He that followeth after righteousness and mercy findeth life, righteousness, and honor." This is man's foremost duty, Matthew 6:33 and it has a promise attached to it, for he that seek, find, (Matthew 5:6; 7:7), if he seeks it according to the Lord's order, and for His glory. Hosea 10:12 also speaks of seeking of righteousness and mercy and it comes only by grace, Roman 4 (entire chapter). Eternal life, true righteousness, and honor are all tied together. Wisdom is always better than might, for strength without wisdom becomes a detriment. Even very weak men may direct the strongest brutes because they have superior wisdom. Man's strength comes from the flesh, but wisdom only comes from God, and it only comes to the submissive.

The man who has so submitted himself to God's will has the ability to overcome the natural man who places confidence in fleshly abilities. "No confidence in the flesh," Phil. 3:3, must be our motto if we would succeed.

Whoso keepeth his mouth and his tongue keepeth his soul from troubles." (Prov. 13:2-3; James 3:2). Jesus taught in Matthew 12:34-37 that words manifest the condition of the heart. A word is a two-edged sword Heb. 4:12 which cuts two ways. When we cut someone down with our words, we do ourselves most harm, for we reveal to the world a bitter and hateful heart. A Proud and haughty scorner is his name who deals in proud wrath." Originally, names were given, not only to designate one from another but also were descriptive of one's character.

All names originally had some meaning. Thus, Nabal's name meant to fool, 1 Sam. 25:25. To manifest proud wrath is to show one's self to be a proud and haughty scorner. Most wrath is proud wrath: it comes because one is stung by a supposed slight. He feels he is not treated with the dignity due to his supposed Peacock state of life.

The desire of the slothful killeth him; for his hands refuse to labor." He is as fit to labor as anyone else, but he has no heart for the necessary labor; yet, his desire for good things is as strong as that of the laboring man, perhaps stronger. Such a situation will kill his self-respect, others' respect for him, his morals (if he tries to obtain things illegally without working for them) and may even kill him physically if he is caught committing a crime in an attempt to get these things without working for them. Covetousness, being idolatry, Col. 3:5, will also kill one spiritually.

The righteous man has his moderate desires abundantly satisfied, and he giveth unsparingly to others of his own property Psalm 37:25-26. Covetousness is a disease which cannot be satisfied: the more it is fed, the more it grows - the only cure for it is mortification (put it to death), Colossians 3:5. This is done by crucifying the flesh and its lusts, Galatians 5:24.

Therefore; living a quite rich life with contentment it is more of gain. The sacrifice of the wicked is an abomination: how much more, when he bringeth it with a wicked mind?" The unsaved person cannot offset his wickedness by sacrifices, for his best religious exercises are hateful in the Lord's eyes. Mere ritualism never pleases the Lord, for it puts more value on man's acts than on God's grace, and is a form of rebellion against God's call, Isa. 66:3-4. Worse yet is when he brings his sacrifice with the idea that these are more valuable than the blood of Christ.

A false witness shall perish: but the man that hears speaks constantly." The false witness is one who lies under oath, and even more solemn sin than ordinary lying. "Heareth," perhaps means hears (with an understanding and obedient heart) what God says about not bearing false witness, Exodus 20:16, and so speaks constantly. However things may appear hopeful for a time for the false witness, he shall ultimately perish, for God cannot tolerate those who resemble Satan by their lies, John 8:44; Rev. 21:8, 27; 22:15.

A wicked man hardeneth his face: but as for the upright, he directed his way." To harden one's face is to rebel—a characteristic reaction of unsaved people—for he will have no one cross him. The saved person, on the contrary, looks to the Lord's direction of his way.

No matter must to be settled by; "What do I want to do?" rather every question ought to be settled by the question: "What would the Lord have me to do?" For; there is no wisdom, nor understanding nor counsel against the Lord. True, many take counsel against the Lord, and defy His purposes, Ps. 2:1-3, but there is no wisdom, understanding nor counsel against the Lord that shall stand, Isa. 8:9-10; Ps. 103:15; 115:5; Acts 4:27-28; 5:39; Eph. 1:11. To set one's will against the Lord Guarantee failure, frustration, and final shame.

The horse is prepared against the day of battle: but safety is of the Lord." Natural helps avail naught if the Lord does not help. Israel often looked to the wrong source for help, Psalm 20:7; Isa. 31:1.

NO SACRIFICE WAS EVER MEANT TO BE A SUBSTITUTE FOR MORALITY AND TO ATTEMPT TO DO SO WAS TO BE GUILTY OF HYPOCRISY - THIS IS TRYING TO APPEAR PIOUS WHILE LIVING UNGODLY.

CHAPTER
TWENTY-TWO

SUMMARY

Proverbs 22:1

A good name is rather to be chosen than great riches, and loving favor rather than silver and gold. "A good name" is not just reputation, which may not truly fit the man, but is rather a character, which is what he really is. A bad man may maintain a good reputation for a time, but eventually, his real character will be known. "Character is better than riches because its foundation is better. In the present evil world, there is much disparity between the rich and the poor, and riches often open doors that are closed to the poor, but both meet together as far as sin, salvation, and judgment are concerned. Because God is the maker of all men, He judges them all "without respect of persons," Roman 2:11. This is why it is better to have a good name before God than to be rich, (v. 1). Understand me. It is good to be rich, but in Christ by His divine Spirit under the tutelage of God Jehovah, Deuteronomy 8:18.

It is wisdom to look beyond the moment of pride and pleasure to see what consequences lie beyond. The motto of the day is: "If it feels good, to do it." This takes no thought for a judgment to come. "It is nature which teaches a wise man in fear to hide himself but grace and faith teach him where. Where should the frightened child hide his head but in the bosom of his loving Father? Those who do not fear the wrath to come, and seek for escape from it in Christ, will pass swiftly into Satan domain. Riches, honor, and life are the chief desires of almost all men, but the problem lies in how they attain them. Too many have no principles about how these are obtained, and so they violate the Scriptural means of attaining them: Our Lord repeated this same order for obtaining these things in Matthew 6:33. Humility and the fear of the Lord always go together, for humility is necessary before one can truly reverence the Lord. Proverbs 15:33 and18:12 have already established this order. Many desire riches so that they will not have to be humble. Just as human flesh cannot resist sharp objects, but is pierced by them, so to rebel against the Lord is to gain nothing but sorrow.

The way of the wicked is as a narrow twisting path through thorns which prick him at every turn, but the Lord makes the way of the righteous a wide avenue without any pricking. This is God's law of sowing and reaping again. Keeping the soul does not refer to one keeping himself saved, which is God's work, Jude 21-24, but rather to his abstention from the evil which would hinder his Christian walk and testimony.

Train up a child in the way he should go: and when he is old, he will not depart from it." Here is God's commission to parents, and none need hope that their child will turn out well if they refuse to obey this law. "Train" in all the other appearances of the word is rendered "dedicated," as in Deuteronomy 20:5. Here it involves: Teaching, Training, Setting a proper example and Discipline for transgressions. Failure in any one of these will almost invalidate the other three. "In order to train a child a right, we must ask God, How and when to do it. As with so many of the Lord's commands, this one has a promise appended to it, which gives hope to faithful parents whose children may be wayward.

V. 7 - The rich rule over the poor, and the borrower is a servant to the lender." Money indeed talks and it often talks with a loud and gruff voice to those who have it not. The poor and the borrower are today protected many bylaws, but it is still true that those with money exercise a lot of influence over those who have it not, and who must borrow. The high cost of homes, cars, etc., often make borrowing a necessity, but many borrows needlessly to buy luxuries when they could practice self-denial for a time, and labor industriously until they have the privilege to buy without borrowing. So many today have borrowed to the utmost limit to the detriment of most families. We need to get back to the principle of frugality, honest labor, and self-denial. Sadly, man steadfastly refuses to believe God's warning that there are consequences to every sin, for he continues to believe Satan's lie that "ye shall not surely die," if ye sin, Genesis 3:4. Often the sinner is angered greatly if anyone brings his sin to his knowledge, but that anger is going to fail—cease to be exercised—when he stands before the God of judgment and freely confesses his sin, as all will be compelled to do, for the record of their sin will then be openly revealed to all, Revelation 20:12.

He that hath a bountiful eye shall be blessed; for he giveth of his bread to the poor." "A charitable man has a bountiful eye, and the same with the single eye (Matthew 6:22), opposed to the evil eye Proverbs. 23:6, the "evil eye" is defined in Deuteronomy 15:9 as one which hardens itself against an observed need and the "bountiful eye" is here defined as the one which gives. God blesses the benevolent person because he so resembles God in this matter. We are given surplus so that we will have to give to others, 2 Cor. 9:8-9.

Cast out the scorner, and contention shall go out; yea, strife, and reproach shall cease." A scorner is one who has disrespect for others, and he takes delight in speaking contemptuously of them, for him egotistically and self-righteously assumes that he is better than they are. Because of his attitude, he continually stirs up contention. He is a leaven, which, if left alone, will contaminate the whole society, but if he is cast out, peace will return, and when he is punished, others will be kept from following his evil way. Good order is necessary for any society, and those who will not conform to it must be put away, else the whole will be corrupted.

He that loveth pureness of heart, for the grace of his lips the king shall be his friend. This is the proper order, for there cannot be grace in the lips if there is not pureness of heart, for evil speaking, scornfulness, etc., comes from a bad heart. Even earthly kings had not use for evil-hearted men who were hypocritical in their speaking. How much more is the Almighty Jehovah Elohim? We have before noted God's hatred of lying in any form. God looks with favor upon true knowledge, and He puts forth efforts and encouragements to preserve it in those who have it. There is never any disharmony between true knowledge and God's Word, for they come from the same source. It is only "science (knowledge) falsely so called," that opposes the truth, 1 Tim. 6:20. But the words that the sinner speaks and which he may think is the truth, God overthrows this because they are against Him.

The slothful man saith, there is a lion without, I shall be slain in the streets." "Many frighten themselves from real duties by imaginary difficulties. For the person who is unwilling to do honest work, any excuse will do ...

The mouth of strange women is a deep pit: he that is abhorred of the LORD shall fall therein." Solomon spoke much of "strange women" in earlier chapters, especially chapter 7. She flatters those who listen to her, promising much, but actually only leading them to the pit of perdition. Those who scorn the Lord's restraining grace will be abhorred by Him and He will remove the restraints and allow them to plunge on to their own destruction. We all owe much praise and thanksgiving to God's restraining grace and this is what any man can ask for, 1King 8:59. Children are not innocent: they are vicious, and the only reason they do not practice as much evil as adults is that they have not learned how yet, but they have all the potential in the hearts that adults have. Parents must discipline as much of this out of a child's heart as possible, Prov. 13:24; 19:18; 23:13-14; 29:15, 17. It is not easy to be a faithful parent.

v. 16. Oppression of the poor has always been a common crime, and will be even in the days of the Lord's return, James 5:1-4. God takes special notice of the cheating of the poor. "Giving" perhaps refers to bribing the rich and powerful, but in spite of this human prudence, one will come to want, for God will not bless such unholy actions. V. 17 -, Solomon was not being egotistical when he styles himself "the wise," for he was conscious that he is the Lord's mouthpiece for this divine wisdom, 1 Kings 3:11-12, and so, that the knowledge he imparts ought to be applied to the heart for a reasonable moral and scriptural values. Wisdom in the heart shall be a pleasant thing, for it does comfort the heart, it leads into the way of blessing, It influences those about us and It honors God. It requires truth in the heart for the lips to be fitted to speak truth consistently. This and the preceding verse reveal a five-fold stage in the complete cycle of truth's work: (I) submitting the ear to it. (ii) Actually receiving the truth. (iii) Applying the heart to do it (iv) Keeping the truth in the heart. (v) Speaking it to others. The truth is never given simply to be hoarded up for ourselves or for our entertainment. We learn that we may teach in all various capacities as it does fit our calling and the Godhead placement.

All spiritual knowledge ought to be presented for the purpose of promoting: A saving trust in the Lord, A daily trust which will build one up in the faith and sustain one under trial and A prophetic trust. For example, a hope in the Lord's return and His final setting a right of all things, this will give us endurance to the end, and this an appeal made to the listener to bear witness to the excellence of the things that have been taught so far. It is acknowledged by many unbelievers that the Bible contains much excellent wisdom and morality, for they like to think they are not as bad as all that, and can eventually work out a plan of salvation for themselves.

V. 22 That I might make thee know the certainty of the words of truth; that thou mightest answer the words of truth to them that send unto thee?" Here then is the purpose of teaching these excellent counsels and knowledge, to have certainty about the truth, to be prepared with truth to give an answer to those who ask about it, 1 Pet. 3:15. Indeed, this is the ordained means of others being brought to the knowledge of truth—through the witness of those who know the truth, John 17:20. No one can adequately witness of the Lord who does not himself know the Lord as personal savior.

V. 22 "Rob not the poor, because he is poor: neither oppresses the afflicted in the gate." The poor are generally also powerless to resist oppression, and so they are considered fair game for the wicked. This attitude often is held even by those in authority, for the "gate" was the place where the official judgment was exercised anciently, and so oppression "in the gate" would be official oppression. But God takes special care for the poor, afflicted and helpless, Deuteronomy 24:12-15; Ps. 35:10; 140:12.

In truth, there is much injustice in this present evil world, and the poor are often oppressed, but this is only because God has not yet taken an accounting. The present life is the testing time when men are allowed enough freedom and opportunity to manifest their hearts conditions, and, under the divine wisdom, to see their shortcomings and their need for divine cleansing and forgiveness of sin. Those who refuse to see and admit this, but go on in their idolatrous pursuit of Mammon will be judged and spoiled as they thought to spoil others for the sake of gain

V. 24 "Make no friendship with an angry man, and with a furious man thou shall not go." People who cannot control their tempers make poor companions for anyone, for they are liable to lash out and do bodily harm any time things do not go to suit them. Generally speaking, angry, furious people are those who were not disciplined as children but were allowed to rule by their temper tantrums. They, therefore, grow up expecting the world to conform to their wishes, and when anyone doesn't, they throw a temper tantrum, as in childhood. Eventually, such a person meets another such, and one or the other is killed when they both try to force their way. Such make poor associates in any realm.

We are all influenced more by our associates than we realize, which is doubtless why our Lord has commanded His people to be a separate people, Ezra 10:10-11; 2 Cor. 6:14-18; Rev. 18:4-5. We learn much by observing, and while we may for a time be deterred for evil by fear, yet to continually see the wicked sin with no apparent punishment may embolden the weak Christian to sin likewise. But we must remember that for the most part, the judgment does not fall until our Lord's return, and so we cannot think that God has no interest in righteousness simply because some are unpunished for their sin in this life.

V. 26 - 27 it is normal and usual for a person to be willing to stand good for those of his own family, and so it may be that this must be understood in the context of the angry and furious man, (v. 24). The earlier verses warned against being surety for so-called friends and strangers: here against being pressured into it by fear of a man's temper. Without a doubt, any acting as surety ought only to be done after much careful thought, Proverbs 6:1 and 11:15.

It was forbidden in Exodus 22:26-27 to take away one's clothing for more than just the daylight hours, for people slept in their clothes for warmth, but apparently it was permitted for a surety to have the sleeping pallet taken away if he could not repay. This would make him uncomfortable, but it would not endanger health like the taking away of his very covering would, but it is intended as a warning of the consequences of careless suretyship. All of these warnings about suretyship assume the natural tendency of many to take advantage of the naïve trusting of good people.

V. 28 "Remove not the ancient landmark, which thy fathers have set." The only references to landmarks in the Bible are here, Proverbs 23:10; Deuteronomy 19:14; 27:17 and Job 24:2. These were the boundary markers so necessary to keep every man's inheritance intrude from others. We can easily see the importance of these when we consider how strictly each piece of land was to be passed on only to the man's sons, Lev. 25:23-28.

There are also spiritual landmarks which must not be removed. There are some Christian Organization called Fanatics and radical classic because they held on to the old doctrines while so many were removing these and following modern doctrines. The infallible of Scripture is our Landmark in many ways.

V. 29 "Seest thou a man diligent in his business? He shall stand before kings; he shall not stand before mean men." The world recognizes the value of a diligent man in business, and it seeks such. Rulers are always on the look-out for such to run their lesser concerns.

We see several illustrations of this in Scripture and in Joseph, Gen. 39:3-6; 41:42; Nehemiah, (2:11; 2:1); in Daniel, Dan. 6:1-3; 8:27. The Lord also values diligence in the spiritual realm, Rom. 12:6-8; 2 Cor. 8:7; Heb. 6:10-12. "Mean" means "obscure." A diligent man shall stand before great men, not just before obscure, unimportant men. The diligent Christian will stand before the King of kings, as his faithful servant, to be rewarded by Him. Are we diligent in the Lord's work?

CHRISTIAN LIFE CONSISTS OF FAITH AND CHARITY – IF THERE IS NO REVELATION SUCH AS DREAM, VISION AND PROPHESY TO YOUR QUESTIONS CLINGS TO THE DIVINE MANUAL – THE BIBLE

CHAPTER
TWENTY-THREE

SUMMARY

Proverbs 23:1

When thou sit to eat with a ruler, consider diligently what is before thee. It was considered a great honor and privilege to be asked to dine with a national leader and even today, good manners are expected of the guest, but anciently if one offended the rules, he could lose his life for it. The delicacies of a state dinner might be a temptation to overindulge and so to offend the host. At any sumptuous meal, it is almost impossible to try a little of every food, however, one may like to. Almost unlimited amounts of all sorts of delicacies would be a great temptation to a common man who barely had enough to make ends meet, but instead of partaking of all of it, it would be better for one to put the knife to his throat to restrain his own gluttony, than to indulge his gluttony and have the king put an axe to the neck, because he was offended at his eating. Self-restraint is always a duty, and it is always better in all realms than going to excess.

Delicacies may be more appealing than ordinary food, but they are generally not as good for a person as the ordinary food is, many people have been destroyed from too much and too rich food than; by too little and too plain food such as bitters and naturals. The context here suggests that, though one might be flattered to be invited to eat with the king, yet the partaking of the king's delicacies does not necessarily mean that he has found acceptance with the king. The meal may end with the guest being hanged as Haman was Esther 7:1, 10, so that one is deceived by the fact that he eats at the king's table.

LIFE APPLICATION:

I ought to attend a wedding one day around 1994. The very day of the occasion my aunt packed all her money and kept, and this restrain me from going. In the night Jehovah Elohim the revealer of all secrets gave me an insight; and I saw myself with those I am sure would be present on that occasion and I discovered that I was given a meat to eat, as I threw the meat in my mouth, they were all jubilating and said I have been caught not knowing that I had not swallowed it, and immediately I notice this I expel the meat out and they were like disappointed. If I had gone to that occasion only God knows what would have happened by eating that meat or one of the delicacies somehow. This is an example of putting the knife on the throat and it also suggests that not all occasion you attend and or if attended the law of moderations need to apply Galatians 5:16.

V. 4 - 5 "Labor not to be rich: cease from thine own wisdom." Wisdom here no doubt has to do with human wisdom that is put out in an endeavor to gain worldly riches. God's command is that all men be content with having a sufficiency of life's needs. Sometimes God gives much more than we need so that our abundance may be a means of helping others, 2 Cor. 8:13-15; 9:8-11.

Superior abundance ought not to be squandered. But; mere riches for riches sake, is not to be sought. "Solomon does not oppose diligence, but anxiety. "Thine own wisdom" is in contrast to the wisdom of God which seeks, not riches, but for righteousness. For riches certainly, make themselves wings' they fly away as an eagle toward heaven." Nothing is more certain than that man cannot possess worldly riches for any great length of time. If riches are not taken away from the man, man is eventually taken away from them by death. This verse finds an N.T. echo in 1 John 2:15-17. These "are not" in that they are so very temporary, and then they fly away through theft, inflation, taxation, poor management, etc. 1 Tim. 6:17-19. The wings they fly away upon are of their own making.

V. 6 - 8 "Eat thou, not the bread of him that hath an evil eye; neither desire thou his dainty meats." Apparently here "evil eye" is used in the sense of an envy eye because of covetousness, as in Matthew 20:15. If so, then it is contrasted with the "bountiful" eye of Proverbs 22:9. Some would invite guests to their table because they feel it is expected of them, yet would begrudge every bite that was eaten. Such ought to be steered clear of, nor should his food be desired, however, delicious it may appear.

The heart, being the motive center of the whole man, determines what he really is. Outward appearances mean little, for hypocrisy is easy to every person, but what he thinks in his heart when no one but God can see, reveals his real character. This host urges his guest to eat and drink, but all the time he is calculating the cost of the food, and he reckons it off more worth than his guest, and the more the guest eats, the more it bothers him. Alas, how often "things" assume a greater importance in some people's minds than people do. How sad that to covetousness some will also add hypocrisy. Sometimes churches fall into this sin also, and begrudge every dollar that is sent to the Lord's work which does not profit them personally. It is uncertain in what sense this is to be taken, whether, you will have reason to wish you could give back the food which was so grudgingly given, or else, in an imperative sense: return the hospitality shown to you with all haste so that you will no longer be obligated to one who so begrudges what he offers. However sweet the words that were spoken at the table, they are lost when one realizes the grudging spirit in which the food was given.

V. 9 "Speak not in the ears of a fool: for he will despise the wisdom of thy words." It is our duty to take all fit occasions to speak of divine things; but, some will make a jest of everything. A wise man is advised not to speak in the ears of such fools. To "speak in the ears" suggests speaking earnestly and personally, for this is not a general conversation with all who are near, but intimates personal dealing with him about his relationship with the Lord. The fool (i.e., the self-confident, unsaved rebel against God) does not appreciate the divine wisdom, and those who try to talk with him about it are generally despised and repulsed by him. He thinks himself self-sufficient, and so in no need of God's grace and mercy, and it is an affront to him to suggest that he does.

V. 10. Remove not the old landmark; and enter not into the fields of the fatherless Proverbs 22:28. The ancient landmarks were placed purposefully to protect land from the encroachments of unscrupulous men, and none would be so apt to be the victim of such as the fatherless, who would seemingly have no one to stand for their cause and to protect them. But God Himself has pledged Himself to be the protector of such, Exodus. 22:22-24; Deut. 10:17-18. It is not only an ungodly thing but also an unmanly thing, for anyone to take advantage of the fatherless and widows simply because they cannot defend themselves.

The following verse shows the solemnity of doing so. For their redeemer is mighty; he shall plead their cause with thee." Prov. 22:23. "Redeemer" (Hebrew. Gaal) was the near kinsman who had a right to redeem anyone who was in debt or had sold his land, Lev. 25:25-26, 48-49. "The Lord is the nearest of kin to the godly and friendless poor Matthew 12:50, in the day of judgment, when men are called to account for their business practices, he who defrauded the fatherless of land or goods find none other than God Himself is the prosecuting attorney to plead the case for the fatherless.

This is Solemn thought! There can be no right obedience where there is no knowledge of duty, and most knowledge is received by hearing and heeding the teaching and preaching of the Word of God. Nor is it enough to receive truth in abstract theory: it must be applied to the heart so as to become a part of one's life. One should receive and apply to the heart these words of knowledge." Instead of rejecting and rebelling against the wisdom spoken, Only the Spirit can apply truth to the heart, but there is the need for one to apply his heart to know the truth; i.e., to seek for the truth, Hosea 6:3.

Many do not know the truth because they do not follow on to know it. In another hands, Parental discipline is not only a duty; it is also a deliverance of the child from an early stage if it is rightly administered: instruction with love in the right way and consistency of life on the parents' side can go a long way in discipline a child. This does not justify brutality to children, but it does require punishment that is stringent enough to put fear into the child. Too many parents only discipline the child enough to make him mad the more, but not enough to make him fearful of disobedience, for if every transgression of parental law is quickly visited with punishment, there will be instilled in the child a sense of impending punishment for transgression of divine law as well.

Most capital crimes are committed by people who have escaped punishment many times for lesser crimes, and whose parents did not discipline them, and so, by experience they come to believe that most of the time one is able to escape punishment. Any spiritual man is going to rejoice to see his children walking in ways of spiritual wisdom, but if he is knowledgeable in the Bible, he knows that this will not come about unless he practices the discipline of verses 13-14 on them; however it may be painful to him at the time. But he must have the child's ultimate good at heart, and not just his own and the child's temporary feelings.

In disciplining children, it is a matter of priorities: As we asks ourselves this questions--which is more important: letting the child be temporarily happy in evil-doing, which will eventually destroy him, or make him temporarily unhappy through punishment which will make him be spiritually wise, and will ultimately deliver him from Satan domain? For a parent to see his child manifesting spiritual wisdom rejoices the heart, for thereby the parent is assured that no permanent evil can ever befall his child, for God's power and wisdom will be operative in the child. Words alone do not prove the possession of wisdom, but where the lips continually speak right things, it is a pretty good indication that God is in the heart.

V. 17 - 21 "Let not thine heart envy sinners: but be thou in the fear of the Lord all the day long." How easy it is to look upon the seeming success and prosperity of the lost and to envy them, not realizing that their prosperity is only for the very limited time of this life, after which they must go away into everlasting perdition. Because they did not fear God in the present life, they must everlastingly experience the fear of the Lord in Satan domain. The fear of the Lord, which moves us to honor and obey God, whatever the cost in this life, is the antidote to envying the prosperity of sinners. Why envy those who are soon to be cut off from God forever? We ought rather pity them. For surely there is an end, and thine expectation shall not be cut off." There is an end to this life, an end to spiritual opportunities, an end of sinful prosperity for the unsaved, and an end of the poverty and affliction of the righteous. And though then end of life in this world will be the end of all good for sinners, it will be just the beginning of good for the righteous Luke 16:19-31

God's justice guarantees retribution to evil and reward for good. Faith in Christ gives us a hope or expectation of glory to come, Roman 5:2, and this cannot be cut off: it rests upon the promise of Him Who cannot lie Revelation 22.

We must not overlook the Divine order here: It is, Hearing the Word, by which faith comes—saving faith and living faith, Rom. 10:17, Wisdom, which must always be based upon the truth, and which must be received first of all in the person of Christ, 1 Cor. 1:24, 30, after which one is qualified to guide his heart in the way of righteousness. Contrast the unsaved man's inability to guide himself a right in Jeremiah 10:23.

Not all tragedy comes through a rebellious refusal to hear God's Word. Often Satan simply gets people so preoccupied with this world that they do not hear, learn God's truth and thereby direct their hearts aright. Let us be warned lest we be ensnared with the things of the world.

In this following verse, two sins are warned against here: drunkenness and gluttony. Immoderation is wrong in any realm; temperance is one of the fruits of the spirit, Galatians 5:23, while drunkenness is one of the works of the flesh, Galatians 5:21. Solomon will speak in more depth about the results of wine-bibbing in verses 29-35. As Abraham Lincoln said, "Liquor has many defenders, but no defense." Nothing good can be said of drinking alcohol as a beverage.

Medically, alcohol has some good uses, but it is a poison, as any doctor will tell you, which, even in a single drink, will kill some cells of the brain. In our nation, overeating also causes more early deaths than almost any other single cause. This reminds us of the story of the prodigal son, Luke 15:11.

Drowsiness is the natural consequence of eating and drinking, especially the latter, and usually one of the first things that happens to an alcoholic is that he begins losing jobs as fast as he gets them, because of absenteeism. Then he starts selling off his possessions to keep himself in drink until he has nothing left but a destitute family and a drinking habit that he cannot control but which is taking him rapidly to Satan domain. Sad condition!

v. 22 "Hearken unto thy father that begat thee, and despise not thy mother when she is old." Children sometimes think that because they have achieved legal age that they are therefore fully equipped for life, and they forget that there is much more to knowledge than merely possessing the theory of it, and parents always, as long as they live, have more experience in life for they are generally twenty to forty or more years in advance of their children in the accumulation of experience. The mother is more apt to be despised by self-willed sons than fathers are, because she does not generally exercise the power and authority that the father does. A parent never gets too old for the respect and honor that his children still owe him Exodus 20:12; Ephesians 6:1-3

V. 23 Buy the truth, and sell it not; also wisdom, and instruction, and understanding." Proverbs 4:5-9. Actually truth cannot really be obtained just by money, for a rich fool is still a fool, however he may spend money to obtain degrees.

Truth is free to all who will seek it legitimately, which is what is meant by buying it—obtain it in honest legitimate ways. And once one has the truth, he should never let it get away for any reason—he must not sell it for any price, for it is infinitely more valuable than anything he could sell it for. "Truth is that by which the heart must be guided and governed, for without truth there is no goodness. We must buy it whatever it costs us; we shall not repent the bargain.

Truth is like the pearl of great price, worthy of our selling all that we have in order to obtain it, for without truth, all else is worthless, but with truth, all needful things will come to us, Matthew 13:46.

Nothing so rejoices the heart of parents as seeing their children living righteously and wisely, for the wiser and more experienced parents knows the dangers and sorrows of living wickedly. There is joy in knowing that by living righteously, they will escape much sorrow and harm. Children are the monuments of parents, and parents enjoy a sort of earthly immortality in their children, but how sad it is when children live wickedly, for they are then a monument to parental failure, or seems so at least. There may be the outward observation of a parent's ways, and a listening to his counsel, but if the heart is not yielded, it avails little. The same thing applies in the spiritual realm: God calls upon each of us to yield our hearts to Him first so that we may learn of Him and follow Him rightly. If the heart, the motivator and regulator yielded to the Lord, the whole man will be also.

V. 27 for a whore is a deep ditch, and a strange woman is a narrow pit." Here is why a young person needs wisdom—there are many moral pitfalls in life, and they are often dressed in very appealing appearances; so much so that he may not recognize the true depth of evil until it is too late if he does not have this wisdom. Young people often have a natural guilelessness and easy to fool that the wisdom of more mature years removes, 1 Cor. 6:15-18, as one might think from the illustrations of the ditch and the pit, (v. 27). Here, the harlot is likened to a wild beast, which is perched on a rock or tree limb, ready to pounce upon anyone who comes by, and so it is an active danger.

The sexual drive is a powerful force, and there is no sin in it as such, for it is given by God for the propagation of the race and for the pleasure of the creature. But it becomes sin when it is misused by taking it out of its ordained realm, 1 Cor. 7:1-7, 28; Heb. 13:4. Those who scorn God's rules, increase transgressions in others as well, and so become doubly guilty: first, of their own sins, and then of those sins, they inspire in others.

V. 29 "Who hath woe? Who hath sorrow? Who hath contentions? Who hath babbling? Who hath wounds without cause? Who hath redness of eyes?" All of these are pointed questions concerning the drunkards. Few things in this world have produced so much heartbreak as liquor. One of Satan's most infamous lies is "Leave it alone and it will leave you alone," for every drunk blight the lives of from one to dozens of people. Nor is any person more contentious than a drunk, who generally thinks he is wiser than all others, and must speak authoritatively on every subject; but few people make little sense in their talking as an intoxicated person, who would not believe when sober that he could speak such senseless babbling.

The drunk also awakens red of eye, his head splitting with a hang-over, and wonders how he got all the scrapes and scratches, yea, and even broken bones.

Proverbs 23:30 - 34

They that tarry long at the wine, they that go to seek mixed wine; this is the answer to the question of verse 29. It is fashionable today to consider wine as not so bad as the "hard liquors," but as a fully socially acceptable beverage, even in some professedly Christian homes, but consider the Divine indictment here set forth. It does not take a large volume of alcohol in drinks to ensnare people in alcoholism; even the drinkers of 3.2% beer can become alcoholics. Better to never take the first drink, and one will never have to worry about how to stop drinking.

Many are ensnared because Satan appeals to their pride with the thought "Only weak people become alcoholics, but you are strong; you can quit anytime you want." This very reasoning, whether conscious or unconscious, shows weakness. V.31 By far the most common explanation of the word rendered "color" is "eye" or "aspect" which probably refers to the glitter or sparkle in the cup of wine. Indeed, the "lust of the eyes" is one of the three principle avenues of temptation, 1 John 2:16. Better then not to even look, than to look and be ensnared in evil. One must consider, not the first result of something, but the end result thereof, to know its real character. "Serpent" is the more common word and sometimes it has a general meaning, but it is clear from Psalm 58:4 where the same Hebrew word is used, that it often referred to a poisonous snake, probably to the cobra, as Numbers 21:7, refers to serpents.

The word rendered "adder" is rendered a Myth Serpent in Isaiah 11:8; 59:5; Jeremiah 8:17. To what kind of snake it refers is not known, except that it too was deadly. These illustrative terms show us the real nature of liquor. Thine eyes shall behold strange women, and thine heart shall utter perverse things. Liquor always has the effect of losing the restraints upon one's lusts so that a person will do and say things under the influence of drink that he would never otherwise do. Liquor often leads to immorality, Gen. 19:31-36; Hosea 4:18. Immoral women often frequent in drinking establishments because of the opportunities to sin there, and drunken men delight to find them there. There is also always much evil and perverse talking at such drinking places.

Good descriptions of the dizziness of the drunk for few things are as unstable or uncontrollable as a body tossed about by the violence of a stormy sea. Worse yet is the agitation at the top of a mast on a boat on a tossing sea. Even so, a drunk staggers and stumbles as he tries to maneuver about; he has surrendered control of himself to a poison that not only disrupts the right function of his brain but actually kills its cells with every drink. And what does he get in return? Nothing but condemnation! Drunkenness produces insensibility to all sorts of insults and hurts at the time, and not until he awakens the next morning, sick, sore, his clothes ruined, perhaps his money taken, etc., does he realize that someone—he remembers not whom, in all likelihood—has taken him for all they could. Yet the habitual drunkard can hardly wait to awaken from one binge so that he can go on another, all the time hardening himself in that which will ultimately kill his body and damn his soul. "Insensibility to correction is the spiritual mortification which precedes death, Isaiah. 1:5, he doesn't want to feel guilty, but he won't seek the remedy for it. Satan domain is his destiny if he continues to deaden his conviction with a drink.

LIFE APPLICATION:

In 1984, I followed one of the elderly Christian mothers for Evangelism and follow-up, and we got to one of those streets off Owoseni Street in Lagos, she decided to go for some group of women to the right and I was lead to entering into a certain beer parlor behind on that same street. Immediately I entered, I humbly greet those men and they responded, and I simply started my conversation with them that 'I brought good tiding of Jesus Christ to them', as I was discussing with them, I just mention that if death should come now and meet them in this beer parlour they will end in Satan Domain, *Taah!!!*, the other man got angry and started raging; mentioning the number of wives he had, that he is powerful, he had charm he can turn monkey to lizard blah, blah, and besides that, ever since his great grandfathers, the Christians have been deceiving that Christ will come; up till that moment, 'a day has not turn to nights'. Then, I told them; all I am saying is that they should give their life to Christ because if death comes that very day their own Christ have come; and I opened Hebrew 9:27 and Revelation 20:12-15, 21:7-8 for them and left to join my Evangelism team, then; they also were through. When we got to the church we gave reports and pray, then dismissed. As I was going back to my house I was like should I pass through same street or another because almost four streets lead to my house from the church, then I made up my mind to pass on the same street. As I was going some people were like pointing at me and muttering as I was wondering what could have happen then two people ran towards me and asked me if I am the girl that came to preach in beer parlour an hour ago and I answered that it was me and what happen, it was then they told me that those men, one of them just died, is like they were drunk one picked bottle and hit it on the one that died and that particular one was the one raging talking like the rich man in the Bible Luke 13.

You see he who refuses to hear the instruction of God Almighty through His messenger hurts himself, most of all, for in refusing to yield divine warning, he dooms himself eternality Proverbs 29:1. If only we would learn from the preceding generations, how much sorrow we would avoid. The truth must be in the heart for it to have any practical bearing on us. In this way only will it be a motivating principle in us. The eyes read it, the mind ponders it, but only the heart can put it into practice.

THE WHOLE OF CREATION, WITH ALL OF ITS
LAWS, IS A REVELATION OF GOD

CHAPTER
TWENTY-FOUR

SUMMARY

Proverbs 24:1

"Be not thou envious against evil men, neither desire to be with them." How easy it is to envy the prosperity of the wicked, when only a moment's reflection will convince us that though they may have much worldly prosperity, they are soon to be cut off, and then they will be eternally separated from God and all good, while God's people, though poor in this world, shall be eternally rich and happy in the hereafter, Psalm 37:1-2, 9-17 Only through short-sightedness and lack of discernment could a Christian ever envy the wicked, but greed often moves us to thoughtlessly wish to be as prosperous as the wicked, yet none of us would wish for their state of condemnation to be on us, and often the two things must go together. V.2 gave the reason for not envying the wicked: they are evil in heart and lips, and so manifest their character as anti-God. He who continually thinks and talks evil is evil, and no profession or pretense otherwise can make any difference.

The true child of God who fellowships with such are going to find that it works out to his detriment; he will never profit any in such a situation.

Though the wicked study the destruction of others, it always falls back upon their own heads, Proverbs. 11:3, 5-6; Job 5:2. This is one of God's basic laws—the law of retribution.

V. 3 – 6. Through wisdom is a house built: and by understanding it is established." The word "house" often refers to the household or family, and while a man may thoughtlessly beget many children, yet they will never become a house of honor to him, nor a blessing to their community, nor faithful servants to God, unless they are taught wisdom and understanding. We have already noted several times in Proverbs God's solemn threats to cut off the "house" of the wicked, and His promise to build and establish the house of the righteous.

"Knowledge" of the Lord and from the Lord, of course, which is always profitable in the long run, and shall ultimately, enrich the home spiritually, and oftentimes materially as well. Riches, just for the sake of being rich, should never be sought. One should continually trust in the Lord who never fails, (1 Tim. 6:17), and if He gives one riches, which He does unto many, then those things ought to be used wisely and for His glory. Note the inclusiveness of this promise: "all precious and pleasant riches." Too often, however, we try to restrict "riches" to gold, silver, jewels, money, etc., but there are many other, more valuable things which may be so designated, such as the riches of God's: Goodness, Roman 2:4, Glory, Roman 9:23, Wisdom, Roman 10:33, Grace, Ephesians 1:7, Mercy, Ephesians 2:4, Good works, 1 Timothy 6:18 and Reproach of Christ, Hebrew 11:26. Wisdom, because it is from the Lord, strengthens people with a mental and spiritual strength which are far more valuable than mere physical strength. Physical strength is of use only in this world, but mental and spiritual strength are of use now, and more especially in the world to come. Wisdom avails where strength cannot, for a wise man can make the strength of the mighty to work against him, Prov. 21:22; Eccl. 9:14-16.

The saying that "A dialogue is mightier than the sword" is based upon the fact that wisdom is mightier than strength. Someone has well said that "Knowledge is power," and so the more knowledge and wisdom that we get, the more power we will have at our disposal. Nowhere do we see this exemplified so well as in the case of David and Goliath, 1

Samuel 17:6; is not a command to make war, but, as the second part of the proverb suggests, "Thou shall make thy war victorious unto thee by wise counsel." Nations generally do not go to war in order to be defeated, but they desire victory, and so they need the wisest counselors that can be found. Wisdom will erect a college or a council of state. Wisdom will be of use, to make an advantageous peace, the more wise counselors there are, the less likelihood of some important factor being overlooked to the defeat of the nation in war.

V. 7. "Wisdom is too high for a fool: he opens not his mouth in the gate." Remembering that "fool" in the Bible refers generally to the unsaved person, and that wisdom is from God alone, we can easily see why the fool does not attain it: he rejects the one source of wisdom, because of his proud belief in his own self-sufficiency. "The gate" was the place of judgment, and also was the place of teaching by the wise men. The fool, because of his rebellion against God's wisdom, is not qualified to speak in the gate, and though he might, in his pride, desire this position, he would not likely attain it in the eyes of the people.

V. 8. He that devices to do evil shall be called a mischievous person." "Mischievous" has a deeper meaning in the Hebrew than our English word, which we generally associate with harmless pranks. The Hebrew word means "a wicked device" (so rendered in Psalm 37:7; Prov. 12:2; 14:17, and "lewdness," Jeremiah 11:15. So far from devising evil being a matter of no consequence, as some seem to think, God denominates it wickedness, for to devise evil in the mind is almost equivalent to the deed, and sometimes is, if he is only withheld from it by circumstances. To even think evil is sin in God's eyes, for thoughts are nearest to the heart—the fountainhead—and manifests its condition. Foolish thoughts, therefore, reveal a fool's heart. The second half of this verse shows that even among men of the world, scornfulness is a hated thing. "Thought" is derived from the same Hebrew root as "mischievous" in verse 8. This verse refutes the idea held so commonly that sin consists only in doing wrong.

V. 10. "If thou faint in the day of adversity, thy strength is small." Adversity is the test of a person's character and endurance. Any kind of a sinner can put on a pretty good show of being a Christian when things are going well, but when adversity comes, it shows where the real strength lies, and who is a genuine, strong, grounded Christian. If one faints in the day of adversity, he reveals that he has not received as much wisdom and knowledge, (v. 5), as he should have, else he would have endured the adversity. "Even Job (4:3-5) fainted in the day of adversity. If thy strength is small, go to Him who 'giveth power to the faint, v 11, if thou forbear to deliver them that are drawn unto death, and those that are ready to be slain. This cannot refer to the justly condemned, for God has ordained that such are to be immediately put to death, Num. 35:31-33; Deut. 17:6-7. "A great duty required of us is to appear for the relief of oppressed innocence. 1 Thessalonians 5:15 expresses a similar thought.

He, who stands by and does nothing to deliver those who are mistreated in their innocence, will one day find himself being mistreated with none to help him. Excuses are easy to find when one does not want to do his duty, but God knows our innermost thoughts, Prov. 16:2; 21:2, and He judges in truth, not just according to outward appearances. He sees and knows when our excuses are lies; dodge. Alas, how often we deceive ourselves with our excuses, but we do not deceive Him who is the keeper of the soul, and who, consequently, knows it better than anyone else.

The last phrase is taken from Psalms 62:12, and is quoted in Revelation 20:12; 22:12, and is variously referred to elsewhere. God deals with people on the basis of their works, not that their works have anything to do with their justification, but because they manifest the ruling disposition of the heart. In the judgment, God always deals in perfect justice, which is "according to every man's works."

V. 13 – 14. "My son, eat thou honey because it is good; and the honeycomb, which is sweet to thy taste." Honey was the most common form of sweetness in ancient times and the land of Canaan was specially adapted for the production of honey, Exodus 3:8, 17; 13:15; Matthew 3:4.

It was a food that almost everyone enjoyed, and science has since found that it is one of the most healthful foods, having already been digested in its production by bees. Solomon is not, however, here teaching on wise dietary practices, but rather uses the honey as a symbol of the sweetness of the Word, as the following verse shows. V. 14. So shall the knowledge of wisdom be unto thy soul: when thou have found it, then there shall be a reward, and thy expectation shall not be cut off."

This likeness of the Word of God to the sweetness of honey is a common metaphor, (Ps. 19:9-10; 119:103). Thus we have here a gracious invitation to partake of a sweetness of divine wisdom; it is, like honey, both sweet to the taste, and also good for one, resulting in blessings to the soul and rewards to the life. "Thus should we feed upon wisdom, and relish the good instructions of it. But this figure of speech also suggests something practical: just as no one can enjoy the sweetness of honey without eating it, so none can enjoy wisdom without a study of, and submission to, it.

V. 15. "Lay not wait, O wicked man, against the dwelling of the righteous; spoil not his resting place." "Dwelling" is more commonly rendered "fold," which suggests a humble dwelling place, but however humble it may be, the wicked had better not lay wait to do evil to the Lord's people for He is the avenger of all such, Luke 18:7-8; 1 Thess. 4:6-8. "Assail him not either by secret fraud or open violence. *It is often the case, that in his contempt of God, the wicked man assaults the Christian since he cannot assault God personally. He may even do evil to Christians in an attempt to thereby convince himself that God either does not exist or that he takes no interest in the affairs of earth. But there is a judgment to come for all who misuse God's people.*

V. 16 – 18. For a just man fall seven times, and riseth up again: but the wicked shall fall into mischief. This expresses the security of the saint: though he may fall many times, yet no fall is ever permanent, for God raises him up each time, Job 5:19; Ps. 37:23-24.

The saint is not secure because of anything within himself; rather he is secure because of God's faithfulness to His promise to keep the believer, John 10:28-30; 1 Pet. 1:3-5. But conversely, the wicked fall into evil with no promised rescue from even one fall, so that his fall is a permanent calamity. Seven, being the number of completeness, suggests a continual rescue from every fall that comes upon the righteous.

What a wonderful and encouraging promise to the saints. In salvation, we lose what we cannot keep in order to gain what we cannot lose. Grace is the basis of the saint's security. V. 17. Rejoice not when thine enemy fall, and let not thine heart be glad when he stumble." These deals with our attitudes toward enemies: we are not to take delight in any evil that befalls any, for it is only the grace of God that prevents it from coming upon us. "Not only are we not to exult in a more severe calamity, but not even in a lighter one of an enemy.

The Christian is to overcome evil with good, Rom. 12:18-21. Exulting over the problems of an enemy generally, stems from a self-righteous spirit. David set a good example in this when he mourned over Saul's death, though Saul had often maltreated him, 2 Samuel 1:17. By contrast, see Obadiah 12.

None of us can perfectly discern the reasons why calamities fall, and this made us think that they always indicate God's displeasure. Therefore, we should not rejoice on enemies calamities lest the Lord see it, and it displeased him, and he turn away his wrath from him. It is not so expressed, but one wonders if the thought is not of turning away the wrath from one's enemy and letting it fall upon the one rejoicing in the calamity. In another word, God Almighty sometimes allows displeasures to come for His glory, sometimes for discipline's sake, sometimes to test one's faith, sometimes to develop patience, etc. The Lord sees our attitudes, however deeply they may be hidden in the heart, and He deals with us accordingly. Hence the need to always maintain a right attitude does matter whether any man knows it or not.

V. 19 - 20. Fret not thyself because of evil men, neither be thou envious at the wicked. Prov. 23:17; Ps. 37:1, 7. "Even that which grieves us must not fret us; nor must our eye be evil against any because God is good. If wicked people prosper, we must not, therefore, incline to do as they do. Envy not their prosperity. No Christian envies the judgment that awaits the unsaved, so neither should someone envy the little earthly prosperity which comes to him, which is so very little at best compared with the torment that he must endure when he dies. If one gained the entire world, what would be in comparison to the spiritual loss if he goes to Satan domain? Mark 8:34-37. Often envy is based upon the egotistical idea that we deserve more than others because we are better than they are; it is a form of self-righteousness.

There shall be no reward to the evil man; the candle of the wicked shall be put out. Prov. 13:9. However, much a wicked man may seem to be accumulating in life, and however care-free he may seem, the discerning Christian knows that he is but a step from death and eternity when he shall be separated from all good, for his feeble, flickering light of physical life shall go out, leaving him eternally in the blackness of darkness. How foolish and futile our envy of sinners will then appear, for Christians not only have eternal life but are also promised rewards for everything they suffer for the Lord's sake. Divine wisdom assures us of this, v. 14; Rom. 8:16-18.

Proverbs 24:21 - 32

My son, fear thou the Lord and the king: and meddle not with them that are given to change. The civil authority is instituted by God for the protection of the good and the punishment of the evil Roman 13:1-10; 1 Pet. 2:13-17. Christianity must never be an excuse for anyone to be lawless, and anyone who thinks that God's grace excuses them from obedience to civil authority or from doing right, is an antinomian - a Christian who believes that faith and divine grace bring about salvation and that it is therefore not necessary to accept established moral laws (an outlaw and or against the law) and this shows that he doesn't really understand grace at all. Here is also a warning to beware of those who are unstable. Many are like weather vanes, blown about by every wind of doctrine, circumstance and emotion. They love innovation for innovation's sake and can never be depended upon since they are, like the ancient Athenians, always looking for something new, Acts 17:21. To run with such is almost as bad as running with those who rebel against God and government, for the results are often the same.

Rebels, whether against God or civil government, are on dangerous ground. Anciently, civil rulers were much quicker to destroy rebels than today, but even in some part of the World today it is not healthy to speak against rulers. The question here suggests the awfulness of the ruin of such. Because of God's long-suffering, many assume erroneously that He takes no interest in the rebellion of men against His will, but judgment day is coming in due time, and then all men will bear witness to the folly of resisting God's will and purpose, part of which is good order in human governments. Only when human government clearly clashes with God's will are we justified in refusing to obey it, and then we must not actively seek to overthrow the government, but only passive resist it Acts 4:18-20; 5:29. Among other things that belong to the wise is not to have respect of persons in judgment. Here are more wise maxims, these showing the other side of the matter. "As subjects must do their duty, and be obedient to magistrates, so magistrates must do their duty in administering justice to their subjects.

Note carefully the application that is made of having respect of persons: it is not good in matters of judgment, and this is consistently the application that is made in the Bible when God is said to be no respecter of persons. We all have the right, and exercise it, to respect persons in the choice of friends, mates, etc., and God does also. In redemption He always has respect of persons, Genesis 4:4; Exodus 2:25.

Election is the sovereign choice of some persons and the leaving of others in their self-chosen state of sin. Whosoever, say to the wicked thou art righteous; shall bring curses from people, in fact; nations shall abhor him. In Proverbs 17:15. No one can really respect him who perverts justice, for he shows that he esteems personal gain (which is generally the cause of his perversion of justice) more than he esteems the truth or people. Just as it is wrong for us to set ourselves up as judges over the wrong that people do so also it is wrong for us to set ourselves up to justify the evil that men do; we have neither the right to condemn right actions, nor to justify wrong actions, for both of them are the perversions of truth. Often people will justify wrong doing in great men in order to find acceptance with them. This is as wrong as if one did it for a monetary bribe. Even unsaved people can see the evil of such perversion of justice, and will scorn such in their hearts. But to them that rebuke the wicked shall be delight and a good blessing shall come upon them. It is the failure to rebuke and punish evil that encourages others to practice it as well.

There is always a cleanse agent value to punishment, but only if it is consistently and immediately exercised upon the offender. Two things are needful to maintain good order in society: Proper laws, including courts that use them rightly, and good law enforcement of those laws. In our land, good law enforcement has been discouraged for several years now by lenient courts which too often turned the criminals loose on technicalities.

V. 26. Every man shall kiss his lip that gives a right answer. Judging from the context, this apparently has reference to giving the right answer in matters of judgment. A kiss has always been a sign of affection, and was anciently employed as much between men as between men and women, Genesis 27:26-27; 29:11. It was sometimes employed hypocritically to make a show of affection where none really existed, 2Samuel 15:5; Matthew 26:47-49; Luke 22:48. In our lesson, the kiss given for right answers suggests that one will be loved for rendering proper judgment.

V. 27. Prepare thy work without, and make it fit for thyself in the field; and afterwards build thine house. Necessary things are to take precedence of those which are for ornament and elegance. Be content with a cottage, and labor strenuously in the field of agriculture, until you have made the necessary money for building a more commodious and elegant house," Solomon's temple was built of stones already hewn and shaped and ready to be set in place, 1 Kings 5:18; 6:7). Also "to build a house" is used in the sense of to marry and beget children. If it is intended in this sense, then the meaning is labor to become sufficiently solvent to support a family before you take on the responsibilities of being a husband and father. "Build a house" is used in this sense in Exodus 1:21; Ruth 4:11; 2 Samuel 7:27. Too many young folks today rush into marriage without any thought of how they will support themselves and their children, and so they often experience many financial problems which often cause the marriage to break up.

V. 28. Be not a witness against thy neighbor without cause; and deceive not with thy lips." This is related to what was set forth in verses 23-26. There it had to do with the magistrates' duty: here it has to do with the individual's duty to court. No one is to bear false witness against another, Exodus 20:16. We are to speak only the truth, and if truth does not require us to bear witness against another, we must keep silent. Sometimes people are irrevocably harmed just by suspicions and insinuations. A half-truth is almost always a whole lie, for what is left unsaid generally is misused so as to give what is said a wrong meaning or a wrong application. Jesus' golden rule of love is "Whatsoever ye would have men should do to you, do ye even so to them: for this is the law and the prophets, Matthew 7:12. If this were always applied, how much evil and sorrow it would eliminate. V. 29. Say not, I will do so to him as he hath done to me: I will render to the man according to his work." This is the golden rule in reverse. It is revenge's law of malice and hate. Revenge does not belong to us, but to the Lord, Proverbs 20:22; Leviticus 19:18; Deut. 32:35; Roman 12:19. "If there be occasion to bring an action or information against thy neighbor, let it not be from a spirit of revenge. Even a righteous cause becomes unrighteous when it is prosecuted with malice.

It is common for men to want "to get even" when someone has done them wrong, or when they believe someone has. But even if there truly has been a wrong done, to get even by doing evil to them would require one's stepping down to his level. To return good for evil, which God requires, is to keep on a much higher level, and is to be like God.

I went by the field of the slothful, and by the vineyard of the man void of understanding. Every man has one temperament or other; according to Tim Lahaye analyses in the area of handling tools and environment which bears witness to the slothfulness of its owner. It is in the nature of all created things to degenerate if not constantly repaired and revived. This is part of the curse brought on by sin. The person who is too lazy to do his or her work will soon find that his place has practically reverted back to the wild, and is of little practical value. Anciently, boundary lines were often marked by walls made of piled up stones, but because these were not cemented together, they easily fell down and so had to be constantly rebuilt or the boundary in time would become indistinct. The overgrowth of weeds would add to the poor appearance of the place.

There is much to be learned from observation, for, as someone has well said, "There is a sermon in every blade of grass." If we were more observant of the mistakes of men, we might not have to continually repeat the same mistakes over and over again in every generation. Even when we do observe the mistakes of others, instead of humbly learning from them and being warned by them, we often self-righteously assume that we could never make such a mistake, and in our pride, we are not profited by others' mistakes. We must remember that, but for the restraining grace of God, we could be and would be, as bad as the worst.

V. 33 - 34. Yet a little sleep, a little slumber, a little folding of the hands to sleep. Note the repetition of the words for rest: three distinct Hebrew words are used, each of which is only "a little." The temptation is never to sleep several hours more, but always only a "little," but it results often in much more than little. Almost all temptation is to do little evil, but when it is set in motion it becomes much. We are afraid of "great" sins, but little sins are tolerated, and they become great. The slothful man becomes poor a moment he always find excuses to work.

Poverty comes gradually, little by little, like a traveler who, even on a great journey, moves only one step at a time, until that poverty becomes as strong and as oppressive as a robber. As one gets into the habit of taking life easy and catering to the body, he becomes more and more caught up in the meshes of practices that lead inexorably to poverty and want. Let us observe the negligence of the slothful and be warned by it. The spiritually slothful man will come to eternal poverty through his failure to awaken to righteousness.

NEVER THINK THAT GOD'S DELAYS ARE GOD'S DENIALS
HOLD ON! HOLD FAST! HOLD OUT! PATIENCE IS GENIUS

CHAPTER
TWENTY-FIVE

SUMMARY

Proverbs 25:1

These are also proverbs of Solomon which the men of Hezekiah king of Judah copied out. Indeed the Lord and His Apostles frequently quote from this section 25:5-7 with Luke 14:8-9; 25:22 with Romans 12:20; 26:11 with 2 Peter 2:22; 27:1 with James 4:13-14.

V. 2 - 3. It is the glory of God to conceal a thing: but the honor of kings is to search out a matter." The Lord reveals such of Himself and His works as are necessary for a foundation for our faith, but He never caters to the carnal curiosity of men about things of no consequence, Deut. 29:29. There is an unfathomable depth to the Lord's counsels, Roman 11:33, and we know of them only what He pleases to reveal to us for our good and His glory, 1Corinthians 2:9-10, but the unregenerate person neither understands nor receives the things of God, for they are contrary to his nature, 1Corinthians 2:14. It is to the honor of the national leader that he seeks to find out as much as he can of the things of God, for this will be for the good of his kingdom, and so will establish his reign. This enables us to remember the absolute power that oriental kings had, we can understand how that; no one could call him to neither account nor examine his heart's processes. Though he could search out matters, yet none but God could search out the king's heart. This is true to a certain extent concerning all men, for the heart is a secret place, but kings' hearts are especially unsearchable: but God is able to turn it according to His pleasure, Proverbs 21:1.

v. 4. Take away the dross from the silver, and there shall come forth a vessel for the finer." This is laid down by way of illustration of the verse to follow. The more that silver is refined, the purer it is, and so the better and more valuable will be the vessel made from it. The Word of the Lord is likened to perfectly purified silver in Psalm 12:6. This is the purpose of many of our trails that come upon us as Christians: it is to purge us of dross, to file the rust off us, to burn out the fears, doubts, lusts, etc. that cumber us. The N.T. often refers to our bodies as "vessels" that need to be cleansed, 1 Thessalonica 4:4; 2 Timothy 2:21.

V. 5. Take away the wicked from before the king, and his throne shall be established in righteousness. Bad subordinates in a government can overthrow much of the good that a good king may attempt to do. Hence, he must take away all such if he would have his kingdom established. Bad men in government are like tarnish on metal: the longer left undisturbed, the more they increase. Fire (which purges the dross from the silver, v. 4) is a common symbol in the Bible for judgment.

V. 6. Put not forth thyself in the presence of the king, and stand not in the place of great men. This is a warning against ambition for worldly greatness. The natural man is a hero-worshipper: he desires to associate with supposedly great people, for he thinks this will somehow rub off on him and make him also great. But our Lord taught that the way to greatness is through humility, not self-exaltation. For better it is that it be said unto thee, Come up hither; that thou shouldest be put lower in the presence of the prince whom thine eyes have seen Luke 14:8-10. Pride always goes before destruction and a fall, Proverbs 16:18, and this includes proud ambition as well. So Jesus taught Matthew 23:11-12. It is better, more for a man's satisfaction and reputation, to be advanced above his pretensions and expectations, than to be thrust down below them, this involves retribution in kind, for it is the man who is so proud that he thinks he deserves to be high up, that is compelled to go lower. The humble man, who thinks he deserves only the lowliest place that is, bidden by the host to go up higher—a fitting reward for humility.

V. 8. Go not forth hastily to strive, lest thou know not what to do in the end thereof when thy neighbor hath put thee to shame." Almost all strife springs from pride, Proverbs 28:25, or from anger and frustration, Proverbs 10:12; 29:22. Strife is one of the works of the flesh, Galatians 5:20, and so it is to be shunned where possible, Roman 12:18; Phil. 2:3, for it is the source of much evil, James 3:16. Many things that are done in haste are repented of at leisure for a long time, for the old maxim "Haste makes waste" is generally true. A quick-tempered person is almost always at a disadvantage with the cool and deliberate person who carefully thinks out his argument before he speaks. Strife should be the last resort, not the first reaction.

V. 9 - 10. Debate thy cause with thy neighbor himself; and discover not a secret to another. Where there is a matter of variance between two people, it ought to be kept confined to those two and settled by amicable discussion if at all possible, Matthew 18:15. In no case should one, out of spite, malice or revenge, reveal the secret of another (so some render it) when that secret has no bearing on the matter of debate, or, when the disclosure of it would be better kept secret. "To tell one's own secrets is folly; to tell our neighbor's secrets are treachery; lest he that heareth it put thee to shame and thine infamy turn not away." Often the hearers of secrets are the proclaimers of secrets also, and what has been received with a promise to tell no one will be broadcast to the four winds, so revealing the original teller of the secret to be infamously unfaithful to his pledge to keep the secret. Or perhaps the infamy (reputation) will be of his maliciousness in revealing secrets out of spite, (v. 9). Whether a revealer of secrets through malice and or out of a love for gossip, the consequences are shameful.

V. 11-12. A word fitly spoken is like apples of gold in pictures of silver. This is another illustrative figure of speech. Apples, as we know them, did not grow anywhere in the region of Israel. Here and elsewhere that "apple" is mentioned in Scripture it probably refers to the quince or citron, which were golden in color, and fragrant to smell. "Picture" has to do with a setting: here perhaps referring to an ornament basket of silver through which the golden fruit could be seen. A fitly spoken word is an appealing thing, whereas a word wrongly spoken can be a revolting and hurtful thing. In another hand, as an earring of gold, and an ornament of fine gold so is a wise man that is reprover upon an obedient ear. This further showing the meaning of verse 11. Wise and appropriate reproof is a beautiful thing, and he who receives this reproof with the right attitude is also a precious person. But, how rare; it is to find someone who will take a deserved reproof with grace and humility. This is the reason why reproof must be spoken fitly—so that it will not unduly antagonize. There is here a mutual responsibility both for the man that reprove and of the reproved.

V. 13. As the cold of snow in the time of harvest, [so is] a faithful messenger to them that send him: for he refreshes the soul of his masters. An unfaithful messenger can distort the message, give it to the wrong one, or not deliver it at all, but the faithful messenger is not false to his duty in any way and so he refreshes the soul of those whom he serves. Alas, how few of the modern ministers of God are faithful messengers. Multitudes have been given false hopes by those who are careless about their duty, just because of negligence, Fame, Power and riches of the world.

V. 14. Whoso boasted himself of a false gift is like clouds and wind without rain. Apparently "false gift" means the promise of a gift which is never given, and so only frustrates the one to whom it is promised. Farmers know how frustrating it is to see clouds form and winds blow, but no rainfall upon the parched and dry earth. Read in connection with verse 13 this may refer to false promises which false prophets and teachers often make, which always leaves the hearers disappointed and frustrated and skeptical of all who claim to be God's messengers. Satan still discredits true messengers with counterfeits.

V. 15. By long forbearing is a prince persuaded, and a soft tongue breaks the bone. Princes, who exercise great power, are nonetheless capable of being persuaded, but it is not so much by power, but by patience, and the little boneless member—the tongue—by mildness is able to break bones. This is a seeming contradiction, but the much spiritual truth is paradoxical. As the tongue, a little member of the body can lead to a big community's uproar, so it was found to be a breaker of bone. In another hands, David placated Saul 1 Samuel 24:9-16 and Abigail smooth-out David's wrath against Nabal 1 Samuel 25:23-33. Harsh words only beget more harsh words generally.

V. 16 - 17. Hast thou found honey? Eat as much as is sufficient for thee, lest thou be filled therewith, and vomit it. In the Promised Land, there was an abundance of honey originally, as there was of other good things 1 Samuel 14:25-26. It was the most common form of sweetening. Its sweetness to the taste would be a temptation to overeat of it. It is not forbidden fruit to thee, and this brings to us a law of moderations. In Proverbs 24:13-14 honey was used as a symbol of wisdom, but it cannot have such a symbolic meaning here since no one can get too much wisdom. It may have, however, reference by way of illustration, to the following verse. Withdraw thy foot from thy neighbor's house; let he be weary of thee, and so hate thee." As fellowship with a neighbor can be very enjoyable, yet too much time spent at his house can cause him to get tired of you, so a parallel is drawn between this and eating too much honey. Almost any two people can be together too much, and so a proper balance is to be maintained between working at home, and visiting with friends. Human friendships can be ruined by presuming too much upon them.

V. 18 -19. A man that bears false witness against his neighbor is a maul, and a sword, and a sharp arrow. These items are all instruments of destruction and death, for such is a false witness. The maul bruises and breaks; the sword cuts and the arrow pierces deeply, so that the bad effects of a false witness are extensive, touching not only a man's outward reputation but also his personal character and being. It would be bad enough that a man should bear false witness against a stranger, but to do so to a neighbor is a most heinous sin. Often the unfaithfulness of a person is not manifest until the worst possible time—a time of trouble—when he may suddenly manifest his true colors by bearing false witness against a neighbor, (v. 18), and treacherously turns on those who had formerly thought him a friend. Such is likened to broken teeth and disjointed limbs—two very painful ailments—both of which may look perfectly normal, yet be extremely painful. We are warned against putting confidence in men— even in men of apparently noble character—for only the Lord is worthy of our full confidence Psalm 118:8-9. The best of men are but sinners who, in a time of trouble, will let us down Psalm 146:3.

V. 20. As he that takes away a garment in cold weather, and as vinegar upon nitre, so is he that sings songs to a heavy heart. Nitre (potash) was mixed with oil and used as soap Jeremiah 2:22, but vinegar on it caused it to boil until it lost its force, and so was of no value as a cleanser. Thus, both the taking away of the coat and the putting of vinegar on nitre defeated the primary purpose of these, and these are illustrative of the folly of merriment to a sad heart. Roman 12:15; 1 Cor. 12:26 show our duty. Circumstances must determine our response in every case, but Matthew 7:12 contain a good rule of thumb.

V. 21. If thine enemy is hungry, give him bread to eat ... to drink Roman 12:20. Cf. Ex. 23:4-5. These two; bread and water, take in all the necessaries of life; and giving them is expressive of all acts of beneficence and humanity to be performed to enemies. The best way to destroy an enemy is to make a friend of him, and this can only be done by being kind to him. Note: there are no conditions to this: it doesn't say: "if he asks for them," nor "if he acts humbly," nor "if you think it will convert him." It is an absolute command. This is part of the law of the Kingdom of God Luke 6:27-36. Spite is not the motive for doing good to enemies, but rather the hope that it will be the means of humbling him and bringing him to repentance for his evil toward us. In any case, if we have the right attitude, the Lord's blessings will be on us, whatever the response of our enemy. Again this is a definite thing: those to whom we have done good may pretend that they are not affected, but it will have its results, and whatever they may be, the Lord is committed to rewarding us for it.

V. 23. The north wind drives away rain: so doth an angry countenance backbiting tongue." In the East, the fair weather came out of the north Job 37:22. So, if one shows that he rejects and scorns slanders of others, he will halt the spreader of gossip. Open ears always encourage open mouths. "If you do not listen to, but frown on, the backbiter, you put him to silence. The receiver of slanders gives forward motion to and shares the guilt of, the slanderer Roman 1:32. There would be no backbiters; if no one listens to them.

V. 24. It is better to dwell in the corner of the housetop, than with a brawling woman and in a wide house. Proverbs 21:9. "Brawling woman" is literally "woman of contentions," the plural suggesting the continual aspect of it. A woman can make a home a heaven or a Satan domain, depending upon her nature. "The roofs of houses in Judea were flat, encompassed with battlements, whither person might retire for solitude, and sit in safety; and it is better to be in a corner of such a roof and be exposed to scorching heat, to blustering winds, to thunderstorms, and showers of rain, than with a brawling woman in a wide house,"

V. 25. As cold waters to a thirsty soul so is good news from a far country." A comparison easily understood, but the spiritual application is blessed: It was the good news of God's grace which sent a Saviour to suffer and die for worthless and Satan-bound sinners that they might be redeemed and made citizens of that "far country.

V. 26. A righteous man falling down before the wicked is as a troubled fountain, and a corrupt spring." This can be taken either in two ways: first, for a righteous man to fall down in his convictions so that he no more rebukes the wicked, but compromises, is to become, no more a fountain of the truth and life John 7:38-39, but one that is troubled and corrupt. Second, for a righteous man to fall down and yield to temptation and sin, is likewise to be a troubled fountain and a corrupt spring, for he sends forth a false and deceptive testimony to those about him, and so he poisons those to whom he should be a fountain of life-giving Truth. We should neither live nor die unto ourselves Roman 14:7-8.

V. 26. It is not good to eat much honey: so for men to search their own glory is not glory." Proverbs 24:13 advised the eating of honey, but 25:16, 27 advises moderation in it, for too much of most things will be bad for one. Here, the metaphor is illustrative of the folly of self-interest. "Glory follows him that seeks it not ... To be humble when glory unsought comes to us, and to attribute all glory to God, is our wisdom. Jeremiah 9:23-24 and Galatians 6:14 show the only legitimate glorying that we can glory in.

V. 28. He that hath no rule over his own spirit is like a city that is broken down, and without walls. Most of the time man has destroyed himself after others had failed to have much influence over him to destroy him. In truth, man is often his own worst enemy. Before modern weapons, most ancient cities relied upon high, thick walls for a defense. The Great Wall of many countries were built to keep out invaders, yet of the several times it was breached, none of them were because of the wall being broken down: all were the result of betrayers within. He who has no control over his own spirit, whether it has to do with pride, (v. 27), lusts, anger, or whatever, has a betrayer within to overthrow the city of his soul. "Prayerful, watchful and self-control is the wall of the city.

IMPURITY IN EVIL TURNS THE MORAL SILVER ITSELF INTO DROSS (ISAIAH 1:22),

CHAPTER
TWENTY-SIX

SUMMARY

Proverbs 26:1

As snow in summer, and as rain in harvest, so honor is not seemly for a fool." Rain in harvest June and July; was very remarkable, so much so that in 1Samuel 12:17 it was considered to be a special act of the Lord. Snow in summer and rains in harvest were both undesired and unseasonable, and so this is used to illustrate the unseemliness of giving honor to a fool; to do so is to seemingly put a premium upon his foolish self-confidence and is to encourage him in his rejection of the Lord. The self-sufficient sinner is almost a hopeless case without encouraging him in it by giving him honor.

V. 2. As the bird by wandering, as the swallow by flying, so the curse causeless shall not come." Many kinds of birds migrate long distances, some even flying from tree to tree annually, being motivated by an internal instinct to do so. These illustrate that when God allows a curse to come upon the fool (v. 3) it is for a reason—his sinful rejection of the Lord. Many people try to curse God's people, 1 Samuel 17:43; 2 Samuel 16:5-13.

"Who can curse, whom God has not cursed? Yea, such shall be cursed themselves; see Psalm 109:17, Number. 23:7-8.

V. 3. A whip for the horse, a bridle for the donkey, and a rod for the fool's back." "Wicked men are compared to the horse and the donkey, so brutish are they, and not to be governed but by force or fear, so low has sin sunk men, so much below themselves.

Though the fool, in his conceit, may think very highly of himself and his intellectual ability, yet in spiritual things he is really brutish, Psalm 32:9; Jude 10, and for this reason, he must be disciplined and controlled as the beast is, by fear, Proverbs 10:13; 10:20. This is the curse that is caused to come by a fool's folly; it never comes without due cause, and that cause is the sinful instinct inherited from parents, Genesis 5:3. The fools are to be treated according to their disposition within the natural phenomenon. Therefore, answer not a fool according to his folly, lest thou also be like unto him."

A Christian can sometimes do the cause of God great harm if he answers a wicked man in such a way as to be like him. This confirms the wicked man's opinion that he is no different than a Christian, except perhaps a little wiser. "Sometimes a fool, or wicked man, is not to be answered at all ... and when an answer is returned, it should not be in his foolish way and manner. For some things; silence is the best answer. In another hand, answer a fool according to his folly, lest he is wise in his own conceit." The first part of this and verse 4 are exactly the same except for the tense of "answer" and the word "not," so that it requires spiritual discernment to know what is taught. "Regard to the difference of times and circumstances harmonizes the seeming contrariety of the two precepts ... The reason added by Solomon draws the distinction. Do not answer when your answer will make thee like the fool: answer when you know that silence will give him a handle for self-conceit and or controlled.

V. 6. He that sendeth a message by the hand of a fool cutteth off the feet, and drinketh damage." Since the character of a message is going to depend on to a great extent upon the faithful character of the messenger, so to send a message by one who is not dependable is folly and will result in damage to the one who sends him. The feet are the means of support, and also of motion, so that to cut them off is to reduce one to a very dreadful condition. To "drink damage" is to be harmed internally. V. 7. The legs of the lame are not equal so is a parable in the mouth of fools." It just a very brief statement to know a man with stroke attacked. So it is when an unsaved man tries to speak the Word of the Lord: the disparity between his own life and conduct and the Word of God which he speaks will be apparent to all, and he will be manifest as a hypocrite. This is what does more harm to the cause of God, and to His true people than almost any other thing—the inconsistent lives of many who claim to be His people, and often even His preachers. The life must teach first, or else one teaches not at all to God's glory. V. 8. As he that bindeth a stone in a sling, so is he that giveth honor to a fool." One did not choose a precious stone to use in a slingshot, for the purpose of the stone was to be cast away, so only stones of not value were used. Thus, the implication here is that all honors that are bestowed upon the fool are wasted, for it is the casting away of a stone. Some understand "bindeth" in the sense of tying it in so that it will not be slung out, and that so it does not accomplish its purpose, but the Hebrew word is a common one which does not imply more than the placing of the stone in the cradle of the sling.

V. 9. As a thorn goeth up into the hand of a drunkard, so is a parable in the mouth of fools." The Hebrew word for "thorn" is also rendered "thistle" an equal number of times and seems to suggest a small thorn, which the drunkard receives without realizing it is there until he sobers. Thus, the fool, though he may speak the Word of the Lord, does not realize what it is, but may actually use it as a pun or a jest, and so his misuse of it results in judgment to him, just as the un-tended thorn in the drunkard's hand might fester and set up blood-poisoning and result in eventual death. It is a solemn thing to tamper with God's Word, Proverbs 30:5-6. The great God that formed all things both rewarded the fool and rewarded transgressors." The common rendering seems preferable, for it shows that the sovereign Creator of all things is also the just judge who shall recompense all according to their works, whether good or bad, (Isa. 3:11; 40:10; 62:11; Rom. 14:10-12; 1 Cor. 3:13-15; 2 Cor. 5:10; Rev. 20:11-15).

V. 11 - 12. As a dog returned to his vomit, so a fool returned to his folly." 2Peter 2:22, was a place verse 11 is called a true proverb. Dogs are almost always spoken of metaphorically in a bad sense in Scripture, Isaiah 66:3; Matthew 7:6; Philippians 3:2; Revelation 22:15. The picture for our understanding in this particular verse is the dog's folly in returning to that which made him sick once, and which is now even more corrupt. It is a most appropriate picture of the awakened but unconverted sinner who reforms his life for a time, then returns again to his sin, 2Peter 2:22. Compare Matthew 12:43-45. It is common for people who have professed salvation, joined the church and apparently lived a Christian life for a time, to one day turn back to the world and continue in their apostasy until death Luke 9:62. Hebrew 10:25-31 speaks of these also and this is in conjunction with the next verse - Seest thou a man wise in his own conceit? There is more hope of a fool than of him. Often; those who return to their folly as in verse 11, do so while persuaded that they are wiser than others who continue to deny their lusts and live the Christian life. The fool who is one through infirmity of nature is more likely to be saved than the self-sufficient, self-righteous man, for if a man but know he is a sinner, there is hope, for Christ death for such, since He died not for the righteous, Matthew 9:13. Pride and self-sufficiency are fatal sins, for they are sins against the very remedy for them.

V. 13 - 16. The slothful man saith there is a lion in the way; a lion is in the streets." Proverbs 22:13. This is how often people scare themselves out of real duties by imaginary evils. Most of our fears never come to pass anyhow, and we dishonor by our unbelief the God Who promises protection to all who trust in Him. "This is an idle excuse; since lions are usually in woods, forests, and not on public roads. There is no lack of excuses to those who are determined not to do their duty and the following verse explains further "As the door turneth upon his hinges, so doth the slothful upon his bed." As the door moves back and forth on its hinges, yet makes no real progress, so the sluggard moves over and over on his bed, yet he never makes any progress toward rising. Some sluggards, like doors with rusty hinges, do little but make noise, talking much but doing little.

There are also many people who are like double-hinged doors—they swing whichever way the least pressure is on them: they are compromisers. The slothful man is unconcern for his own welfare as understood in v. 15.

And if at last, the lazy man gets out of bed, (v. 14), yet; he is still lazy—so much so that he prefers to go hungry rather than earn his food. Today we would say that he stands with his hands in his pockets, but anciently pants were unknown, and lazy men stood with their hands in the folds of their robes. Though; there will always be poor people, Matthew 26:11, because some are not good managers, and others are just plain lazy. Unfortunate people ought to be helped, but not lazy people, 2Thess. 3:10-11.

A lazy man won't want to take the slightest trouble for the most necessary things," A lazy man was also rendered as a sluggard and these are wiser in their own conceit than matured men that can render a reason." "Sluggard" is the same Hebrew word rendered "slothful" in verses 13-15, so that the subject is the same as in these verses. Seven is the number of completeness or totality. His conceit apparently over his ability to get out of honest labor, and he considers himself wiser than all others who are honest supporters of themselves. His slothfulness is the cause of his good opinion of himself.

V. 17. He that passeth by, and meddleth with strife belonging not to him, is like one that taketh a dog by the ears." "Meddle" is more commonly rendered "be worth." "Instead of being a mediator and peacemaker, he takes on one side, and acts the angry part, as in; blows things up into a greater flame, and enrages the one against the other, Dogs were not meant to be picked up by the ear, nor do they appreciate it, and would generally snap at those who tried, and so a person might be bitten. It is the blessed duty of all to be peacemakers, Matthew 5:9, but at the same time, we are warned against being busybodies, 2Thessalonia 3:11, 1Timothy 5:13, 1 Peter 4:15.

A busybody generally involves self-righteousness and conceit and more also like a mad man who casteth firebrands, arrows, and death, in other to deceived his neighbor, and saith, Am not I in sport? Here we are shown the harm that lies even in what may be considered innocent jesting. However; much "fun" one may consider it to be to cast firebrands and arrows in the air, the truth is, there is potential and likely death in each one, and it matters not that one may say that it was all done in fun if one is wounded or killed by these. So is the man that deceived his neighbor, and saith, Am not I in sport?" The point made is here is that every deception—yes, even "white lies" —has the potential of great harm to others. 2Peter 2:13 described the unsaved as those who sport themselves with their own deceiving; they deceive themselves about the innocence of their sporting. Sin is always more deadly than any person could realizes. Satan does camouflages.

V. 20 - 22. Where no wood is; there the fire goeth out: so where there is no talebearer, the strife ceaseth. "Talebearer" is also rendered "whisperer." He is a Satan postman, constantly stirring up strife by running back and forth with whispers and insinuations about what each party has said. He keeps the strife going by making "statements which either he or someone else has invented, reveals what ought not to be told, tells it to someone to whom especially he ought not, either by additions and or subtractions Strife will die out eventually without fresh fuel, but almost every community has some who delight to refuel strife. In other words, as coals are to burning coals, and wood to fire; so is a contentious man to kindle strife." "Coals" refers to charcoal, and is a different word than that rendered "burning coals." Both charcoal and wood are a fuel which kindle easily and quickly; so the contentious man is one who readily kindles strife. He cannot get along with others and he delights to stir up others to be like himself. He is an incendiary, delighting in the flames of anger and hatred, Proverb 15:18; 29:22. One may but ask this question - Why do some people delight in strife? The answer was because the Prince of peace has never entered their hearts to give peace, and so their nature is warlike, Psalm 120:6-7; 140:1-3. Divine wisdom in the heart produces peace, James 3:17-18.

In another hands, the words of a talebearer are as wounds, and they go down into the innermost parts of the belly Proverbs 18:8. They wound the credit and reputation of all people involves, including themselves if at all they have conscience. "Innermost part of the belly" speaks of the depth of the hurt that can be inflicted by a sharp word, a slander or other of the talebearer's merchandise. The talebearer considers his tales no more harmful than scattering feathers, but they are as hard to retrieve as feathers scattered a week before in a high wind. Such tales however fall with the weight of iron and cause deep wounds in those affected by them. People are accountable for their words, Matthew 12:34-37.

V. 23 - 26. Burning lips and a wicked heart are like a potsherd covered with silver dross. Considering the context here, the lips are apparently burning with professions of love—i.e. ... with great pretensions, but without the corresponding reality. A potsherd was a piece of broken pottery which was of little value, Isaiah 30:14. It's natural worthlessness would not be materially increased by covering it with silver dross, which was also worthless, but would make it appear more attractive from a distance. Here, Jesus' most scathing denunciations were directed against hypocrisy. Matthew 23:13-15, 23-33. This reminds us of Cain's hypocrisy whereby he covered his hatred of Abel as he acted friendly to him until he got him out in the field where he killed him v. 24 compare Genesis 4:8. However, it is also true that one's speech will betray his heart's condition and true feeling.

It takes a pure heart (purified by grace) to speak pure truth, and if the heart has not been purified, the speech matters but little. Therefore, when he speaketh fair, believe him not: for there are seven abominations in his heart." Some Jewish expositors believed these seven abominations were those mentioned in Proverbs 6:16-19, but some of them could not possibly have been in the heart. Seven being the number of completeness or totality, the thought is that, however fair and sweet his speech may be, that is no proof that he may not be totally corrupt in heart, for fair speech is often a pretext for an abominable heart, (v. 24).

It is sad, but we often have to be somewhat tested people until we know that they are dependable, since so many evil people hide behind fair speeches. Most crooks or lawbreaker are very convincing and or smooth speakers. They amount to nothing since their hatred is covered by deceit, and their wickedness shall be showed before the whole congregation." To hate a fellow creature is one sin, but to hide that hatred under a guise of fair speech and apparently benevolent feelings is to add sin to sin, and to be guilty of hypocrisy on top of hatred, which is on top of a refusal to repent of the original hatred and an unforgiving spirit. Sin may only be removed by the blood of Christ, but God also requires, in conjunction with this, the confession and forsaking of it, Proverbs 28:13; 1 John 1:9, and he who is too proud to confess his sin will one day have it revealed and reviewed before all the world, Roman 14:11-12; 1 Corinthian 3:13. The great congregation" probably refers to the universal gathering of saints, sinners and ministering spirits at the last great judgment Day Rev. 20:12.

V. 27. Whoso diggeth a pit shall fall therein: and he that rolleth a stone, it will return upon him. This Solomon had learned from his father David, Psalm 7:15-16. This is again the Divine law of retribution, Galatians 6:7-9. This is the practical working out of the hatred that he hid in his heart in verse 24-26. "The mischief which a wicked man labors hard at, as men do in digging a pit, or rolling a stone, in time revolves upon themselves; the measure they mete out to others is measured to them. The outworking of such retribution is a part of God's providence—His making of all things fulfill their original purpose and working all for the good of His own people, Roman 8:28.

V. 28. A lying tongue hateth those that are afflicted by it; and a flattering mouth worketh ruin. If one did not hate them, he would not lie to them, and so, mislead them and cause them trouble. Some ancient eastern versions render the first phrase "A lying tongue hates the truth." Which is also true, whether this is meant here or not? And a flattering mouth is almost as bad as a lying mouth, for it works ruin, as Satan's flattery did to Eve, Genesis 3:4-5. Probably more people have been ruined by flattery than by criticism, for it is a sweet and desirable poison. God hates flattering lips, for flattering is a form of lying.

THE REFORMATION OF THE COURT WILL PROMOTE THE REFORMATION OF THE KINGDOM, (PS. 101:3, 8),

CHAPTER TWENTY-SEVEN

SUMMARY

Proverbs 27:1

Boast not thyself of tomorrow; for thou knowest not what a day may bring forth. Man not only does not control the future: he doesn't even know what it holds, and so he is not to boast even of the next following day as to what he will do, either of good or of bad, or what he will be, nor of what opportunities he will have. Most people die even while yet expecting to live and fulfill other desires. "Death is certain to all men, as the fruit of sin, by the appointment of God; and there is a certain time fixed for it, which cannot be exceeded; but of that day and hour no man knows.

Men ought to always be prepared to stand before the Lord at any time He calls, for one day He will. And v. 2, further, explain the limitation of men as in ascribing unnecessary honor to themselves. "Let man praise thee, and not thine own mouth; a stranger, and not thine own lips." From the danger of boasting of future opportunities, Solomon passes to the folly of boasting of one's own deeds or Excellencies, which is usually disgusting to others.

To praise others is to attract them but to praise self is to run all others off. "To be commended by others, by any but a man's self, is to his credit and reputation; but nothing more hurtful to it than self-commendation; see 2 Corinthians 10:18," Many, however, have the philosophy that: "He that raise not his own horn, the same shall not be raised." This is sometimes true, but a man may not be the one to be raising it.

V. 3. A stone is heavy, and the sand weighty: but a fool's wrath is heavier than them both. A fool's wrath is often directed against others since it is a characteristic of the unsaved to hate others, (1 John 3:10-18). Hate always does more harm to the hater than to the hated. In fact, a fool's wrath may or may not eventuate in the physical death of the hated one, but it certainly results in the spiritual death of the hater, (Job 5:2), for hatred, wrath, etc., are all works of the flesh, (Gal. 5:20), but the first fruit of the Spirit is love, (Gal. 5:22). The heaviness of this wrath will sink the fool to the bottom of the pit: this is simply a matter of spiritual gravity.

V. 4. Wrath is cruel and anger is outrageous; but who is able to stand before envy? "Outrageous" is so rendered only here: more commonly it is rendered "a flood" or "overflowing of waters," which pictures it as unexpected, powerful, overwhelming, destructive, etc. The second half of the verse shows envy to be similar to these things. "All mankind in Adam fall before the envy of Satan; for it was through the envy of the devil that sin and death came into the world … Abel could not stand before the envy of Cain; nor Joseph before the envy of his brethren … and, where it is, there is confusion and every evil work, James 3:14, 16. Envy is a work of the flesh, Galatians 5:21 and part of the unregenerate life, Roman 1:29, but it is also a pitfall of the saved as well, Galatians 5:26; Roman 13:13-14

V. 5 - 6. Open rebuke is better than secret love. When a brother sins, it is an act of charity to rebuke him in love Leviticus. 19:17, but in so doing, care must be taken not to do so proudly nor self-righteously less one also be ensnared Galatians 6:1. Jesus directed such to be done privately Matthew 18:15. He does not forbid public rebuke on occasion, 1Timothy 5:20, nor does it mean that rebuke must always be public. Rather open rebuke, as distasteful as it is to us, is shown to be better than a secret love which is not moved to seek for the betterment of the loved one by rebuking his sin. It is both the privilege and the duty of believers to endeavor to convert fellow saints who err to the truth, James 5:19-20, but we must always practice Ephesians. 4:15, and this is to say faithful are the wounds of a friend, but the kisses of an enemy are deceitful."

A wound is always painful, but it may be necessary to correction, and so it ought to be appreciated, as proceeding from love. Alas, how many false shepherds care not for the sheep, but heal them with a false peace, Jeremiah 8:11.

A true friend is always interested in the ultimate and best interests of his friend, not just in temporary ease, Psalm 141:5. No greater illustration can be found of deceitful kisses than in Judas Iscariot, Mark 14:43-45; Luke 22:47-48. A kiss doesn't always mean love, nor does a wound make one an enemy.

V. 7 - 8. The full soul loatheth a honeycomb, but to the hungry soul, every bitter thing is sweet. Nothing improves one's appreciation of food like having to do without for a while. Picky eaters generally have too much luxurious food, and would have a better appetite if they had to go hungry a little

Sin has caused us all to be too often dissatisfied when we ought to be very thankful for what we have. Pride makes us think we deserve more and better than what we receive. As a bird that wandereth from her nest so is a man that wandereth from his place. A bird that moves too frequently or too long from the nest can cause the eggs not to hatch, or the eggs or little ones to be devoured. This illustrates the danger of loss that may come to the man who, through dissatisfaction with his place or lot, frequently moves about. How easy it is to look about and to desire the "greener pastures," not realizing that they may be "artificial territory," and so, not so desirable, 1Corintian 15:58; 1Peter 5:9-10. This can be likening to a young man or woman that has many bedmates and or has too much attachment to materials gains not to settle down on time in the will of God in marriage.

V. 9. Ointment and perfume rejoice the heart: so doth the sweetness of a man's friend by hearty counsel. Ointments and perfumes (or incenses, as it is rendered over fifty times) were widely used, probably made necessary by the infrequency of bathing, as compared with our times. This was not the Temple ointment and incense, which was forbidden for common use, Exodus 30:9-10, 33-38, but was common ointment and incense. These odors were delightful, and so are used to illustrate the blessedness of good counsel by a friend. The marginal reading "counsel of the soul," is preferable, for it shows this to relate the spiritual counsel. See Jesus' counsel for lukewarm churches in Revelation 3:18.

V. 10. Thine own friend and thy father's friend forsake not; neither go into thy brother's house in the day of thy calamity; for better is a neighbor that is near than a brother far off." Our father's friends should continue to be ours also after our father has died. Solomon followed this counsel, 1Kings 5:1-7. His son Rehoboam, however, rejected this counsel, and lost ten of the tribes, 1 Kings 12:1-16.

One should not always be dependent upon family alone for counsel, but should have friends who will also give counsel when needed. "A sincere friend is to be preferred in adversity to a brother that is not a true friend 1 Kings18:24. Joseph found more kindness with strangers than with his brethren. Jonathan's friendship afforded David's sympathy which his own brethren did not. Rehoboam forsaking his 'father's friends' cost him the most of his Kingdom 1 Kings 12:6-8. My son, be wise, and make my heart glad, that I may answer him that reproaches me. Nothing so gladdens a parent's heart like having a wise child, and well-behaved children give parents much to answer the reproaches of those who may accuse him of being too strict, being a poor parent, or of having a foolish son. Children are the products of the parents, and will generally reflect upon them either good or ill, according to the teaching and examples are given them. In every parent's life, there will come a reaping time for what has been sown in the children.

V. 12. A prudent man foreseeth the evil and hideth himself; but the simple pass on, and are punished - Identical to Proverbs 22:3. It takes spiritual discernment to see through Satan's camouflage and recognize evil. The truly wise man will betake himself to Christ, who is the city of refuge, the stronghold, the rock, in the clefts of which the people of God hide themselves.

V. 13. Take his garment that is surety for a stranger, and take a pledge of him for a strange woman - Identical to Proverbs 20:16; such a man that is a Surety for a stranger; will be stripped of all he has, and have not a coat to put on. Therefore, there is advice to be wise.

V. 14. He that blesseth his friend with a loud voice, rising early in the morning, it shall be counted a curse to him." The loud voice, the early rising to bless suggest that he is a sycophant and flatterer, with ulterior motives for his supposed blessing, and this will raise suspicion in the one so praised that there are sinister reasons for this, instead of receiving what he desired from the one blessed, his blessing may be accounted a curse instead. Also, sometimes to heed such "blessings" may become a curse to the one so praised, as it was to Herod, Acts 12:22-23.

V. 15 -17. A continual dropping in a very rainy day and a contentious woman are alike. See Proverbs 19:13 and notes. Men can tolerate much trouble from without, but what can one do when the home life is miserable: there is not much place to retreat to for refuge and comfort. Home is the one place where men expect to be able to retreat to when trouble arises and to find peace and comfort, but if one is here regularly faced with a warfare, it is like a badly leaking house in a very rainy day—no better than the outside. "Contentious is the same word used in Proverbs 21:19, and that rendered "brawling" in Proverbs 21:9 and Proverbs 25:24.

Contentiousness springs from a spirit of discontent, bossiness, and self-righteousness, and marks a woman who is out of her God-given realm and whosoever hideth her hideth the wind, and the ointment of his right hand, which betrayed itself. Loved ones often try to keep the evils of such a contentious person from being known by outsiders, but such a person will proclaim her own shame so that it is as hard to conceal as a howling wind or the strong smell of ointment. The Wind howls all the more from being pent up in a tight place, and so a woman with a bitter spirit becomes all the more contentious from attempts to restrain her. Iron sharpened iron; so a man sharpeneth the countenance of his friend." As a file is used to sharpen an edged tool, so friends sharpen friends

It is often true that a man is known by his friends, and not only known by them, but also comforted and encouraged in good or evil, according to the character of his friends. Hence, it is extremely important that we use great care in choosing friends, for they will shape our attitudes.

V. 18. Whoso keepeth the fig tree shall eat the fruit thereof: so he that waiteth on his master shall be honored. This has to do with rewards of being faithful, patience and longsuffering; these are fruits; the Fig tree of the Holy Spirit and also a reward of exhibits them. It was a law that the caretaker of fields and orchards were to have priority in the eating of them, 1Corinthian. 9:7; 2 Timothy 2:6. These principles are carried over into the spiritual realm also, which is what is intimated in the second part of this verse. Jesus promised this in John 12:26. "If even he who keeps a fig tree is rewarded with a share of its fruits, surely he that has the more honorable office of waiting on his master shall be honored by that master. But we must also remember the limitation of 1Corinthians 3:8: our rewards will only be according to our "own labor," not the labor of others.

V. 19. As in water face answereth a face, so the heart of man to man. The reflective properties of water are used to illustrate that men's hearts are all the same—sinful and rebellious—until God's grace changes them, and then all the saints' hearts are the same—purified by grace and submissive. The sinful sameness of all men's hearts is declared in Romans 3:9, 22-23. Because of universal sinfulness, man can never rightly judge of himself by comparing and contrasting himself with other men; the true standard is found by looking into the mirror of God's Word. "The law is a glass, in which the enlightened person sees not only the perfections of God, the nature of righteousness, but also his sin, and the sinfulness of it; this glass neither magnifies nor multiplies his sins, but sets them in a true light before him, by which he discerns the nature of his or her life.

V. 20. Satan domain and destruction are never full; so the eyes of man are never satisfied." Some things cannot be satisfied, Proverbs 30:15-16. Satan and destruction never run short of space for sinners, Isaiah 5:14, so that none will ever be turned away. Man's lustful eyes can never be satisfied because of his sinful heart is not satisfied. Sin, as has been said, has created a "God-shaped vacuum" in man, and nothing but God can satisfy that. Sin can oversupply but it cannot satisfy. Only the Lord can fully satisfy, and this will be done at His return in glory, Psalm 17:15; 65:4; Jeremiah 31:14.

V. 21. As the refining pot for silver and the furnace for gold; so is a man to his praise. "Refining pot" refers to a crucible which was used to smelt and test ores and metals. Praise may be a test of men. "The meaning is, either a man is known by the persons that praise him, according to what their characters are; if he is praised by good and virtuous men, he may be thought to be so himself; and if by wicked men, he may be concluded to be so likewise; see Proverbs 28:4.

V. 22. Though thou shouldest bray a fool in a mortar among wheat with a pestle, yet will not his foolishness depart from him. This shows the innate depravity of the unsaved person who has been hardened through many years indulgence in sin. The rod of correction used in youth drives foolishness from a child's heart, Proverbs. 22:15, but when one is allowed to grow up without discipline or spiritual training, the result will be incorrigibility when maturity is reached, and he is hardly able to be turned from his wickedness. Only God's sovereign grace can do it. Such are described in Isaiah 1:5-6; Jeremiah 5:3-4 and 13:23. God alone can change the nature of the sinner into a holy nature.

V. 23. Be thou diligent to know the state of thy flocks, and look well to thy herds." "The calling of the shepherd is here particularly mentioned, because valiant, honorable, innocent, and useful; but the same diligence is to be used in all other callings and businessmen are employed in, that they may provide for themselves and their families. This is an especially applicable admonition for pastors since the very word "pastor" means a shepherd, and church members are called "sheep" and the church a "flock." However, this was a common figure of speech for leaders long before churches existed, Isaiah 56:10-11; Jeremiah 23:4, but Jesus Christ is the ultimate good Shepherd, Psalm 23:1; Isaiah, 40:10-11; John 10:11-16; Hebrew 13:20; 1Peter 2:25. For; riches are not for ever: and doth the crown endure to every generation. It is but common sense to be diligent in one's business while the opportunity for profit presents itself, for things will not always remain the same. It is noteworthy that the unwise shepherds before referred to, made this very mistake, of thinking that things would always be as easy and as profitable as they then were, Isaiah 56:12.

Many people today who are too young to remember the great depression of the olden time think that things can never be different than they now are, except that perhaps they will become even better. Sad mistake! Churches today ought to use wisely the riches the Lord gives them, for the day may come when they will not have the money to support missions as they now have.

There are crowns to be earned. V. 25 - 27, is another argument for the pastoral calling; for it shows that God has caused the earth to spontaneously bring forth pasturage for flocks, making it one of the easier and less involved callings. Canaan was especially well adapted for the pastoral life, and most of the people of Israel were shepherds. Modernization and mechanization have complicated life and has especially promoted sin by gathering people into towns where sin and crime most thrives.

Rural people are generally the more conservative in religion. The lambs are for thy clothing, and the goats are the price of the field. Here is a further argument for the country life: under bad conditions a pastoral family can practically live off the land, and can get by comfortably when a city family is starving. Sheepskin garments have been common since earlier times, for even modern garments have hardly surpassed the warmth and practicality of woolen garments. "Goats" refers to he-goats which were sold, while the nannies were generally kept to increase the herd. Thus, the price obtained for the he-goats could be used to rent or purchase land, pay taxes, etc.

And thou shalt have goats' milk enough for thy food, for the food of thy household, and for the maintenance for thy maidens. The herds not only provide milk but also butter and cheese, besides meat, so that there is both a sufficiency and a variety. The flocks and herds supplied all their needs in those days, without superfluous luxuries. Though without most of the luxuries of our day, we doubt not that these ancient people were as happy in many ways, and even happier in some, than most modern people.

The secret of true happiness is not in having much, but in trusting the Lord for our needs, and being content with what He gives us, 1Timothy 6:6-10. Life does not consist in the abundance of the things that we possess, Luke 12:15. May God give us the grace of contentment!

STICK TO THE BOOK OF PROVERBS AND FIND THE BEST ADVICE IN THE WORLD.

CHAPTER
TWENTY-EIGHT

SUMMARY

Proverbs 28:1

The wicked flee when no man pursueth: but the righteous are bold as a lion." "Wicked" is singular, but "flee" is plural: they all flee as one man, but "righteous" is plural, and "are bold" is singular: they are each one individually bold as a lion. Those who fear God with a reverential, filial fear, need to fear nothing else; but those who refuse to give God the fear due to His majesty, must necessarily fear many other things, for man has an inbred sense of judgment to come upon all who have not been reconciled to God, and nothing—not psychology, not religion, not atheism—can remove that fear. Peace of mind and heart comes only by justification, Roman 5:1.

V. 2. For the transgression of a land, many are the princes thereof: but by a man of understanding and knowledge the state thereof shall be prolonged." Sin is not only a reproach to a nation, Proverbs 14:34, but it also undermines the stability of a nation, and will eventually cause the nation to be destroyed, Genesis 15:16; 1 Kings 21:26. Multiplied transgressions of the land cause there to be a succession of rulers, as one overthrows another, or as the people put out one bad ruler, only to have another equally bad take his place. A good ruler, who has spiritual understanding, however, will prolong the office. "National sins bring national disorders ...

V. 3 - 4. A poor man that oppresseth the poor is like a sweeping rain which leaveth no food." A person who has been poor and then gains some riches often has a neurotic drive to get more and more riches, and never gets over the insecurity of his poor days, with the result that he oppresses those who are like he used to be. Rain is necessary for growth and fruitfulness, but a sweeping rain causes the only destruction; so a poor man who comes to power, so far from being compassionate toward those like he used to be, may be a worse tyrant than a man who has never known poverty.

They that forsake the law praise the wicked but such as keep the law contend with them. With verse 3, this shows the real nature of the oppression of others—it is a forsaking of the law, and actually, justifies and praises the wicked. Men tend to justify and praise those like themselves so that one manifests what kind of person he is by those whom he praises, Roman 1:32-2:3. Only those who themselves keep God's law are going to have the convictions necessary to rebuke transgressors. "Wicked people will speak well of one another, and so strengthen one another's hands in their wicked ways in other to seared the conscience - Evil men understand not judgment: but they that seek the Lord understand all things Deuteronomy 4:5-6; 1 Corinthian 2:14-15; 1John 2:20, 27. By nature, man can understand natural matters, but spiritual things can only be understood by a nature regenerated and indwelt by the Holy Spirit. "Natural" in 1Corinthians 2:14 is rendered "sensual" in Jude 19 and is defined as "having not the Spirit." Being devoid of the Spirit, evil men cannot understand the truth, but those who seek the Lord, understand, for they are regenerated and taught by the Spirit. It takes a submissive attitude to know the truth, John 7:17.

V. 6. Better is the poor that walketh in his uprightness, than he that is perverse in his ways, though he is rich Proverbs 19:1. The world's philosophy is that riches are the ultimate end to be striven for, while morals and righteousness are incidentals which are to be tolerated only if they do not hinder the acquisition of wealth. However, such a philosophy overlooks the solemn question of Luke 12:20, for it ignores the fact that there is a righteous and holy God before whom everyone must one day appear and be judged for all unrighteousness.

V. 7. Whoso keepeth the law is a wise son: but he that is a companion of riotous men shameth his father." No one can perfectly keep the law of God, and so none can be saved by the law, but to delight in the law of God gives evidence of love and respect toward God, Psalm 1:1-2; Roman 7:22-25. It is always wisdom to keep God's law since there is no profit in rebellion, Psalm 19:7-11. Because it prescribes how one is to conduct himself, the law will keep one from evil associates. "Bad companionship is opposed to keeping the law".

V. 8. He that by usury and unjust gain increaseth his substance, he shall gather it for him that will pity the poor." "Usury" means to bite. It was forbidden to the Israelites, Exodus 22:25; Deuteronomy 23:19-20. He that exacts too much of his brethren, will gather it only so that another, more generous person, may use it rightly. "The meaning is that things should be so overruled by the providence of God, that what such a greedy man gets in his dishonest way should not be enjoyed by him or her; but should be taken out of his hands, and put into the hands of another, that will do good with it, by showing mercy to the poor; see Job 27:16-17.

V. 9. He that turneth away his ear from hearing the law, even his prayer shall be an abomination." This may refer to the law of increase, v. 8, but it is a general rule which applies to all law, to violate which brings wrath, Zechariah 7:8-12. Some think to sanctify thievery by prayer, but this proverb shows the folly of such reasoning. Jesus illustrated this very thing by the lives of the Pharisees, and He called it hypocrisy, Matthew 23:14, for to say one thing and to do the opposite is hypocrisy, Proverbs 23:2-5. When one's prayer becomes an abomination to God, he is a hopeless case.

V. 10. Whoso causeth the righteous to go astray in an evil way, he shall fall himself into his own pit: but the upright shall have good things in possession. It is common for wicked people to try to lead others astray also as if numbers would make sin right, and nothing so rejoices the heart of sinners like being able to point his finger of accusation at a sinning saint (which is often why they try to lead them astray). But God's promise is that; the sinner shall fall into his own pit, Proverbs 26:27; Psalm 7:15. The elect cannot be totally or finally deceived, Matthew 24:24. However, the wicked may try to lead the righteous astray there will yet be a goodly inheritance for them. "They are heirs of God, and joint-heirs with Christ, and shall inherit all things; they have all good things in Christ, with him and from him now," [Gill]. See Acts 26:18, Romans 8:17; Revelation 21:7.

V. 11. The rich man is wise in his own conceit, but the poor that hath understanding searcheth him out." "Those that are rich are apt to think themselves wise, because, whatever else they are ignorant of, they know how to get and save; and expect that all they say should be regarded as an oracle and a law - Many think that possession of wealth proves God's blessings on them, but they forget that Satan claims the right and ability to give the things of the world to those that please him, Luke 4:5-7. The poor but righteous person, however, having spiritual understanding, is able to search out the flaws in his reasoning, so as to distinguish between true and false riches.

V. 12. When righteous men do rejoice, there is great glory: but when the wicked rise, a man is hidden." Righteous men can only rejoice when there is spiritual prosperity, and so it is a glorious season when such is the case. When wicked men rise to power then the righteous must hide themselves from oppression and persecution. See also verse 28. Spiritual men have always been persecuted by carnal, though religious, men, Galatians 4:28-31.

V. 13. He that covereth his sins shall not prosper: but whoso confesses and forsake them shall have mercy." "God may cover a man's sins, and it is an instance of his grace, and it is the glory of it to do it, but a man may not cover his own: it is right in one good man to cover the sins of another, reproving him secretly, and freely forgiving him; but it is wrong for a man to cover his own, only one thing can adequately cover sin—the blood of Christ, Ephesians 1:7; Hebrew 9:14; 1Peter 1:19; 1 John 1:7-10; Reverend 1:5. The Romanic Confessional is manifestly wrong, for while it requires confession, it does not require the forsaking of sin, but rather makes a profit from the repetition of sin Roman 6:1-4.

V. 14. Happy is the man that feareth always: but he that hardeneth his heart shall fall into mischief." Not a quaking terror of God, but rather a fear lest we dishonor and offend Him. David confessed that he was most unhappy when he sinned against God through a lack of fear and then tried to cover his sin, Psalm 32:3-4. He hardened himself against the Lord and got into deeper trouble. Only by confession was he forgiven, (v. 5). Hardening one's heart leads only to more trouble, Proverbs 29:1 and it manifests a devilish attitude. When the heart is out of fellowship with God, no part of man is right with Him.

V. 15 - 16. As a roaring lion and a ranging bear; so is a wicked ruler over the poor people. Rulers will act according to their ruling disposition, just as do other people, and if he is wicked, he will act so. Here, he is pictured as a wild and voracious animal, tyrannizing over those who cannot resist. This is a contradiction of the very purpose for rulers, which is to protect the weak and to punish the wicked. Tyrants are frequently compared to lions, Jeremiah 4:7, and 50:17; 2 Timothy 4:17; and the man of sin, the wicked ruler and great oppressor of God's poor people, is compared to both; his feet are as the feet of a bear, and his mouth as the mouth of a lion, Revelation. 13:2. The prince that wanteth understanding is also a great oppressor: but he that hateth covetousness shall prolong his days." "Wanteth" means "lacketh." Any person who does not understand the doctrine of God's just retribution for all sin is apt to think that if he escapes civil detention and punishment he is alright, and so he will be a great oppressor if he has the civil power to do so. The divine qualifications for rulers are that they must: (1) Be men of ability, (2) be God-fearing, (3) Be men of truth, (4) Hate covetousness, Exodus 18:21. Covetousness—either of greater possessions or of greater power or of greater praise—is generally the cause of a ruler's tyranny. Covetousness, so far from promoting one's welfare, actually shortens his life, for it is a form of idolatry, and draws down God's wrath upon those who tolerate it, Colossians 3:5-6.

V. 17. A man that doeth violence to the blood of any person shall flee to the pit; let no man stay him." God had, from the earliest, decreed capital punishment for murder, Genesis 9:6, and the murderer is destined for Satan domain because, by slaying one made in the image of God, he has come as near to slaying God Himself as he is able. To even hate another without a just cause is to manifest that one is unsaved, 1John 3:15. God's command is to not uphold (more common rendering of "stay," as in Psalm 41:12 nor justify the murderer nor hinder the penalty from being executed upon him. Numbers 35:33-34 is very clear in this matter, for the murderer is not to be pitied, Deuteronomy 19:11-13, 19-21.

V. 18. Whoso walketh uprightly shall be saved: but he that is perverse in his ways shall fall at once. See Proverbs 10:9. "Safe" may be a preferable rendering, for Scripture is clear that no one is saved by his own efforts. This contrasts the upright man with the perverse man and the violent man of verse 17. Walking uprightly is always the safe path, but no one is upright except by the grace of God. "Not that his upright walk is the cause of this; the moving cause of salvation is the grace of God; the procuring cause, our Lord Jesus Christ, the only Author of it; but this is a descriptive character of the persons that are and shall be saved, a twisted walk reveals a corresponding character and forecasts a permanent fall to Satan domain.

V. 19 - 20. He that tilleth his land shall have plenty of bread: but he that followeth after vain persons shall have poverty enough Proverbs 12:11. In the beginning of the race, this was man's decreed labor—to work at his trade, whatever it might be—but it only became a tiresome and burdensome things after sin entered into the System and world of Man Genesis 2:5-9; 3:17-19. This is the only promised means of having a sufficiency of life's needs, and he that follows those who promise shortcuts to wealth will sooner or later be brought to poverty—spiritual poverty, if not material poverty. The money ritual, The Extortionists, the prostitute and all those who thought they are smart to get riches, Fame and power outside 'The All-knowing God – Jehovah Elohim would find themselves to blame 'Had I Know' Mathew 16:26. Yet; a faithful man shall abound with blessings: but he that maketh haste to be rich shall not be innocent." Faithfulness, whether to God or to men will be rewarded, and so this is the way of blessings, for even if men do not reward the man who is faithful, yet the Lord will. "Mammon" was the personification of riches, (Matthew 6:24; Luke 16:9), and many people make an idol of it. "When man hastily, or in a short time, becomes rich, though he cannot be directly charged with fraud and injustice, yet he is not innocent in the minds of men, or free from their suspicions and jealousies of him.

V. 21. To have the respect of persons is not good: for a piece of bread that man will transgress. Proverbs 18:5; 24:23; Leviticus 19:15; Deuteronomy 16:19; James 2:1-2. When one is ruled more by what he thinks of persons than by truth, he will easily transgress the truth for his friend's sake, and this is a sin. Truth must always determine our reaction to any circumstance, not our feelings, pro or con, for those involved. Once a compromise is allowed for any reason, there is no stopping place.

V. 22. He that hasteth to be rich hath an evil eye, and considereth not that poverty shall come unto him See v. 20, Proverbs 23:6. For; "an evil eye" He who, through a desire to be rich, begrudges all that others receive, and especially if it seems to detract from his possessions, considers not that poverty comes, not from liberality, but from greediness, Proverbs 11:24-26. When our giving is for the glory of God we cannot out give God: He will repay us.

V. 23. He that rebuketh a man afterward shall find more favor than he that flattereth with the tongue Proverbs 27:5-6. The rebuke of sin is a duty, Leviticus 19:17, but love and tact must be used, for at best, rebuke is bitter at the time. "Reproves may displease at first yet; afterward, when the passion is over and the bitter physic begins to work well, will love and respect them.

V. 24. Whoso robbed his father or his mother, and saith, It is not transgression; the same is the companion of a destroyer. It is a sin for children to not provide for parents' needs in their latter years, Matthew 15:3-6, how much more so is it sin to actually rob them? It matters not that he may argue that the inheritance will eventually be his anyhow, for it is not his until they die, and so to take it before that is a robbery in the eyes of God. "Sins against parents are greater than against others.

V. 25 – 26. He that is of a proud heart stirreth up strife: but he that putteth his trust in the Lord shall be made fat." The proud heart here is literally "an enlarged heart," but not in a good sense; it is puffed up in pride and self-trust, and such egotism always despises others, Luke 18:9, and so they stir up strife. This is unprofitable, but to trust in the Lord is always a blessing, Jeremiah 17:5-9.

The fountain of pride is trust in self and unbelief towards the Lord (v. 26); the fountain of humility is 'trust in the Lord. In the peace offering to the Lord from His people, a choice portion of the animal (the breast or the thigh) lifted or waved before the LORD. Afterward, that choice portion of the meat was for the priest and his family, and was considered holy - so it had to be eaten in the *holy place*. This part of meat offering was considering the best portion, and so according to the line of verses above "to be made fat" means to have the best of prosperity Number 18:8-10.

Therefore, He that trusteth in his own heart is a fool: but whoso walketh wisely, he shall be delivered. Because the natural heart is wicked above all things, and there is no good in it, to trust in it is to incur God's curse for idolatry, Jeremiah 17:7-9, for self-trust, is a departure from the Lord. But whoso trusts in the Lord (the alternative to trusting in self) shows that heavenly wisdom has come to him, and he shall be delivered, not only from God's curse but also from all evil, Psalm 84:11-12. This was Paul's persuasion, Rom. 8:35-39.

V. 27 - 28. He that gives unto the poor shall not lack: but he that hideth his eyes shall have many a curse. Proverbs 19:17; 22:9. God pronounces a blessing on benevolence to the poor, for such resembles His own benevolence. Jesus taught that good deeds shall be rewarded with good, Luke 6:38. The natural man fears that he will be in want by giving; the reverse is the truth. The covetous man, however, closes his eyes to others' needs, and while he may pray "God bless you," he will not be God's instrument to bless. Such puts a question mark over one's profession of salvation, 1 John 3:17-19. The curse may be both from men and God. When the wicked rise, men hide themselves: but when they perish, the righteous increase." Similar to verses 12; Proverbs 11:10; 29:2. Reemphasizing that wicked ruler is blight to the nation. When the wicked are in power, the rich often hide lest their riches be taken away, and the good hide lest they are persecuted for their righteous example, 1 John 3:12-13. Men's characters may be known by their response to good and evil, and by their treatment of others. Christians are to pray for their leaders, even if they are wicked men. God can set up or put down men as it pleases Him, Psalm 75:6-7.

GOD ENTERS BY A PRIVATE DOOR INTO EVERY INDIVIDUAL AND IF GOD SHUTS ONE DOOR, HE OPENS ANOTHER

CHAPTER
TWENTY-NINE

SUMMARY

Proverbs 29:1

He that being often reproved hardened his neck shall suddenly be destroyed, and that without remedy. This is a solemn warning against obstinacy in sin. There comes a time for every rebel against God's will when it crosses the point of no return, and God turns him over to his own wickedness and he is beyond hope of repentance, Proverbs 1:23-33. Rebellion against human reproof is one thing, but against the Lord is something else again, 1Samuel 2:25. The metaphor is taken from oxen, which kick and toss about, and will not suffer the yoke to be put upon their necks. Such a one shall suddenly be destroyed; or broken; as a potter's vessel is broken to pieces with an iron rod, and can never be put together again; therefore, such persons shall be punished with everlasting destruction.

V. 2. When the righteous are in authority, the people rejoice: but when the wicked beareth rule, the people mourn Proverbs 28:12, 28. A righteous rule is always a blessing to all the people under it, and only the depraved would desire to have it otherwise. As an illustration of these two states, contrast Esther 3:15 and 8:15. As a general rule, the government of a king will correspond to his own character, and so accordingly, it will be a blessing or a curse to those under him.

V. 3. Whoso loveth wisdom rejoice his father: but he that keepeth company with harlots spendeth his substance. One's love for wisdom will be manifest in practicing wisdom. Knowledge may be only theoretical, but wisdom is always practical, and one must love wisdom before he will put it into practice. Solomon has already warned of the folly of going in unto strange women Proverbs 2:10, 16; 5:3-10; 6:23-26; 7:1-5. He who keeps company with harlots is dominated by his fleshly lusts, and he will come to deadly infections and or sickness, spiritual ruin as well as financial. There is an evident contrast between him who loves wisdom, and him who lusts after harlots. Wisdom may be applied to gospel wisdom 1Corinthians 1:19-21 or to Christ the Wisdom of God 1Corinthian 1:24 or to wisdom in general.

V. 4 - 5. The king by judgment establishes the land: but he that receiveth gifts overthroweth it. Gifts, in all other 75 appearances, used of offerings of some sort; here, it is a bribe offering. God has always hated the taking of bribes, Ezekiel 45:9. Righteous judgment always tends to establish a nation, but unrighteousness in high places discourages the people, and, in effect, teaches them by example to do evil. In other hands, a man that flattereth his neighbor spreadeth a net for his feet. There is a big difference in flattery and honest compliments: the latter are good to encourage one in righteousness. It is everyone duty to aid his neighbor; this one cannot do by casting a snare before his feet, even if it is done in the name of compliments. Flattery is almost always self-serving, i.e., in the hopes of gaining something from him thereby. Flattery involves the elating of one's pride by telling him lies about himself.

In the transgression of an evil man there is a snare: but the righteous doth sing and rejoice. One sin always leads to another, and with every sin that a person does, he becomes more entangled in sin, and while one may think that by yielding to temptation he is getting his desires, he is actually enslaving himself, 2Peter 2:19, and transgressions never lead to true, lasting happiness. On the other hand, the righteous, while apparently denying himself many things that seem to be desirable, shall sing and rejoice while the wicked mourn. This does not refer to vindictive rejoicing, although the saints will in time rejoice in God's perfect justice to their persecutors, Psalm 58:10-11.

V. 7. The righteous considereth the cause of the poor: but the wicked regardeth not to know it. In the light of verses 2, 4, 12, 14, etc., righteous may refer to a righteous ruler. Neither the rich nor the poor the mighty nor the weak were to be favored in judgment, but the ruler was commanded to judge righteously, Leviticus 19:15. The sad thing about wicked people is that not only do they not do right, they do not even want to know about righteousness; it makes them feel guilty to know what they ought to do. Special blessings are upon those who consider the poor, Psalm 41:1-3. All are spiritual paupers before God, and we must deal kindly with others if we would have the Lord deal kindly with us.

V. 8 - 9. Scornful men bring a city into a snare: but wise men turn away wrath. Scorners are those who hold in contempt the reproofs, (v. 1), and warnings of wrath to come; when they are rulers, they bring the whole city into danger by their attitude, for unbelief is infectious, and so wrath comes upon the city because of wickedness. Wise men, by warning a city of coming wrath, may bring the city to repentance so that they will be delivered, Jonah 3:4-10. Wrath must fall where there is unrepented sin. A wise man contendeth with a foolish man, whether he rage or laugh, there is no rest. Whether the wise man treat the fool with haughty disdain, or with good nature, the result will be the same, that is to say, the fool will not cease from his strife or folly. The design of the proverb is to show, that all labor to reclaim a fool from his folly is lost, let a man take what methods he will. See Proverbs 12:15; 21:2. There is no one so hard to move from his position as the one who conceitedly thinks that he knows everything, and so he will not be corrected.

V. 10. The bloodthirsty hate the upright: but the just seek his soul. The bloodthirsty are those who hate others, and who either kill them, or would do so if they had power to do so, 1John 3:11-15. One day bloodthirsty men will be given their own blood to drink as a judgment, Isaiah 49:26,

Revelation 16:4-6. By contrast, the just, instead of seeking for the blood of the wicked, seek to deliver him from his blood-guiltiness by pointing him to Christ. The just, whom the bloody men hate, seek their soul, pray for their conversion, and would gladly do anything for their salvation.

V. 11. A fool uttereth his entire mind: but a wise man keepeth it in till afterwards. Solomon taught that there is a time to keep silence and a time to speak, Eccl. 3:7. An adage in the east proverb says: While the word is unspoken, you are master of it. When once it is spoken, it is master of you. In the fool, there is a direct connection between his mind and his mouth: whatever he thinks, he speaks without consideration as to whether it is fit or proper. Conversely, a wise man holds his tongue, meditates on his thoughts, edits and revises them, and casts many of them into the black pit of oblivion because they are not fit to see the light of day.

V. 12 - 15. If a ruler hearkens to lies, all his servants are wicked. When a ruler heeding to lies told to him by his servants, it encourages them in this, as well as in others. Just as lying lips are not becoming to a ruler, Proverbs 17:7, so neither is it wise for him to allow liars to remain in his company and relationships. David practiced this, Psalm 101:7. As is a prince, such are his courtiers; his example has a great influence upon them. God has decreed that liars shall not abide in his presence, Revelation 21:8, 27; 22:15. Behold then how enormous a thing a lie must be, because White lies are still lies. The poor and the deceitful man meet together: the Lord lightened both their eyes. Proverbs 22:2. Though so opposite in many ways, yet they must meet together so far as sin is concerned, Roman 3:23, judgment is for both, and they are both accountable to God, for He lightened every man that cometh into the world, John 1:9, so far as individual responsibility is concerned. We see the Lord both in men and in their circumstances. It is practical hypocrites to regard God as the Creator of the man and as having nothing to do with the man surroundings.

The king that faithfully judgeth the poor, his throne shall be established forever Proverbs 20:28; 25:5. Emphasizing God's delight in justice of all mankind, the poor is least likely to have defenders, for there is little worldly profit in it. But God delights in this, and promises blessings to those who do so. But the faithful discharge of kingly duties will pay eternal dividends for any ruler, as the rod and reproof give wisdom: but a child left to himself bring his mother to shame. though; already referred to, Proverbs 19:18; 22:6, 15; 23:13-15. Both the rod and reproof are necessary, for without the fear of a rod, a child will not heed reproof. When a rod is used, it must be clear to the child that this is for correction sake, and not just the result of anger. In other words, the children of God grow wiser by the corrections and chastisements of their heavenly Father, which are always for their good; and he is a man of wisdom that hearkens to the rod and to him that has appointed it, and learns the proper instructions from it, Micah 6:9.

V. 16 - 17. When the wicked are multiplied, transgression increaseth; but the righteous shall see their fall. So many parents in resignation of their duty to teach and correct their children has caused an increase in wicked adults, and, consequently, of transgressions. An undisciplined child always grows into an irresponsible and self-centered transgressor. Character is never developed through self-indulgence, but always through discipline and self-denial. Transgressors are ultimately going to fall, and the righteous, though they may be persecuted unto death in this world, will see their fall, Psalm 58:10; 59:10; Isaiah 66:24. In other words, Correct thy son, and he shall give thee rest; yea, he shall give delight unto thy soul. It is sad when parents permitted themselves to be nagged and tantrum into yielding to children selfish desires. Scriptural discipline produces children of character which delight the souls of parents, for they thereby give promise of being the godly parents for eternity, and not just belonging to them for this short life, after which they would be separated from them and cast into hell for being wicked.

V. 18. Where there is no vision, the people perish: but he that keepeth the law, happy is he. Vision is not used subjectively (of something seen in the mind), but rather is used objectively of a knowledge of duty. By vision understand revelation. Where the connection between the natural and the supernatural is cut off, destruction is the necessary consequence. The word perish, however, does not etymologically in this case mean destruction; a more literal rendering would be: Where there is no revelation the people run wild; that is to say, each man is a law unto himself, Nature's light is not sufficient to lead men away from destruction: apart from God revelation (the Bible) they will destroy themselves, Jeremiah 10:23. In proportion as a people loses its faith in revelation it falls into decay.

V. 19. A servant will not be corrected by words: for though he understands, he would not answer. So Job servant reacted, Job 19:16. Reference is to wicked servants, for a good servant obeys immediately, and as the preceding verses show, Solomon is dealing with the wicked and rebellious of several classes. There are many who serve wholly from a spirit of fear, and if there is no fear, they are slothful. If the master challenges their sloth, they silently sulk in their rebellion. Many professed Christians do this very thing when the Word challenges their slothfulness.

V. 20. Seest thou a man that is hasty in his words? There is more hope of a fool than of him. In Proverbs 18:13. Impulsiveness is seldom good, for every matter needs to be well thought out before one speaks to it. There are two classes of people: one always has something to say; that is, he is a wise person whose counsel is always a blessing. The other always has to say something; i.e., his egotism compels him to speak to every matter, though he may not have the most basic knowledge of it. He is always a disease to any society. Even other kinds of sinners have more hope than the egotistical compulsive talker.

V. 21. He that delicately bringeth up his servant from a child shall have him become his son at the length. Abraham servant was his heir apparently until God blessed Abraham with an heir, Genesis 15:1-6. Childless couples used to often make a servant their heirs and doubtlessly many servants hoped for this very thing, and to be treated nicely might encourage his hope.

V. 22. An angry man stirreth up strife, and a furious man aboundeth in transgression. Causeless anger is a fruitful cause of many other sins, for he who has no control over himself and his passions will be subject to many defeats by Satan, Proverbs 25:28. Anger is only a symptom, for it shows an attitude toward others. Strife is one of the works of the flesh, Galatians 5:20, and while there is an anger which is not sinful, Ephesians 4:26, most anger and fury is sinful for it is a result of giving place to the devil. A man pride shall bring him low: but honor shall uphold the humble in spirit. This thought has often been before us in Proverbs, 15:33; 16:18; 18:12, and our Lord also taught this, Luke 14:11.

The sum of the proverb in both parts is the same with the words of Christ, often used by him, Matthew 23:12, Luke 14:11, and 18:14. It is one of the Lord unavoidable laws that those who seek to exalt themselves will be put down, while those who humble themselves will be lifted up in honor. How low man (Anthropos) pride can bring him may be seen in the first act of pride and in its consequence, Isaiah 14:12-15. Pride was the devil original sin, 1Timothy 3:6, and all who are like him in pride shall dwell in hell with him. To sin as the devil did is to partake of his condemnation.

V. 24 - 26. Whosoever is a partner with a thief hateth his own soul: he heareth cursing, and believeth it not. Thievery is a sin whether one is the actual thief or whether he only profits from the theft, and he acts as if he hated his own soul, for he damns his own soul for the sake of a few possessions for the body. According to this, the man who fences stolen property is as guilty as the thief. Perhaps this one is a silent partner with a thief in that he compromised for the sake of gain, and did not bear witness against the oath made by another.

The fear of man bringeth a snare: but whoso putteth his trust in the Lord shall be safe. He may be ensnared because of his fear of the thief whom he heard making false vows, or he may fear the material loss if he witnesses against him, (v. 24). Many fear to trust their supply wholly to the Lord but think they must stoop to all sorts of human exigencies in order to have a sufficiency to live. Many give excuses to sin on the plea that they must live. Many seek the ruler's favor: but every man judgment cometh from the Lord. Another reason why none ever need compromise for the sake of possessions: if we are pleasing to the Lord, we need not the ruler's favor to have what we need. If we delight in the Lord, He will give us our desires, Psalm 37:3-5. Jehovah Elohim is the true and primary source of all decisions: nothing happens to save by His permission Proverbs 21:1. By Him, too, we shall be ultimately judged. Therefore commit thy cause to Him, 1Corinthian 4:3-5.

V. 27. An unjust man is an abomination to the just: and he that is upright in the way is an abomination to the wicked. Birds of a feather, stick together.

There has always been a mutual enmity between the seed of the woman and the seed of the serpent, Genesis 3:15. God saints, however, does not self-righteously attribute the difference between himself and the wicked to himself, but realizes that it is God grace alone which makes him differ from the wicked, 1 Corinthian 4:6-7, and so he gives all glory to God, 1 Corinthian 1:26-31. According to this proverb, there is no place for mutual friendship and fellowship between the just and the unjust, James 4:4; 1John 2:15. What is our attitude toward sin? Is it an abomination to us? Do we give reverential to Godhead and His Commandments?

GOD EVEN USES CHASTISEMENT TO TRAIN US IN RIGHTEOUS
AND GOD'S LOVING DISCIPLINE WILL PAY OFF IN THE END

CHAPTER THIRTY

SUMMARY

Proverbs 30:1

The words of Agur the son of Jakeh, even the prophecy: the man spake unto Ithiel, even unto Ithiel and Ucal." As with all eastern names, these names each had a meaning: Agur means "collector," while Jakeh means "obedient." Ithiel means "God with me" Matthew 1:23, and Ucal means "the mighty one" Isaiah 9:6; Rev. 1:8. Because of the meaning of these names, some think that there is a reference to God, but the names most significant of this are the names of the pupils of Agur, so that perhaps it is not so much an address to the Lord as a prophecy about Him. "The name Ithiel is identical in meaning with Immanuel, the number only being changed, —God with me; and Ucal signifies the mighty One. And judicious interpreters have translated the clause, 'the man speak concerning God with me, even God with me, the mighty One.' But, aside from this interpretation, the passage has several things unquestionable and conclusive on the subject of which we treat (The Triune Creator– Divine Godhead) … His theme is the nature of God, of whom he speaks in the plural number: —the Holy Ones …

The authors of the last two chapters are Agur Ben Jakeh and King Lemuel, of which we know nothing more than what is written here. Both these chapters are called "prophecies" so that they are Divine utterances, whoever were the human instruments of writing them. They would not be in the canon of the Bible if they were not inspired of God.

V. 2. Surely I am more brutish than any man and have not the understanding of a man. It is actually a mark of spiritual wisdom for a man to see himself as nothing in God's eyes and as incapable of knowing God apart from a revelation from Him. Human pride and vanity may exalt human ability, but a knowledge of God makes us feel our nothingness and inability and moves us to desire from Him spiritual understanding. In the beginning, the man was very knowledgeable, but he lost much of this wisdom as it relates to God when he fell into sin. "Agur refers to the corruption and blindness of man's nature, in divine things, as contrasted with the knowledge of God which man possess before the fall, as also with the purity of the Word of God (vv. 4-6).

V. 3 - 6. I neither learned wisdom nor have the knowledge of the Holy. In truth, one must become a fool in his own eyes and in the eyes of the world before the Lord will impart spiritual wisdom to him, 1Corinthian 3:18-20. "Holy" is plural, actually having the same ending in Hebrew with Elohim, the word for the Triune God, has. It may refer to holy things, but more likely it refers to the Holy Ones —the Trinity of God, all of whom are called "Holy" in Scripture, v. 4 Who hath ascended up into heaven, or descended? Who hath gathered the wind in his fists? Who hath bound the waters in a garment? Who hath established all the ends of the earth? What is his name, and what is his son's name, if thou canst tell?" Here are seven questions that no atheist or agnostic can answer, yet; the Word is sufficient to reveal Him; the answer to us, even as Agur does in verses 5-6. These questions remind us of the questions the Lord asked Job in Job 38:1.

There is an invisible power that ascends and descends on the earth by staircases unseen," there can be but one answer to these questions— God—but who can know Him fully in His nature as revealed by His names? Only those who receive a divine revelation of Him and of His

Son, Matthew 11:27; John 1:18; 6:46; 8:19. Every word of God is pure: he is a shield unto them that put their trust in him." Psalm 12:6-7; 18:30. Agur teaches the same basic truth as 2 Timothy 3:15-17. Here is the sufficiency of the Word of God for all our needs, and it is sinful to seek for spiritual light elsewhere. "When men add their own fancies or their own inventions to the divine testimony they are guilty of felony; the addition is but so much subtraction, for it perverts the meaning, it lessens the force, it modifies or destroys the original authority,"

Therefore, we have to be careful the attitude we show to the commandment of blessed Jehovah Elohim. Add thou not unto his words, lest he reproves thee, and thou be found a liar." Deuteronomy 4:1-2; Revelation 22:18-19. It is a solemn thing to tamper with the eternal Word of God, for the eternal destiny of souls depends on upon its faithful proclamation in its original purity. Many people corrupt the truth: some by withholding it, Jeremiah 23:30, and misinterpreting it, Jeremiah 23:31. Others by substituting other things for it, Jeremiah 23:32, and making human traditions or creeds superior to it, Matthew 15:1-6. Alas how much of this is done in the modern religious world. Men manifest their character by their attitude toward the Word of God, Isaiah 8:19-20.

V. 7 - 9. Two things have I required of thee; deny me them not before I die. This is a sensible request. "Request" is not to be understood in the sense of a presumptuous demand, but rather, this is the language of faith in a benevolent Father. Agur simply practices what we are encouraged to do by the Lord—come boldly unto the throne of grace and ask for whatsoever we have faith to claim, Hebrew 4:16; Matthew 21:22; Mark 9.23, James 4.2-3; 1 John 3:22.

Remove far from me vanity and lies: give me neither poverty nor riches; feed me with food convenient for me." Vanity is self-deceit, while lies have to do with the deceiving of others: both are dangers to be avoided, and both poor and the rich are subject to them. Hence, Our Saviour taught us to pray "Lead us not into temptation but deliver us from evil," Matthew 6:13. No one wants to be poor, and very few are capable of rightly handling wealth without coming to depend upon it instead of on God, for it is a snare to the unwary, 1 Tim. 6:9-10, 17.

We are admonished to be, as Agur was, Godly with contentment with a sufficiency, 1 Tim. 6:5-8. "Food convenient" is literally "food of my alliance," i.e., a daily ration, like the manna in the wilderness, Exodus 16:4-5, 16-18. "It seems to be the same that which Job calls his necessary food, and Christ, our daily bread: Are we content with only a sufficiency for our needs? Lest I be full, and deny thee, and say, who the Lord is: or lest I be poor, and take the name of my God in vain." This was the very response that Pharaoh's power and riches evoked in him, Exodus 5:2. Too much dependence upon material things can keep even a believer from trusting to God's providence. Likewise, extreme poverty may make one do evil in stealing, and then try to cover up the theft by taking an oath that he has done no evil, so taking God's name in vain. Indeed, for any professed Christian to do evil is to take God's name in vain, for God's name is upon him by profession and all that he does reflects either good or bad on God. We need to learn to fear sin in every condition, for sin is still sin whether we commit it through excessive riches or excessive poverty.

Accuse not a servant unto his master, lest he curses thee, and thou be found guilty." Roman 14:4 is good advice in most instances. However, there are instances when fidelity to truth and righteousness requires the exposing of evil deeds. Care should be taken; however, not to falsely accuse another, whose curse pronounced upon one's meddling may be ratified by God, who deals justly with all. "But when conscience requires faithfulness in exposing sin, there the servant's delinquency is to be told to the master Genesis 21:25. It is only false or trivial charges that are a reproach. We must remember that we are also servants of our God, and we will one day have to give an answer for all of our deeds Roman 14:10-13. Are we faithful to Him that has called us?

V. 11. There is a generation that curseth their father, and doth does not bless their mother." Here begins the first of seven quatrains (four-line poems). "These four generations are but one. This is Agur's view of the age in which he lived, or it may be his summary of human nature as it had come under his own observation. Obviously from the parallelism, to not bless is almost the same as to curse. It is not enough that children do not curse and revile their parents: God requires that they bless them (obey, honor, respect and care for them).

The duty of honoring parents (not just obeying them, which may be done hatefully) is basic to worship of God, as is shown by it being one of the ten commandments, Exodus 20:12; Matthew 15:1-9; Ephesians 6:1-3.

In other words, there are still other Generations by one way or the other that involves in one evil deeds and other as mention in the next verses. There are generations that are pure in their own eyes and yet are not washed from their filthiness. Here the sin is that of willful blindness and self-righteousness—two of the hardest barriers to overcome, and they prevent many people from being saved for none will take a bitter medicine if he is not convinced that he has a fatal illness, Roman 10:1-4.

A person is not justified, however, according to his own estimate of himself, but according to God's estimate, 1Corinthian 4:3-5. The self-sufficient person always thinks himself to be righteous, even when he is in the height of sin. The extreme filthiness of this self-righteousness is to be seen in that the same word is rendered "dung" in 2Kings 18:27 and Isaiah 36:12. So much for man's righteousness, Isaiah 57:12; 64:6.

There is a generation, O how lofty are their eyes! And their eyelids are lifted up." Pride is the sin here referred to: it is one of the seven abominations in Proverbs 6:17. Pride may take many forms, depending on what it centers in: Possession—pride (wealth), Position—pride, People—pride (heritage), Piety—pride, Potential—pride (ability). All such ignores the fact that all that anyone is or has that is good, is from the Lord, to whom all glory should go, Deuteronomy 8;18; Isaiah 26:12; 1Corinthian 15:10; Philippians 2:13; James 1:17; Jeremiah 9:23-24. There is a generation, whose teeth are as swords and their jaw teeth as knives, to devour the poor from off the earth, and the needy from among men." Here the sin is greedy, greed without conscience as to how one obtains the desired things. They are violent, and have no pity for the poor and needy. It is frightening, not only how nearly all these descriptions fit our times, but how they are almost universally practiced without restraint, rebuke or regret. But there is a judgment to come.

V. 15 - 16. The horseleech hath two daughters, crying Give, give. There are three things that are never satisfied, yea; four things say not, It is enough. Insatiableness is set forth under the figure of some sort of blood-sucking insect. There is a curious progression here from a single horseleech to its two daughters, to three things to four things. Perhaps this suggests that greed is never satisfied, though it continually increases.

There is always enough to satisfy that everyone's needed, but there is never enough to satisfy another's greed. The grave; and the barren womb: the earth that is not filled with water; and the fire that saith not, it is enough." "Grave" is Sheol in the Hebrew, and refers to the unseen world, as does the Greek Hades in the New Testaments It is sometimes used for the place of the departed spirits, and sometimes for the place of dead bodies. "It is not full, it waits for more; nor will its mouth be shut till the last enemy, death, is destroyed; Proverbs 27:20.

The second insatiable thing is a barren womb, for especially among the Hebrews, barrenness was considered a reproach and a sign of God's disfavor, and so women constantly sought to conceive until they had had at least one child; some of them were very ill-tempered about it, Genesis 11:30; 16:1-2; 25:21; 29:31; 30:1-3; 1Samuel 1:2, 5-19. The thirsty earth is the third insatiable thing. In a desert land, where the soil is sandy, the earth can soak up a lot of rain before it begins to puddle. Fire is the fourth insatiable thing, for the more it is fed, the more it grows and the more fuel it demands.

V. 17. The eye that mocketh at his father, and despiseth to obey his mother, the ravens of the valley shall pick it out, and the young eagles shall eat it." Often when a child dares not outwardly disobey its parents, will look insolently at them. God will not even tolerate this, but warns of judgment to come upon all disrespect shown to parents. The birds of prey especially like the eyes of dead things, and attack them first. That one's body is prey to the carrion birds suggests that one will come to an ignominious and untimely death. Ephesians 6:1-2 warns that disrespect to parents will cut short one's natural life. God had hedged parental authority about with His own authority.

V. 18 - 21. There are three things which are too wonderful for me, yea, four which I know not." Here the "three ... yea, four" has to do with wonders on top of wonders. In every area of life there are marvels beyond the understanding of even the wisest of men in that area of knowledge.

God alone is the master of the wonders of the universe and He alone has the key to unlock the secrets of them to us, through the Power Gifts: Word of Wisdom, Word of Knowledge and Discerning Spirits and most confirm; especially in His Divine Words – The BIBLE. If He chooses not to reveal them to us, then the best theories of men are eventually proven to be only so much foolishness. We know only what He reveals to us, Deuteronomy 29:29.

Those three things mention above are: The way of an eagle in the air the way of a serpent upon a rock the way of a ship in the midst of the sea; the way of a man with a maid. Not one of these leaves a track behind to show where it has been, yet all are stately and wondrous in nature.

The first three of these are easier to understand than the last. The Hebrew for "man" means a mighty man, a hero, and the word for "maid" is more commonly rendered "virgin," as in Isaiah 7:14. Apparently it has to do with the influence in courtship that a hero has. We all know how the girls are awed by the football hero: they see reasons for admiration that no one else sees.

In connection with the verse which follows, this suggests that this influence is misused. Such is the way of an adulterous woman; she eats, and wipes her mouth, and saith, I have done no wickedness." "Such" shows a definite reference back to verse 19, but whether the reference is to her adultery being like the fornication of the mighty man, or whether it only means that she is as mysterious in wicked designs as the mighty man is in his honorable courtship is uncertain.

Notice the five appearances of "way" here. As mysterious as are the ways of nature, so mysterious are the ways of sin in its working. The adulterous woman, like the adulterous man, tries to cover up her evil, and denies that she has been faithless to her husband. Most people are not concerned with sin, but only with being caught at it, which shows that what they fear is not evil, but only its punishment. This is the wrong attitude.

V. 21 – 23. For three things the earth is disquieted and for four which it cannot bear. These things are intolerable because they are all contrary to good order in society. Any person, who is out of his place, and acting contrary to orderliness in society, will cause irritation in others. God is a God of order, and any disorderliness is manifestly not from Him, 1Corinthian 14:33, 40.

V. 22. Those three things mentions in v. 21 are: For a servant when he reigneth and a fool when he is filled with meat. Slaves were generally not fitted to rule, not having the advantages of the necessary learning and training, and being due to being in subjection, when they came into power, they had the tendency to misuse their power, and to lord it over all who were under their authority, Proverbs 19:10; 28:3. So often power goes to the head of the former servant, just as money goes to the head of the former poor person, and they both become obnoxious to all their associates.

The fool—i.e., the self-sufficient wicked man—never becomes so wicked in his self-sufficiency as when he has an abundance of material possessions to make him feel secure. Luke 12:16-21 illustrates such a person. Perhaps the reason why God does not give riches to more people is because they not only would trust in them, but would also become rude and overbearing toward others not so well off as they are. For an odious woman when she is married; and an handmaid that is heir to her mistress." "Odious" has to do with hatefulness, which she conceals before marriage, but which is then revealed and her true character is known.

The security that she thinks she now has as a married woman makes her cast off all restraint and treat everyone badly. Likewise, a former maidservant who has become heir to her mistress may make herself unbearable to those about her. So did Hagar, Genesis 16:4. We are to endeavor to be peace-makers, not peace-breakers, Matthew 5:9; 1 Pet. 3:10-11.

V. 24 - 28. There be four things which are little upon the earth, but they are exceeding wise. "These words distinctly teach that wisdom is not measurable by physical magnitude. The large man may be a little man. Even in nature, greatness is traced to God, and He is the source even of instinct in the beasts.

The ants are a creatures not strong, yet they prepare their meat in the summer. In Job 12:7-9 declares that there is wisdom in all of nature if we will but read it and learn from it. Everything has its lesson.

The locusts have no king, yet go they forth all of them by bands. These are natural locusts, not the infernal locusts (demons) of Revelation 9:1-11, which have a king over them. Locusts are called God's great army in Joel 2:25 because they do His bidding in executing judgment upon the wicked.

The lesson to be learned from the locusts is that of orderliness in unity, for they go forth in "bands." God has never intended for His people to be loners and isolationists: He has commanded them to fellowship and work together for mutual good. In this dispensation, it is His will for every saved person to be an active member of one of His true churches, Acts 2:41-47. Every person has a different ability, but all are to use their abilities in the church according to His Divine Principles and Commandments, 1 Cor. 12:4-13. The spider taketh hold with her hands, and is in king's palaces. Some think this refers to a type of lizard. The Hebrew word appears nowhere else in the Bible, so that it is uncertain to what it refers. Does this mean skill: this skill will have its reward? Does it mean patience in working out elaborate and beautiful results: then here is progress - getting into king's houses, into high places, into palatial position? The spiritual application is that there are heavenly rewards for earthly efforts, Matthew 6:19-21; Luke 18:22. Hence, we ought to keep to our task of serving the Lord regardless of the discouraging obstacles.

V. 29 - 33. There be three things which go well, yea, four are comely in going, and this has to do with great stateliness in motion. It is well, where possible, to have grace in our motions, as well as grace in our manners.

In a spiritual sense, there is the need for comeliness in going. "Every man is set upon an ascending line of human life. We never find God calling a man downwards, diminishing the volume of his manhood, checking his good aspirations, putting him low in the scale of his being.

Every good gift from above is to enrich our Life to Eternity. In other words, God loves towards man and His calling is always for the man well being and always to the Top, to be the Head and not the bottom or tail Deuteronomy 28:13, Jeremiah 29:11, 3John 1:2,

Man originally to walk in his life with sense of His divine majesty; yet; this is part of God's benefits to man - and a righteous man is as bold as lion. A lion is strongest among beasts and turneth not away for anything. It is probably partly because of this fearless, regal behavior that the lion is called the king of beasts. Any of the cat family has a grace about their movements, but the lion, being the largest, multiplies this grace.

The Bible often speaks of the bold, fearlessness of the lion, and the believer is likened to him in this, Proverbs 28:1. This animal is also used as symbol of Christ at His return to earth because He will then be regal, fearless, and overpowering, Revelation 5:5.

A greyhound, an he goat also; and a king, against whom there is no rising up." As the marginal reading shows, there is uncertainty as to what the first animal is, whether a greyhound, a horse, or some other animal. Certainly both the greyhound and the horse are majestic. The he-goats; these were often used as leaders of flocks, Jeremiah 50:8, and they also had a certain majesty about them. Kings, in their power, were sometimes likened to the goats that would push with the horns, Daniel 8:5-8. Kings are mentioned last as majestic beings, especially those who are absolute sovereigns, against whom none can successfully rise. Beauty of dress and pompous ceremony is one thing, but absolute power is another, and the latter will awe almost anyone. Christ is to return to earth soon in such majestic power, and He will be at the head of a great army of saints. Then He will be King of kings and Lord of lords, Revelation 19:11-21. May He hasten that day to come?

If thou hast done foolishly in lifting up thyself, or if thou hast thought evil, lay thine hand upon thy mouth. It may be that this should be read in connection with the last part of verse 31. If there is no rising up against an earthly prince, woe to him then that strives with his Master

However, this may be a general warning against any form of wrong-doing against God's majesty. Every sin that a man may do is a lifting up of himself against the Lord's will, and even that evil which is not actually acted out, but is only thought, is still sin, and it is known by the Lord, and man is held accountable for it, Psalm 94:11.

The mouth is the place of exit for thoughts, as they become words, and so man is to control the mouth. When once a person realizes his contemptibility in God's sight, he will cease to try to justify himself, and will lay his hand upon his mouth, as Job did, Job 40:4.

Surely the churning of milk bringeth forth butter, and the wringing of the nose bringeth forth blood: so the forcing of wrath bringeth forth strife. Agitation is necessary to turn milk into butter, and it takes violence against the nose to cause it to bleed, which actions are used to show that the violence of wrath only begets more wraths. This then is the opposite of what is shown in Proverbs 15:1, and is the same as that in Proverbs 15:18.

How then can one overcome wrath? "The wise way is (v. 32), 'Lay thine hand upon thy mouth. Even if we are absolutely sure we are right, (which we are not always sure that we are), sometimes the best thing to do is to silently walk away from an angry and argumentative person.

God's people have been called to be peacemakers, not to win every argument that they may happen to get into. Often the refusal to argue over a point may make more of an impression than the winning of that argument. Wrath and strife are works of the flesh, Galatians 5:20, and must never be confused with that striving for the mastery in 2Timothy 2:5. He is to strive against sin, especially in himself, but he is not to strive with men, but must be gentle unto all men, 2Timothy 2:24.

A TRUE LOVE FOR GOD MUST BEGIN WITH
A DELIGHT IN HIS HOLINESS

CHAPTER
THIRTY-ONE

SUMMARY

Proverbs 31:1

The words of king Lemuel and prophecy that his mother taught him "Lemuel" has the meaning of "devoted to God," and this, with him being called "son of my vows," (v. 2), suggests that his mother was a godly woman who had prayed much for a son, and had then, like Hannah (1 Sam. 1:11, 27-28), devoted him to the Lord, when he was born.

The whole of this chapter is a "prophecy" or divinely given utterance. We may infer what a Biblical prophecy is from 1 Corinthians 14:3: it is a speaking to men for their edification, exhortation, and comfort, whether it is futuristic or not. This prophecy was given thru Lemuel's mother, and she taught it to him. One reason that some think that Lemuel was another name for Solomon – perhaps his mother's pet name for him—is that Lemuel's mother's teaching here parallels Solomon's father's teaching in 4:4, except that they differ in the subject matter.

Few people realize the great influence that mothers have on the condition and destiny of the world through their teaching of their children. It will be great in good or great in evil, according to the mother's heart's condition. "This is a fine example of maternal influence. This chapter is as mysterious, as far as its author is concerned, as the previous one. Some suppose this King Lemuel to be Solomon, but the evidence for this is rather slim. Others suppose him to have been an Arabian or a Chaldean king, and in support of the latter, it is noted that there are some Chaldean words here used.

However, there is no way to be certain who King Lemuel was, for the Scripture is silent beyond what is written here. It is enough that god has included this portion in the inspired canon; it is, therefore, profitable for our study. This chapter is in two sections; verses 1-9, dealing with vices to be shunned and virtues to be practiced, and verses 10-31, a description of the ideal woman. These latter verses were perhaps drawn up by Lemuel's mother either as an instruction to her daughters, as the foregoing verses were to her son or as a direction to her son in the choice of a wife

What, my son? V. 2 and what the son of my womb and what the son of my vows? She feels the greatness of her task in teaching truth to him who is to rule over others, for she knows that according to the soundness or rottenness of her teachings he will do good or evil to his subjects. The next available verses are one of the constant warnings to a wise young man and it says - "Give not thy strength unto women, nor thy ways to that which destroyeth kings." This is not a prohibition of marital pleasures which are, throughout the Bible, pronounced right and good, Proverbs 5.10-19, 18.22, 1 Corinthian 7.1-6, Hebrew 13:4, but it is a forbidding of illicit relations with other women, a sin that kings seem to be especially prone to because their position and power often make them immune to human laws protecting the virtue of women. This warning has been a recurrent theme in Proverbs and elsewhere, Proverbs 5:20-21; 7:26-27; Deuteronomy 17:17; Nehemiah. 13:25-27; Hosea 4:11; Hebrew 13:4.

The desires of the flesh are a powerful drive, but God has made full provision for these, by permitting to every man one wife and to every woman one husband, and not even kings were exempt from this law, though many have transgressed it, Matthew 19:3-6.

It is not for kings, O Lemuel; it is not for kings to drink wine; nor for prince's strong drink. The danger in drinking any kind of alcoholic beverages is not in the first or second drink, but in the fact that excessive amounts take away one's reasoning ability, and loses all inhibitions so that no evil is too great for one to do while under alcoholic influence. But inasmuch as alcohol is addictive, and more so to some people than to others, the wise person will never take even the first drink, and so will never have to worry about becoming addicted to it. No one ever sets out to become an alcoholic, but because of its addictiveness, by the time one realizes the danger he is in of becoming an alcoholic, he is often beyond the hope of recovery by human abilities.

In other words, he ought to heed this warning lest they drink, and forget the law, and pervert the judgment of any of the afflicted." Here is the reason for rulers to abstain: if he cares not about himself, yet he is commanded to have a concern for the office he occupies.

The Levitical priests were forbidden to use alcoholic beverages while ministering in the Tabernacle, Leviticus. 10:9, and the prophets and priests both during Isaiah's ministry were charged with erring through drinking, Isaiah. 28:7. Kings and princes, being the rulers of the land, are especially accountable for the maintaining of law and right judgment, Deuteronomy 17:18-20, yet however well they might know the law, they would not be apt to rightly practice it if they were drunken. It is a sad fact that our national lawmaking and governing bodies often operate in an alcoholic stupor. "Give strong drink unto him that is ready to perish, and wine unto those that is of a heavy heart." Here are legitimate uses for alcoholic beverages; not for pleasure, but for medicinal stimulants. It is clear from Luke 10:34; 1 Timothy 5:23 that wine was anciently used as a medicine because of the alcohol in it. It was also used as an antidepressant, Judges 9:13; Psalm 105:15, and to deaden pain in those who were dying. Mark 15:23 was probably based on this verse. There our Lord was offered drugged wine while on the cross, but he refused it, lest it is thought that He endured the cross only in the strength of the drugs.

He did receive sour wine (vinegar) as He was dying, Mark 15:35, but this was not alcoholic. When grape juice was processed at too high temperature, instead of fermenting and becoming wine, it soured and became vinegar. V. 7. "Let him drink, and forget his poverty, and remember his misery no more." "It is not to be understood that there is sanction here of strong drink as a beverage, but rather the medicinal use of it as in the case of Paul's advice to Timothy to take a little wine for the stomach's sake.

V. 8 - 9. Open thy mouth for the dumb in the cause of all such as are appointed to destruction. The reference is probably not to those who are naturally mute through some physical infirmity, but to those "who cannot speak on their own behalf, either through want of elocution, or knowledge of the law; or people took for granted by their persecutors. To "open thy mouth" means to speak for these, to rise as the patron of those who are unable to defend themselves. God has always had a special concern for the poor, the widow and the fatherless, and He honors those in authority who imitate Him in this virtue.

It is not common with the world to defend those in whom is no profit, but God commands rulers to deal justly with all people, whatever their social status may be. Open thy mouth, judge righteously and plead the cause of the poor and needy. This is an explanation of the preceding verse, a case of Hebrew parallelism. These kings duties are the same in essence as that set forth in Leviticus 19:15 and Deuteronomy 1:16-17.

Since a ruler represents God, by whose permission he rules, Proverbs 8:15-16, any injustice in judgment will reflect back on the Lord, and people will wrongly assume that God ratifies such evil if He does not immediately bring judgment upon the offending ruler, which He often cannot consistently do because He has other purposes to fulfill through him. No doubt about this and the preceding verse must be considered in connection with the warning against strong drink, for nothing so corrupts justice like a judge who is addicted to alcohol.

Proverbs 31:10 - 31

Who can find a virtuous woman? For her price is far above rubies. There are many theories as to whom this refers. We believe that this is a description of the ideal woman, for it is but natural and needful that, having so often spoken earlier of the "strange woman," Divine revelation should now reveal the ideal woman to us. Matthew Henry calls this section "a looking glass for ladies. Next follows a full-length portrait of a virtuous woman or wife.

1. The heart of her husband doth safely trusts in her, so that he shall have no need of spoil. "Spoil" has to do with the goods taken in warfare, or by violence, and the ideal woman is such a manager that her husband can trust her to make do with what he brings in, and will not constantly nag him until he resorts to violent means to satisfy her greed for worldly possessions. He trusts her wise management of the household so that he needs not to try to do his work and hers both. He earns the living, and she makes living worthwhile. This particular verse confirms the divine roles of man and woman in the family setting.

2. She will do him good and not evil all the days of her life. A good wife will do good for her husband, and not just in the bright, flowery days of the honeymoon, but in old age as well, when life may be drab and dark. "The idea here set forth for the woman is fine and represents her at her best and most influential business, viz. that of making a home. It is interesting to note that the average women are most happy and best adjusted when she is doing well for her family. It seems to be a part of the basic make-up of women. It is this basic goodness toward him that continually stirs the man fortunate enough to have such a wife, to trust in her (v. 11). She is worthy of his trust in her. She seeketh wool, and flax, and worketh willingly with her hands. Wool and flax were the raw materials from which woolen and linen garments were made. She did not wait for her husband to bring it home to her, but she sought for it and worked with it to make their necessary garments. She is not like some, who have too much idle time, and so are easily ensnared in evil because they do not occupy themselves in household duties, that is why in some community women that do not have something to do; the idle women sit on the street to gossip, cause trouble for the innocent one that either busy or

not having their kind of life and subsequently they form coven of witchcraft. There was an adage that says, "An idle mind and hand is a devil workshop." One of the modern blessings which may easily become a curse is the easy availability, too much leisure time, sometimes gives women and allows them to get involved in things dishonorable and dangerous.

3. She is like the merchants' ships; she bringeth her food from afar." Perhaps the imagery is drawn both from the exotic nature of the food and also from the fact that there are loads of it. Note the plural: it is not just one shipload, but regular good things that she provides. There is something quite magical and impressive in woman's economy … No one knows how it is done. A good cook can cause a family to eat like kings, even on a limited budget, and can serve all sorts of foreign goodies with daintiness.

4. She riseth also while it is yet night, and giveth meat to her household and a portion to her maidens. Wives often are the first risers of a morning, and have the meal almost prepared before anyone else is awake. Two duties are here shown: (1) Feeding the household and (2) Allotting the tasks to each, for "portion" is rendered "task" in Exodus 5:14. Thus, she has the task of "guiding the household," 1Timothy 5:14, so as to make it operate in an orderly manner. "She applies herself to the business that is proper for her. It is not in the scholar's business, nor the statesman's business, nor husbandman's business, that she employees herself, but in woman's business.

5. She considereth a field, and buyeth it: with the fruit of her hands she planteth a vineyard." Diligence and economy are both involved here. She may save a few coins here and there from her budget, perhaps make some profit on her sewing (v. 13) until she has the money to purchase additional property, and then she works to make that field fruitful and profitable.

In a very literal sense, one can plant a vineyard, for if one has only the cuttings from the annual pruning of grape vines, he can plant these and they will root and become new plants so that no expense is involved, only labor with the hands. Most plants can be acquired and multiplied without cost if one is willing to work with his hands.

6.   She girdeth her loins with strength, and strengtheneth her arms." "The allusion is to the girding and tucking up of long garments, worn in the eastern countries when any work was set about in earnest, which required dispatch," [Gill]. Diligent physical labor, so far from harming a person, actually contributes to strength and health, while majoring on illness generally contributes to its increase. "She has all the delicacy and even weakness of a woman, but the life of constant activity and cheerful toil preserves her health and increases her strength. Idle women, who lounge their days away in constant murmurings over their ailments, speak contemptuously of her.

7.   She perceiveth that her merchandise is good: her candle goeth not out by night. The word rendered "perceive" is more commonly rendered "taste," so that perception by actual experience is here meant. She actually tests her merchandise, and she is not content with poor merchandise, but she labors to make it good, though it may keep her up late at night and cause her to awaken early in the morning, (v. 15). She takes pride in producing something that is valuable, though it may take extra effort to make it so. Anything that is worth doing is worth doing right, and the person who is not willing to do a good job is really wasting time even starting the job.

She layeth her hands to the spindle, and her hands hold the distaff. This refers to a spinning mechanism with which the wool and flax were spun into thread for cloth. Generally, the right hand rotated the wheel of the apparatus while the left hand held the staff upon which the thread was wrapped as it was produced. This speaks of the resourcefulness of the ideal woman, for she not only made her own clothes but also even produced the cloth for them, back in the days before commercial textile mills were invented. This may sound terribly complicated to modern minds, but even so recently as a hundred or so years ago, our own pioneer mothers often spun their own cloth on spinning wheels.

"The spindle and the distaff are here mentioned as her honor, while the ornaments of the daughters of Zion are reckoned up to their reproach, (Isa. 3:18)," [Mathew Henry].

8. She stretcheth out her hand to the poor; yea, she reacheth forth her hands to the needy. Stretcheth out (or rather, openeth wide) her hand' is a phrase implying prompt and liberal giving: the opposite of shutting the hand Deuteronomy 15:7, 8, Note the repetition of "hands" in this and the preceding verse. She is not afraid of manual labor of any sort. The ideal woman recognizes the N. T. principle that we are given wealth that we may share it with others, 2Cor. 9:8-11. "Her liberality is very extensive, reaches to many, and at a distance; it is done with great cheerfulness and readiness: to do good and communicate, is her pleasure. She is blessed because she is benevolent; God heaps blessings on her that she may help others. Too many people think that they get only so that they may keep it for self.

9. She is not afraid of the snow for her household: for all her household are clothed with scarlet." "Scarlet" could be Warm garments, but the idea may be thick or double clothing for all red colors are called "warm colors." "Snow was not uncommon in Palestine and the neighboring country, and its coming was prepared for by the wise and wise mother. Clearly the idea is that the ideal woman is one who prepares for the needs of her family before they arise, and it matters not what her critics may say behind her back, for her own works testify of her that not only are her husband and children adequately clothed, but that she herself is clothed with strength and honor, (v. 25).

10. She maketh herself coverings of tapestry; her clothing is silk and purple." Nor is she clothed only in the simplest and poorest of materials, but by her prudence, she is able to have the finer materials for her clothes. Rich clothing is not, in itself, a sin, though it may be made sinful by having the wrong attitude toward it. "This

shows that the prohibition of 'costly array' 1Timothy 2:9; 1Peter 3:3 is leveled against dress being made the instrument of pride and vanity. Some, interpreting 1Peter 3:3 in an absolute sense, would have us believe that women are forbidden any ornamentation, jewelry, hair styling, etc., but if this is interpreted as an absolute prohibition of any such, then so must we interpret "putting of apparel" in an absolute sense also, as forbidding wearing any clothes. The New Jerusalem, of which earthly wives are typical, Ephesians 5:22-27, is to be gloriously arrayed Revelation 21:9-21.

11. Her husband is known in the gates when he sitteth among the elders of the land. This speaks of the dignity of this woman: she is the wife of a city judge, for the gates were where courts of justice were held, and cases of the dispute were heard and settled. He is known, not only by the clothes he wears, but for his wisdom in judgment, of which his wife is a partaker, and for his exercise of authority over his household, in which she shares. They both reflect well on the other. Every married couple will reflect on each other for good or for ill, according to their character. Here, the suggestion appears to be that his wife reflects well on him in his official position.

12. She maketh fine linen, and selleth it; and delivereth girdles unto the merchant. This was all superior workmanship and had a reputation. Considered in the context here, it may be that her husband is known in the gates as the one who sells what his wife has made above the needs of the family, for the gates were also the places of selling. In which case, he would be known as the husband of "that woman who makes such good and dependable items of clothing."

13. Strength and honor are her clothing, and she shall rejoice in time to come." All material clothing will eventually wax old and deteriorate, but she who is clothed in such divinely given garments as strength, honor, and righteousness Isaiah 61:10 shall never be found naked in God's eyes. The strength and honor that are here mentioned are not things of the body, but are virtues of the

mind and the soul, and this is what gives her confidence to face the future with joyous hope, and not with trembling fear. Her rejoicing is based on repentance, (v. 30).

14. She openeth her mouth with wisdom, and in her tongue is the law of kindness." Alas, how many open their mouths in frivolity and foolishness, never speaking that which is to the edifying of the people of God, but often that which is destructive. The tongue is truly the index of the heart. "When she opens her mouth, for it is not always open, she expresses herself in a discreet and prudent manner; as well as speaks of things not foolish and trifling. The tongue is not to be a free and loose member: it is to contain and be controlled by the law of kindness. Here is one of God's laws that we seldom think of keeping, yet this is involved in that "Golden law" of Matthew 7:12. To those who hope to be saved by keeping the law it must be asked, Have you kept this law continually and perfectly, for that is what is required if one hopes to be saved Galatians 3:10-11. Self-salvation is an impossibility: it is part of the devil's theology. It is not enough for one to speak wisdom: he must also speak it with kindness.

15. She looketh well to the ways of her household, and eateth not the bread of idleness." The household is her particular province, and the ideal woman looks well to it, for what matters if she excels in outside matters if she neglects that which she alone is accountable for, and which she alone can rightly manage. Our generation has seen many mothers forsake the home to earn money to raise the standard of living, and the consequence has been a generation of rebellious and neurotic children who do not appreciate nor deserve the higher standard of living. And every mother who has abandon her God-given responsibility for the household is accountable to God for the moral and spiritual wrecks she causes by her absence from the home during the formative years of the children. But even if one stays at home, she must not be guilty of neglect through idleness. There is much truth in the old saying that "Man works from the sun to the sun, but woman's work is

never done." There is always working needing to be done in the home.

16. Her children rise up, and call her blessed; her husband also, and he praiseth her." While children seldom realize the value of such a mother at the time, yet in the years to come they shall appreciate her efforts in the home. "When they reach mature age, they bless her for her early training of them. "The laborer is worthy of his hire," Luke 10:7, and the faithful woman is worthy of the praise of her children and husband. It is wrong to fail to praise any who serve well.

17. Many daughters have done virtuously, but thou excellest them all." Some think that these are the words of the children and husband of such a woman, or at least, of the latter. In any case, it is clear that the Bible commends those ladies who faithfully fulfill their responsibilities to God and to their families. Such far excels all other women, whatever their other accomplishments may be. A godly and faithful wife and mother accomplish more than the mightiest and greatest queen who ever reigned, and her rewards will be infinitely greater.

18. Favor is deceitful, and beauty is vain: but a woman that feareth the Lord, she shall be praised." "A well-favored look, a graceful countenance, a balance and proportion of parts natural or artificial beauty, are vain and deceitful. At best, natural, physical beauty is brief, and it may cause pride, vanity, egotism, etc., but a reverential fear of God does only good to the one who has it. Here is the secret of this woman's faithfulness: she has a deep reverence for the Lord, and she does all things "as unto the Lord," Colossians 3:22-24, such a woman as this is the kind that every young man ought to seek for a wife. Often family and friends forget to praise the faithful woman, but in the end, her own works shall praise her in the day and place of judgment (Suggested by "in the gates," the place of judgment).

However, this is no excuse for any of us to neglect to properly compliment and praise others for a job well done. Woman's best work is often done in silence and without observation, but her highest praise is when the seeds sown in silence have grown into flowers of loveliness and fruit that are sweet to the taste, The portrait of a true woman is drawn, not to be admired, but to be reproduced in living character.

A VIRTUE AND GODLY WOMAN CAN ONLY BE FOUND IN THE LORD BY HIS DIVINE DIRECTION – GENESIS 24.

Printed in the United States
By Bookmasters